Call My Name, Clemson

HUMANITIES AND PUBLIC LIFE
A Collaboration with the University of Iowa
Obermann Center for Advanced Studies
Teresa Mangum and Anne Valk, series editors

Call My Name, Clemson

Documenting the Black Experience in an American University Community

RHONDDA ROBINSON THOMAS

UNIVERSITY OF IOWA PRESS, IOWA CITY

University of Iowa Press, Iowa City 52242
Copyright © 2020 by the University of Iowa Press
www.uipress.uiowa.edu
Printed in the United States of America

Design by Kristina Kachele Design, llc

Printed on acid-free paper
Library of Congress Cataloging-in-Publication Data
Names: Thomas, Rhondda Robinson, author. | University of Iowa Press.
Title: Call my name, Clemson: documenting the black experience in an
American university community / Rhondda Robinson Thomas.
Description: Iowa City: University of Iowa Press, 2020. | Series:
Humanities and Public Life | Includes bibliographical references and index.
Identifiers: LCCN 2020006582 (print) | LCCN 2020006583 (ebook) |
ISBN 9781609387402 (paperback: acid-free paper) |
ISBN 9781609387419 (ebook)
Subjects: LCSH: Clemson University—History. | Fort Hill Plantation
(SC)—History. | African Americans—South Carolina—History. |
African Americans—South Carolina—Intellectual life.
Classification: LCC LD1061.C3 T56 2020 (print) | LCC LD1061.C3 (ebook) |
DDC 378.009757/23—dc23
LC record available at https://lccn.loc.gov/2020006582
LC ebook record available at https://lccn.loc.gov/2020006583

For Lucretia Wannamaker Earle
and Rachel King Williams,
my great-great-grandmothers,
who were born into slavery in South Carolina
but who lived long enough to
experience freedom after the Civil War

A Schedule of Slaves with
nd ages —

№ 1	Sawney	aged	59	№ 34	M...
2	Tilla	"	50	35	Le...
3	Ned	"	25	36	Sa...
4	Nicholas	"	18	37	Ed...
5	Jonas	"	16	38	Pe...
6	Jim	"	12	39	Is...
7	Matilda	"	10	40	C...
	Chapman	"	8	41	Ch...
	Moses	"	22	42	H...
	Jargar	"	23	43	Ha...
	Lucinda	"	5	44	C...
	Armstead	"	3	45	N...
	Binah	"	3	46	Ri...
	Tom	"	1	47	Ph...
	Cato	"	2	48	Lu...
	Baby	"	1	49	Gr...
	Daniel	"	37	50	Ga...
	Rosanna	"	32		
	Willis	"	21		
	Peter	"	12		

Contents

Foreword

DURING THE SUMMER of 2019, a *Washington Post* headline warned, "Some White People Don't Want to Hear about Slavery at Plantations Built by Slaves." The article reprinted social media posts by tourists visiting former plantations, now open as museums, where the history of slavery is included in the narratives and displays. The comments are a case study in what critical race theorists call white fragility. Seeing artifacts and accounts of enslaved people's lives and of the violent, racist social and economic structures on which nineteenth-century American society was built, many of the visitors questioned the truthfulness of the docents' accounts of plantation life. Others reacted with defiance and anger, intent on defending nineteenth-century white Southerners from what they perceived as defamation. In effect, the comments voiced these tourists' objections to hearing a version of the past that contradicted both their expectations for museums and their understanding of American history, including sanitized, sentimental, and very white versions of life in the South.

That such remarks would be considered newsworthy enough to warrant a prominent newspaper article is unexpected, but the discomfort the reported remarks revealed would surprise few contemporary Americans. Despite the passage of more than 150 years, the Civil War lives on in the United States through stubborn disagreement over the meaning and impact of the country's "great sin and shame," as Frederick Douglass characterized slavery.[1] The disparate ways Americans understand the causes of the Civil War and its tenacious legacies have only grown more visible in recent years. We see the conflict over the past and its continuing power in local fights over the fate of Confederate monuments; in the audacity of neo-Confederate militia groups; in Congressional debates over reparations; in classroom lessons about slavery that cruelly single out and objectify Black students; and in the growing number of colleges and universities confronting their own indebtedness to slave labor. Even historians and journalists argue about the causes and consequences that centuries of laws, leaders, wars, and rebellions have had on enslaved people and slavery, as we can see in responses to the 1619 Project, an online resource created by the *New York Times* in 2019 to mark the arrival of the first enslaved Africans in Virginia four hundred years ago. Ours is a painful history for Americans to tell and to hear. However, for many Americans, the process of documenting, authenticating, interpreting, and acting on the history of enslaved people, slavery, enslavers, and the structures of belief and greed that supported this brutal system is a moral imperative.

Rhondda Robinson Thomas's important new book, *Call My Name, Clemson*, directly confronts the history of slavery through a place-based study that illuminates the complexities of this global system through a local lens. The book presents a riveting account of Thomas's research on the plantation, enslaved laborer, sharecropper, convict laborer, and Black wage-worker history of Clemson University. Her work also documents important ways that some Americans do wrestle—and others might—with our collective past.

For centuries, the impact of slavery on Clemson and, more generally, on higher education in the United States has been a history hidden in plain sight. Although seldom acknowledged, the labor of enslaved people created wealth for whites who endowed colleges and universities across the country. Today, the names of those same slave owners adorn campus residence halls, academic buildings, and classrooms. Some colleges and universities are, in fact, named for prominent slaveholders, Civil War generals, and other early defenders of slavery and white supremacy.

Clemson, like other esteemed schools, is built on land soaked in the sweat and blood of enslaved peoples. In the South, enslaved people constructed countless college and university buildings. They sometimes worked on the campuses or were brought to campus in service to their owners and to administrators, faculty, and students at southern and northern universities. They were cooks, stable hands, domestics, and valets. Many universities prosper today thanks to profits made in the past through the buying and selling of humans. In both the North and the South, profits from slavery were used to help build schools. Many of the endowments that fund current institutions originally came from merchants involved in the slave trade or from northern textile owners who accumulated wealth from cotton or sugar grown and harvested by thousands of enslaved people in the Carolinas, Mississippi, Louisiana, Alabama, or the Caribbean. Other higher education institutions were, like Clemson, built on the sites of historic plantations after the Civil War. In these and many other ways, slavery and higher education have deeply entwined histories.

At the turn of the twenty-first century, this resolutely ignored history is asserting its claims on our national attention, thanks to the efforts of scholars, including Rhondda Thomas; to the activism of students; and to the involvement of descendants and local community members. Earlier institutional histories celebrated growth and progress. However, since the early 2000s, slavery and justice initiatives initiated by administrators, such as Ruth Simmons at Brown University, followed by protests demanding greater transparency, accessibility, equity, and inclusion have joined with emergent public humanities practices and scholarly and community efforts. Activists, scholars, students, alumni, descendants, and community members are now working to uncover the complex and broad complicity of American institutions that benefited from the slave trade, plantation slavery, Jim Crow, displacement of indigenous people, and other oppressive practices. As schools have begun to face this ugly history, they have also been forced to reckon with its continuing impact on people's lives. One result has been undertaking the reparative work of establishing connections with historically Black communities; another result has been asking what restorative justice might entail.

Call My Name, Clemson charts the efforts at Clemson University in South Carolina to make visible a more comprehensive, inclusive, and truthful institutional history. Rhondda Thomas shares the unexpected path she followed to Clemson and the pressing weight of history that compelled her to begin a multi-year search—undertaken in collaboration with students, faculty, staff, alumni, descendants, and community members—for the roles first of the enslaved and then of additional groups of African Americans (sharecroppers, convict laborers, and wage laborers) in the building of Clemson. The original Fort Hill Plantation property on which Clemson stands was initially Cherokee territory, making this history all the more powerful and central to the longer, deeper story of the Americas.

We are honored to publish *Call My Name, Clemson* as part of the Humanities and Public Life Series. Thomas's story is a layered history of nation building. It documents the slow process by which institutions confront their part in that history and accept the responsibility to make tough changes. At the same time, it is a deeply personal account of the impact of her research on many individuals on and off campus, none of whom were more deeply affected than Thomas herself. In this way, the project she describes represents the best of publicly engaged humanities scholarship. From an archival project begun as Rhondda Thomas's mostly solitary effort to investigate the history of her new employer, this project grew into a multi-tendriled effort that connected Clemson with a larger history it had worked hard to ignore. Ultimately, Thomas's research process reconnected the university to a community on which it had turned its back. Throughout the book, we hear the voices of many who participated and many whose lives were affected by this project.

In addition, *Call My Name, Clemson* positions this particular project within a broader context of public scholarship. Thomas's reflections on public history projects and their methodologies will be immensely helpful to the growing number of scholars and communities seeking to develop such projects together. Situating her research at Clemson in relation to many similar and current investigations into colleges and universities' slave histories, Thomas nonetheless convincingly argues for the uniqueness of the Clemson community and its past.

We believe readers will find inspiration and guidance in *Call My Name, Clemson*. We deeply appreciate the vision it offers for public humanities practitioners who seek to create more honest, just, and inclusive campuses and communities.

—*Anne Valk and Teresa Mangum*

Narrative is radical,
creating us at the very moment it is being created.
—TONI MORRISON

Preface

ALTHOUGH I WAS born in South Carolina, I did not grow up in my home state. My family left when I was about two years old, drawn by the prospect of better teaching jobs for my parents in southeast Georgia. Until fairly recently, most of what I knew about South Carolina revolved around stories about my family, whose roots stretch back at least six generations on both the paternal and maternal sides. Leaving South Carolina enabled me to travel to the West Coast, and there, before I became a teenager, I visited a university, which inspired my dream of becoming a professor. Fulfilling that dream brought me back to South Carolina in 2007 to teach early African American literature at Clemson University, where my education about the state's long and complicated history began.

That educational process led to the development of my research project, "Call My Name: African Americans in Clemson University History," which tells the stories of hundreds of African Americans who figure large in the history of the higher education institution. These stories include those of enslaved people who had labored on Fort Hill, John C. Calhoun's plantation, where Clemson was established in 1889; freed men, freed women, and children, who had worked as sharecroppers on the land during Reconstruction; incarcerated laborers, aged thirteen to sixty-seven, who erected the university's earliest buildings; wage workers, who were employed in a variety of jobs, and cooperative extension employees; musicians like Duke Ellington and Ray Charles, who performed at segregated social events; and students, faculty, and staff who came to Clemson during the first quarter century of desegregation.

Call My Name, Clemson also shares stories about the experiences of African Americans in the city of Clemson and nearby towns that developed around Clemson University and the institutions, organizations, and communities they created during the antebellum period and after Emancipation. These include narratives about free and enslaved Blacks who lived and labored in settlements and on nearby plantations and farms; about houses of worship such as Clemson's Abel Baptist Church, established in 1868—in whose cemetery are buried Thomas and Frances Fruster, who were enslaved on Fort Hill, and Willie Earle, the last recorded lynching victim in South Carolina—and Pendleton's King's Chapel African Methodist Episcopal Church, organized in 1860; about social venues like Keese Barn, a country store–antique shop–eatery operated by Ben Keese, which served as the social center of the African American community, and Littlejohn's Grill, a nightclub-restaurant-hotel owned by entrepreneurs Horace and Gertrude Littlejohn, where Black musicians including James Brown, Count Basie, and the Supremes performed and where travelers could find safe accommodations during the Jim Crow era; about educational institutions such as the Seneca Institute, the Silver Spring School, the Central Colored School, and the Calhoun Elementary School; and about the Abel and Cadillac Heights neighborhoods. Additionally, the project documents the development of civic groups like the National Association for the Advancement of Colored People (NAACP) chapters that led local efforts for equal opportunities and the Jane Edna Hunter (JEH) Society that enabled African American females to tend to the needs of women and girls as well as those of the larger community. The JEH Society was named for Hunter, a native of Pendleton, South Carolina, who founded the Phillis Wheatley Association (PWA) in Cleveland, Ohio. The PWA provided housing, job training and placement, and recreation for Black women and girls who moved North seeking a better life during the Great Migration of the early twentieth century.

Drawing on the African diasporic call-and-response tradition, I created the Call My Name project to offer the public opportunities to collaborate with me and my research team to fill out the stories of African Americans for whom records are frequently missing, misleading, or marginalizing. Call-and-response is a group nurturing and affirming experience, a "collaborative improvisatory" tradition that enables communities to engage collective meaning-making that preserves the speaker's voice while eliciting diverse responses from listeners.[1] This research process also evokes the practice of

Clemson cadets engaging in roll call; Clemson professors calling the names of students in their classes when taking attendance or participating in discussions; and the Clemson president calling the name of every graduate before each one walks across the stage to receive a diploma. I believe public history projects like Call My Name that examine the racial histories of universities work most effectively when academics adopt an interdisciplinary methodology and actively seek and value the contributions of community members at every stage of project development. In calling the names of African Americans in early Clemson history, my team and I are inviting an array of people to assist in documenting their stories, honoring their lives, and acknowledging their contributions to the university's development.

In this book, four story lines illuminate the intricacies of documenting the history of African Americans at Clemson. The first details the development of the Call My Name research project. The second highlights critical moments in my life narrative as a sixth-generation South Carolinian. The third recollects my experiences in working with local community partners to document this history. And the fourth outlines the protracted process that led Clemson University trustees to authorize the researching and sharing of the institution's complete history. I present this narrative within a call-and-response framework in the book. Each section begins with a "Call" that represents the voices of individuals whose stories and experiences are being documented and shared by the Call My Name project, including a descendant, enslaved persons, a musician, a convict laborer, students from the integration generation, and the granddaughter of a notable Clemson alumnus. A "Response" follows each "Call," written by individuals who are contributing to the Call My Name project, including a professor, three research assistants, a student, an alumna, and me. Within the Call and the Response passages, italicized words or phrases are repeated, each repetition inviting readers to reflect and respond to the narratives. Interspersed between the Call and Response pieces are the chapters that detail how Call My Name and the Clemson University History Projects came to be. As the story has evolved, I have experienced how "narrative is radical," according to Toni Morrison, "creating us at the very moment it is being created."[2] Recovering and creating narratives about African Americans in the history of Clemson University and nearby communities has enabled me to add new chapters to my own South Carolina story. Other participants in the project have experienced a new or renewed sense of belonging in a community located in a pervasively white and conservative area of the Palmetto state, where Clemson is located.

The complex narrative that unfolds in this book involves far more people and events than I have space to address. I hope that others will publish writings and produce media that also examine public engagement with Clemson University and local community history.

Call My Name, Clemson, always.

Bringing the gifts that my ancestors gave,
I am the dream and the hope of the slave.
I rise

—MAYA ANGELOU

advances made to them subject to the elec
of the authorities having jurisdiction of the

It is understood that each company shall ca
and attend to the stock they work and if no
punctually at the time designated (Sundays
ted) the company so offending shall forfeit
of fifty cents for each offence to be deducted
the share of the crop coming to said compan

January 5th 1874

William His Johnson
        X
       mark

Samuel his Dangerfield
       X
      mark

John His Harkill
     X
    mark

Moses His Sherman
      X
     mark

Witness

John C. Hea

Frank His Vance
      X
     mark

Pinckney His Cuningham
         X
        mark

David his English
      X
     mark

James X Jackson
      mark

Nicolas his Jackson
        X
       mark

his

Call: The Black Fruster Family's Clemson Connection

ERIC YOUNG

I didn't learn that some of my ancestors had been enslaved on American statesman John C. Calhoun's Fort Hill Plantation, where Clemson University was built, until nearly twenty years *after* I graduated from Clemson in 1995.

While growing up in Upstate South Carolina, neither my mother, Pamela Webb, nor my maternal grandmother, Juanita G. Webb, talked much about family history. As a child of the Jim Crow era, my grandmother had been instructed to stay out of trouble and focus on working hard and becoming self-sufficient, a mindset she passed to her children. When I asked my grandmother about our ancestors, she would change the subject. I especially remember an incident during my senior year of high school when a white historian, W. J. Megginson, came to our neighborhood to interview my maternal great-grandmother, Leah Fruster Grier.

"Somebody up there is talking to Mother," my grandmother said cryptically. "They want to know something."

The something was our family history.

When I attended my grandmother's eighty-second birthday dinner in 2014, I heard her express how proud she was of her children, grandchildren, and great-grandchildren. She said she could not have imagined we would come this far considering where we had come from. Her reflections sparked my curiosity. This time I insisted that she tell me about our family.

I was soon listening to the recording of my great-grandmother Grier sharing our family history for the *Black Heritage in the Upper Piedmont of South Carolina Project* that Megginson had completed in 1982 and 1989–1990.[1] Her grandparents, Thomas and Frances Fruster, had been enslaved on the Fort Hill Plantation.[2] As I learned new information about my family, I wondered if it was true. Could these references be about another family? As I begin to confirm the details I was gathering through census records, primary documents, and conversations with my grandmother, I felt a sense of pride and regret. I was proud that my ancestors helped create a university where I obtained an education that was inaccessible to them. A dream they may have had was a reality for me. But I wish I had known my family history much earlier. Maybe I could have achieved more while I attended Clemson. Instead, I acted like a typical student: get in and complete degree. Who knows? Maybe I could have been more involved and brought about greater change, like helping to increase the Black student population.

While I was afforded the opportunity to earn a degree from Clemson, my grandmother Webb couldn't attend because she grew up when the university was segregated. Instead, she began working at Clemson at age sixteen. When her mother became so ill that she could no longer keep her job in the Clemson College laundry, where she had labored for thirty-seven years, my grandmother was allowed to work in her mother's place to help earn a living for their family. She would attend classes at the Pendleton Elementary School during the day and then work at the laundry in the afternoon and early evening, folding sheets and towels. And at the end of each work week, my grandmother took the sealed envelope with her paycheck and gave it to her mother.

I've often wondered about the origin of the inner strength, character, discipline, perseverance, endurance, integrity, diligence, and conscientiousness exhibited by members of my family. Now I know.

My grandmother's story is just one of many personal narratives that explain how my family dynamic was established and has progressed. Her story motivated me to dig deeper and find out more about our family history. This journey of discovery has permanently changed my perspective about myself, my family, and my community.

When I attempt to imagine my grandparents' sacrifices to remain at peace, stay together, and carry on during the Jim Crow era, I am convinced they were laying a foundation for their descendants to be proud of and to build on. They were people of integrity and strength, char-

Thomas and Frances Fruster standing on the front lawn of Fort Hill. Jane Prince, Thomas Green Clemson's housekeeper, is on the front porch, ca. 1883. Courtesy of Clemson University Libraries' Special Collections & Archives.

acteristics that inspired their descendants to achieve success in many endeavors.

We are the Fruster family, and our history is rich and strong considering how far we've come since our enslaved ancestors toiled on the Fort Hill Plantation. Thomas Fruster (sometimes also called Jim or John) and Frances Benson-Fruster (sometimes also called Fannie or Frannie) are most notably known for a picture taken of them, seemingly frozen in time, while standing on the front lawn of the Fort Hill Plantation house sometime after the Civil War.

Over the years, this picture has become an iconic symbol of *The African American Experience at Fort Hill* brochure, as well as events such as Clemson's Black History Month Celebration.

But the Frusters are much more than what an iconic photograph can represent. Thomas Fruster was born in approximately 1817; Frances Benson-Fruster was born about 1832. They married around 1845 when they were twenty-eight and thirteen, respectively. At the end of the

Civil War, both gained their freedom on the Fort Hill Plantation, where they had labored. Both were later employed by Thomas Green Clemson and Clemson College, Frances as a housekeeper and Thomas as a farm hand who worked with horses. According to the 1880 US Census, their union yielded thirteen children, with eleven described as living that year.[3] Thomas was identified as a farm laborer, and Frances was a homemaker. Neither could read or write. They were some of the first former enslaved persons to own property near Walhalla, South Carolina, before 1900. They were also lifelong members of the Abel Baptist Church in Calhoun (later Clemson), South Carolina. Thomas Fruster died in 1902. At the time, he and his wife had been married fifty-seven years. His gravestone reads "Died November 14, 1902. Aged 85 yrs. *A Consistent Member of Abel Church for Thirty Years.*" Frances Fruster died about five years later. Her gravestone is inscribed "Died April 26, 1907. Aged 75 yrs. *Wife of T. Fruster.* Gone But Not Forgotten—Blessed Are Those Who Die in the Lord." Thomas and Frances Fruster, as well as many other members of the Fruster Family, are buried in the Abel Church Cemetery.[4]

My family and Clemson University should embrace and celebrate the strong lineage of my ancestors and their documented ties to the legacies of the Calhoun and Clemson families as well as to Fort Hill and Clemson College. There is so much more for Fruster descendants to accomplish and establish through our service and efforts to help others. Indeed, my family epitomizes the lines from Maya Angelou's poem "Still I Rise": "Bringing the gifts that my ancestors gave / I am the dream and the hope of the slave / I rise."[5] My ancestors Frances and Thomas Fruster lived long enough to begin seeing both their hopes and dreams for better lives for their descendants fulfilled.

Over the years, many Fruster family members have worked at Clemson and in the nearby community. Early on, they were employed as housekeepers, childcare providers, railroad workers, plant laborers, cooks, and skilled laborers. My grandmother, with only a tenth-grade education, for example, held many jobs on the Clemson campus and in Pendleton, South Carolina: a cook at the Clemson College dining hall; a server and baker at the Clemson House Hotel; a server at Dan's Sandwich Shop in Clemson, South Carolina; a caretaker for Clemson football player Bobby Gates's children; a housekeeper for Clemson football player and coach Covington "Goat" McMillan and his wife, Edith McMillan; a housekeeper for former Clemson football coach Les Herrin; a housekeeper for the city of Clemson Holiday Inn owners James and Chrystelle Ensley; a piano-part maker at the Pratt Read Corporation in Central, South Carolina; a childcare provider for Judge Walter Cox's children; a janitor at the segregated Calhoun High School for white students; a housekeeper for Clemson professor of architecture Joseph L. Young; a housekeeper for Clemson College YMCA associate secretary Nash N. Gray; and a caregiver for her parents, as well as for the Pickens County Nursing Home.

My ancestors' labor and sacrifices enabled the next generation of Fruster family members to earn degrees and receive professional training certifications from an array of higher education institutions, including Clemson University, Anderson University, Jacksonville University, University of South Carolina Salkehatchie, Tri-County Technical College, University of South Carolina Upstate, Walterboro's hospital nursing program, Presbyterian College, University of Texas–Arlington, Truman State University, Prairie View A&M University, Howard University, Ashford College, Central Piedmont Community College, and Academy of Somatic Healing Arts School of Massage Therapy.

Some of the notable accomplishments of Fruster family members to date include the following:

» Frusters were among the first Blacks to own property in the Calhoun area before 1900.[6] Many family members still live on Fruster Street in the city of Clemson.
» Jimmy Fruster and Henry Clay Grier were the first Black Americans to own cars in the city of Calhoun area.[7]
» Veterans included great-uncles James R. Fruster Jr. (SC CPL 156 Depot Brig) and Gay Fruster (SC CPL CO B371 Infantry, Purple Heart), World War I, and grandfather James H. Webb (SC SGT US Army), World War II.
» My mother, Jennifer Webb-Dawkins, Ronald Webb, and Rachel Brown were the three African American children selected to desegregate the all-white Pendleton public schools as a result of the South Carolina Equalization Project in 1966 before the official integration of area schools in the early 1970s.

» Kimberly A. Young-Brooks, my sister, was the first Black female officer of the South Carolina State Future Farmers of America (FFA), 1989–1990.
» Jennifer Webb-Dawkins was the first Black music director for the South Carolina State FFA Convention held at Clemson University, 1989–1991.
» Donald Lawrence & the Tri-City Singers with Eric D. Young, and Michael A. Young (my brother) were nominated for Grammy awards (2013, 2007, 2006, 2000, 2002, and 1995). Besides receiving recognition from Dove (2019), they won a Soul Train award (2003), the National Association for the Advancement of Colored People Image Award (2014), and Gospel Stellar awards (2019, 2018, 2013, 2012, 2006, 2003, 2002, 2000, 1997, 1995, and 1993), including Youth Project of the Year in both 2019 and 2012. The single, "Deliver Me (This Is My Exodus)" from the 2019 Donald Lawrence and the Tri-City Singers album of the same name, featuring Le'Andria Johnson, has achieved #1 Gospel Radio Airplay, #1 Gospel Digital Sales, and #1 Gospel Streaming Songs.
» Some Fruster family members are known for appearances and credits on big screen movies, soundtracks, national TV shows, and advertising campaigns and commercials.
» Brian Grier (cousin) was inducted into the Daniel High School Hall of Fame, 2017.
» Jeff Fruster (cousin) has been head football coach at Daniel High School, Six Mile, South Carolina, since 2016.
» Michael A. Young (brother) is a recipient of the Anderson University Alumni Achievement Award 2016 and has been a member of the Anderson University Board of Directors since 2016.
» Fruster descendants have attained influential careers in ministry, the music industry, banking, nursing, education, human resources, marketing, project management, live event production, theater, and fashion.
» Family members reside in South Carolina, North Carolina, Georgia, and Texas. Some have lived as far away as San Francisco, New York City, and Lisbon, Portugal.

Truly, we are the dream and the hope of the enslaved—our enslaved ancestors Frances and Thomas Fruster.

Just two years after learning about my family history, I was given the opportunity to come back to Clemson University with my extended family and participate in the History in Plain Sight event and the Call My Name campus tours and programs, which have given my family history a heartbeat and legs to move forward and inspire others. Considering where our family began, it's hard to believe my ancestors' dreams and visions of a better life, education, and outlook for their descendants have become a reality. The process of researching and uncovering the heritage of my maternal grandparents and their ties to the Calhoun and Clemson families, the Fort Hill Plantation, and Clemson University has been unique, inspiring, and motivating and has filled me with pride.

Indeed, the heritage of Thomas and Frances Fruster and the entire Fruster family is rich and strong.

Response: Hush, Oh, Hush, Somebody's Calling My Name

RHONDDA ROBINSON THOMAS

Hush, oh, hush
Somebody's calling my name
Hush, oh, hush
Somebody's calling my name
Hush, oh, hush
Somebody's calling my name
Oh, my Lord,
Oh, my Lord
What shall I do?
"Somebody's Calling My Name," Negro Spiritual

I needed to know their names.

I had arrived at Clemson University as a postdoc without the benefit of a campus visit. About five minutes into a tour of my workplace on the first day of my new job, Michael LeMahieu, my colleague in the English department, asked me to look toward the center of campus.

What else did I need to see? I wondered.

We had already stopped by a cluster of structures around which my life at Clemson would revolve: our eight-story office building, Strode Tower; red brick classroom building, Daniel Hall; and marble white Robert Muldrow Cooper Library. But LeMahieu insisted that we continue walking on that hot, humid August day, across a bridge toward Death Valley, the football stadium of the Clemson Tigers, located on the other side of campus.

"I don't see anything," I responded as I gazed up the hill toward a cluster of trees.

"Bend your head down and look again," he insisted.

When I followed his instructions, I saw a large, stately, two-story white wooden house with green shutters and oversized pillars situated behind the trees.

That looks like a plantation house, I mused to myself. *Why is there a plantation house in the middle of campus?*

Although I was born in Spartanburg, South Carolina, about sixty-four miles north of Clemson, I had never heard of the university until I began job hunting while completing my doctoral studies at the University of Maryland in the spring of 2007. Having come of age in the 1960s as the Jim Crow era was ending, I'd listened to my parents, Earle and Naomi Robinson, share many stories about Allen University, their

Fort Hill, the former home of John C. and Floride Calhoun and Thomas Green and Anna Calhoun Clemson and their families, is located in the center of the Clemson University campus, 2019. Photo by author.

alma mater, and about Benedict College in Columbia, South Carolina, where other family members and friends had earned their undergraduate degrees during the 1950s. Both Allen and Benedict are historically Black higher education institutions. Allen, the oldest Black higher education institution in South Carolina, was originally named Payne College in honor of African Methodist Episcopal (AME) bishop and educator Daniel Payne and was located in Newberry, South Carolina. Administrators moved the university to Columbia, South Carolina, in 1880 and renamed it Allen, in honor of Richard Allen, a founder of the AME Church. Benedict was established in 1870 by Bathsheba Benedict and the Baptist Home Mission. But I didn't know anyone who had attended or graduated from Clemson. I'd seen the university once when my husband and I drove through campus while we were house hunting earlier that summer. My plan was to teach early African American literature courses, complete my dissertation-to-book project, and find my dream job at another university—anywhere but in South Carolina. But about halfway through that fall semester, my department chair, Lee Morrissey, offered me a tenure-track position as an assistant professor of English. I accepted, deciding to live in my home state again for the first time in more than forty-five years.

My Southern Roots

My family had moved from South Carolina to southwest Georgia in the early 1960s when I was about two years old. We had not planned to relocate, but my daddy could not find a teaching job in the state's segregated public school system that provided a salary large enough for him to support his family—my mother, older brother Donald, and me. I would later learn South Carolina's separate but unequal public education system had been established during the 1895 state constitution convention convened at the behest of Clemson trustee and US Senator Benjamin R. Tillman. His racist policies and practices were designed to drive African Americans out of South Carolina, where the formerly enslaved were the majority after the end of the Civil War. Nearly half a century later, those policies were still affecting my family. Although many of my relatives had moved from South Carolina to the North and West during the Great Migration seeking better opportunities, we headed farther South to live in Blakely, Georgia, where my daddy's sister Herdisene Theresa Robinson Harris and her husband, John R. Harris, also educators, worked at the local segregated public Washington High School as guidance counselor and principal, respectively. The Early County seat, Blakely is a town whose claim to fame is having the only Confederate wooden flagpole—erected in 1861—still standing in the United States.[1] The flagpole is situated in the town square near the county courthouse alongside a Confederate monument titled "Lest We Forget" that the United Daughters of the Confederacy installed in 1909:

A TRIBUTE OF LOVE, TO THE NOBLE CONFEDERATE SOLDIERS WHO CHEERFULLY OFFERED THEIR LIVES IN DEFENSE OF THE RIGHT OF LOCAL SELF-GOVERNMENT, AND TO THOSE WHO FOUGHT AND SURVIVED.[2]

Some of those Confederates who fought and survived their futile effort to preserve the right to create a slave society returned to Blakely and embraced Jim Crow policies and practices. Their settlement in Blakely ensured that housing options for my college-educated, school-teacher parents and their family, nearly a century after the Civil War ended, were limited to renting structures like our first home, located just outside the city limits: a wooden two-story house painted yellow and propped up on bricks. Within a few years, my parents saved enough money to purchase a blue-and-white striped, rectangular shaped mobile home that they set up within a trailer park where other Black professionals lived. The trailer park was located across the street from the segregated Washington Elementary and High School for Black students, where my parents worked and my siblings and I attended school. Our school and home were adjacent to the segregated neighborhood pool, tennis courts, and community center that had been established for Black residents. By the time I turned ten, we moved to Atlanta, Georgia, just before Blakely's public schools were integrated in 1970—sixteen years after the US Supreme Court *Brown v. Board of Education* ruling that had outlawed segregation. There my parents had secured better teaching jobs at Berean Junior Academy, a historically Black elementary-middle school operated by the Seventh-day Adventist Church.

Now I was seeking my first teaching job as a university professor. But I had no desire to move back to South Carolina, the state where daddy had been unable to build a successful career in education. The summers were stiflingly hot. And the career options seemed incredibly limiting for an African American woman who, at about age eight, had begun dreaming of becoming a professor after meeting people from all over the world while exploring the beautiful Stanford University campus in California, where her daddy was completing a master's degree in mathematics.

And yet here I was back in hot, humid South Carolina.

I turned to my colleague seeking an explanation I hoped would not confirm my fears.

LeMahieu's answer perplexed and baffled me: "That's the Fort Hill plantation house. Clemson is built on John C. Calhoun's Fort Hill Plantation."

Why hadn't anyone informed me, during or after the interview process, that I would be working on a historic plantation? How could I have missed such a significant fact when I had diligently searched the university's website for information about my new employer?

John C. Calhoun's Fort Hill Plantation Becomes Site of Clemson University

I would soon learn that in 1825, Calhoun relocated his family to the Upper Piedmont area of South Carolina, situated about forty-five miles northwest of the Abbeville District, where he was born and much of his family still resided. The Eastern Band of the Cherokees had lived in the region before Scots-Irish colonists began arriving in the early 1700s. The Cherokees eventually forged a fragile coalition with the British, depending on them for limited protection as tensions between the colonists and the loyalists increased. Tensions led to raids, battles, and wars, culminating in the American Revolution, during which colonists burned down the Cherokee settlement named Isunigu, later called Esseneca, located on the land where Calhoun would establish Fort Hill.[3] In the 1785 Treaty of Hopewell, the Federal Government took possession of most of the Cherokee's territory except for designated hunting grounds, which the Cherokees gradually lost as the South Carolina government allotted and sold plots of land that would become Greenville, Anderson, Pickens, and Oconee counties.[4]

From the late eighteenth to early nineteenth centuries, prominent white South Carolinians such as Brigadier General and US representative Andrew Pickens, Major and SC state representative Samuel Taylor, US senator John Ewing Colhoun, and American statesman John C. Calhoun established towns, farms, and plantations where enslaved and free people of African descent labored until the end of the Civil War. Like the thousands of enslaved Africans who created prosperous rice and indigo plantations in the South Carolina Lowcountry, transforming Charleston into an economic powerhouse, those who labored in the Upcountry were forced to perform the backbreaking work of preparing land for habitation and cultivation. Yet these working-age enslaved persons comprised only about 10 to 20 percent of the population compared to more than 50 percent in other parts of the state. A small group of free people of color also lived and labored in the Upstate primarily as farmers, laborers, or craftsmen. They likely were migrants to the Piedmont region in search of new opportunities: forced to resettle for legal or political reasons, they had been manumitted by their former owners or had purchased their own freedom. Several free Blacks, including Daniel Burdine, Lydia Holly, Lucinda Holly, and Benjamin Roberts, were enslavers, owning one or two enslaved persons.[5]

By the time John C. Calhoun moved his family from the Dumbarton Oaks estate in Washington, DC, where he was serving as the US vice president, into the four-room parsonage on the property then known as Clergy Hall for the nearby Stone Church, South Carolina's Upcountry Pendleton District was a well-established area. In 1809, Calhoun's mother-in-law, Floride Bonneau Colhoun, had purchased the property through her white male agents from Stone Church pastor James McElhenny. Enslaved carpenters owned by the Calhouns remodeled the house and added ten rooms and large white pillars. After Floride Colhoun's death in 1836, her daughter Floride, Calhoun's wife, inherited the 1,102-acre property but soon relinquished her dower rights to the land that her husband would name the Fort Hill Plantation.[6] By 1850, seventy-five enslaved persons labored for the Calhouns as domestics, field hands, drivers, carpenters, blacksmiths, gatekeepers, seamstresses, lady's maid, and valet. They planted and harvested a variety of crops, including wheat, corn, oats, cotton, beans, peas, rice, fruit, and potatoes. They also made butter, sheared sheep, and maintained formal gardens. Field hands lived in interconnected barracks-like quarters made of granite stone about a quarter mile from the plantation house, while those who labored as domestics stayed in cabins built closer to the Calhouns' residence.[7] The aforementioned Frusters were among the first African Americans I saw trapped in post-Reconstruction time in the photograph of them standing in front of the Fort Hill Plantation house. How long did they stay in the area after Emancipation? Did any family members still live near the university today?

After the Civil War, some southerners sought to preserve a nostalgic view of Calhoun and Fort Hill. In 1881, for example, *Century Magazine* published "The Calhoun Summer Home," a local color story by white American naturalist Ernest Ingersoll about Calhoun's "ancestral acres," infusing his narrative with historical anecdotes and vivid details about the old manse. Ingersoll muses, "In these days of the decadence of all that make such a place glorious and its owner an autocrat, the half-deserted mansion has become a point of pilgrimage for those whose imaginations still cling to the old order of things, and of curiosity to others, who care to see a relic of former pride."[8] Ingersoll not only asserts that both Old South loyalists and history buffs made the pilgrimage to Fort Hill out of interest in Calhoun's legacy; but through his evocation of "the old order of things," he intimates that nostalgic visitors also wanted to visit a historic site where enslaved African Americans had labored for one of America's influential proponents of involuntary servitude.

What my new colleague did not know was that I had no desire to make a pilgrimage to a historic plantation, since many administrators of these sites have clung "to the old order of things" well into the twenty-first century. In fact, I had an unnatural fear of historic plantations, imagining that if I stepped into that space, I would be sucked into a vortex of time travel to the antebellum South, like Dana Franklin in

Octavia Butler's neoslave narrative *Kindred,* and become enslaved. My first and only visit to a historic plantation had taken place in the early 1990s while I was teaching in the departments of English and communication at Columbia Union College (now Washington Adventist University) in Takoma Park, Maryland. After my students and I began discussing books like the *Narrative of the Life of Frederick Douglass, an American Slave* in my Introduction to Research and Writing course and I overhead students talking about books such as Harriet Jacobs's *Incidents in the Life of a Slave Girl* and Toni Morrison's *Beloved*, which they were reading in my fellow professor Debbie Brown's African American Literature class, my interest in visiting a plantation was piqued. I booked a tour of the James River plantations in Virginia, expecting to gain intriguing insights into plantation history, especially about the lives and labors of enslaved African Americans.

I was sorely disappointed. As we walked the grounds of the beautifully landscaped and well-maintained historic plantations, I heard detailed descriptions of structures that had been built by enslaved carpenters, artwork and antiques that had been purchased with profits from the labor or sale of enslaved persons, and fine southern cuisine that had been prepared by enslaved cooks—without any acknowledgment from the tour guides of the people whose forced labor had bankrolled Virginia slave owners' conspicuous consumption. As our group left the outdoor kitchen of the second plantation house situated on the banks of the James River, I asked one of the guides for information about the enslaved persons who had cooked and served the meals. He seemed flustered as he stammered out something about a kind master who had freed his enslaved persons before the Civil War and quickly changed the subject to the fancy toilets that had been built for the family next to the big house. As we walked up the driveway to the final plantation house, which the guides had informed us was a popular wedding venue and bed and breakfast inn, several white women began waltzing as if they were wearing hoop skirt dresses at an antebellum ball. If they were southern belles in their *Gone with the Wind* fantasy, then who was I? I vowed never to visit another historic plantation.

But now I was working at a university that was built on a plantation: ardent proslavery American statesman John C. Calhoun's Fort Hill Plantation no less.

Clemson University's Public History
Omits History of Slavery and Its Legacies

Shortly after I began my new job at Clemson, I searched the
university's website again, looking for details about its history I had
missed when I had investigated the institution as a potential employer.
I soon discovered references to the university's having been built on
Calhoun's Fort Hill Plantation, but the specifics were difficult to find as
they required a series of four clicks: Home > Visitors/Parents > History
> Places > Fort Hill. There the persistent internet user would find this
description:

> Fort Hill was the home of John C. Calhoun, South Carolina's
> pre-eminent 19th century statesman, from 1825 until his death
> in 1850. The antebellum plantation home, office and kitchen are
> furnished mostly with family artifacts. . . .
>
> Thomas Green Clemson, Calhoun's son-in-law and founder of
> the University, envisioned "the preservation of the home of the
> illustrious man who spent his life in the public service of his coun-
> try." Thomas Clemson willed that Fort Hill "shall always be open
> for the inspection of visitors."[9]

I wondered if Thomas Clemson had me, an African American female
professor, in mind when he thought of Fort Hill's future visitors. The
university honors its founder's wish to keep the house open for tours.
As recently as 2015, the institution characterized the Fort Hill plantation house as the "*heart* of Clemson University," intimating it is the
most significant place on campus or the source of Clemson's vitality
(emphasis mine).[10] I would later learn that Clemson cadets, the United
Daughters of the Confederacy, and others had described the house as a
"shrine" to John C. Calhoun during the university's earliest decades.[11]
Eventually the Department of Historic Properties added a link on the
Clemson website to the "History of African Americans at Fort Hill:
1825–1888," an out-of-print brochure. Of the enslaved African American population at Fort Hill, the writer asserted: "Since [they] left no
written record, their perspective is unavoidably voiceless in history.

However, reports of visitors and family letters have given insight into understanding the lives of slaves, who later became freedmen at Fort Hill."[12] What information was included in these secondhand reports? Why weren't those insights acknowledged or incorporated into the Fort Hill tours?

In recent years, African Americanist literary scholars and historians have increasingly challenged the "unavoidably voiceless" argument regarding the recovery and documentation of early African American life. In "Life beyond Biography: Black Lives and Biographical Research," literary scholar John Ernest asserts, "This is a field in which one comes to expect short biographical entries—when you can find one at all—that include the inevitable phrase 'little is known'"[13] or "unavoidably voiceless" as in the case of enslaved African Americans at Fort Hill. Scholars fail to search diligently, limit their research to traditional archives, and believe white lives matter because records about them have been meticulously kept while Black lives must be discovered, often only through relationships with or connections to white historical figures. Ernest recommends that scholars avoid the confines of the linear narrative when researching Black life and instead seek to "capture the complexities of the biographical subject's world, the cultural contexts that any individual inhabits, the complex relation between background and foreground that we witness whenever we examine an individual life."[14] Clemson University would seem to be the perfect place to implement Ernest's approach, particularly because its historians and other scholars and authors have well documented the local, regional, national, and global contexts that enslaved persons who labored on Fort Hill inhabited.

Thus, if some information about enslaved African Americans at Fort Hill was available and Clemson University considered the Calhoun's plantation house to be the "heart" of the campus, why hadn't any of the Department of English faculty members who interviewed me mentioned the university's intimate connection to Calhoun's plantation? Why hadn't having access to primary documents about enslaved life and culture been a selling point for my accepting the offer to teach early African American literature and develop my scholarship agenda at Clemson? Why had my new English department colleagues waited to break the news until after I had accepted the job offer, purchased a house, signed a contract, moved to South Carolina, and come to campus for the first time a few weeks before classes began? I would later learn that this was standard practice for the Department of English. Another of my new colleagues informed me that he had not been offered a tour of the Fort Hill plantation house either. None of the recently hired professors who had come to Clemson for campus visits as part of the candidate review process had visited the historic home.

I was stunned yet intrigued at the possibility of incorporating the history of slavery on the Fort Hill Plantation into my classes. Since I was to be stuck on Calhoun's plantation for three years, I decided to include tours of the plantation house in my American and African American literature courses. Surely whatever information the Department of Historic Properties staff had gleaned from reports and letters about enslaved people would be shared in the tours of the house. That fall I scheduled a tour for my early American literature students. But when I announced the campus field trip in class, they vehemently protested.

"The house is cursed," they insisted. "Any student who crosses its threshold won't graduate."

"Well, I'm going to initiate break-the-curse tours," I responded.

They all went on the tour; they all have graduated.

But on that day, my students learned only about architecture, artwork, and antiques on their Fort Hill tour, just as I had experienced during the James River plantations tour I'd taken more than a decade earlier. The guide did not mention slavery. And my students did not question this omission. A few weeks later, I went to the house dressed casually and took the tour alone without identifying myself as a Clemson professor. Once again, the guide did not talk about the enslaved people who had labored on Fort Hill. At the end of the tour I asked why not. The docent rather sheepishly replied, "Because it's too controversial," not because enslaved people "left no written record." He then proceeded to tell me about the Sons of Confederate Veterans, who visit the house annually, perpetuating the "Lost Cause" mythology of heritage and honor in the War between the States. After devoting seven years in graduate school to the study of early African American literature and investigating slavery as one of its central themes, I discovered that my new employer, Clemson University, deemed the subject of slavery to be too taboo to talk about during tours of Calhoun's plantation house. I soon learned that Clemson preferred characterizing enslaved African Americans owned by the Calhouns and Clemsons as "servants" and Fort Hill simply as a "historic house" or the "John C. Calhoun's home."

The decision of Clemson's Department of Historic Properties to advertise Fort Hill as a historic house in its publicity brochures contributed to the continued marginalization of a story that informs the complicated relationship between the history of slavery and the development of higher education institutions in South Carolina. The land on which Clemson was built is where a slaveholding American statesman forged a bond with his slaveholding diplomat son-in-law that led to the founding of a segregated college for white males on a South Carolina historic plantation. As members of the Clemson community, we were encouraged to view Calhoun simply as an influential antebellum politician for whom the Honors College was named in 1981. We were encouraged to admire Clemson University founder Thomas Green Clemson, for whom the institution itself and college town were named, as a man who significantly influenced American politics and to minimize his roles as a slaveholder and Confederate officer. We were encouraged to honor both men and their families: "It's because of the . . . families' generosity and vision for the future that Clemson University came to be," even though the school had been established for the *white* sons of South Carolina.[15] Soon after my arrival at Clemson I would also learn that the University's most iconic building, Tillman Hall, had been named in honor of self-avowed white supremacist Benjamin "Pitchfork Ben" Tillman, whom the University extolled as an influential South Carolina politician and farmers' advocate and who was also a Clemson lifetime trustee. A political research center was named the Strom Thurmond Institute in honor of segregationist and Dixiecrat presidential candidate Strom Thurmond, whom the University recognized for the distinction of being the longest serving US senator and a Clemson alumnus.[16] Indeed, we were encouraged to talk about these illustrious men so long as we didn't connect them to their practices and the legacies of slavery, white supremacy, and segregation in South Carolina, across the nation, and around the world.

A Schedule of Slaves with their names and ages —

No	Name	aged		No	Name	aged	
1	Sawney	aged	59	34	Mary	aged	23
2	Tilla	"	50	35	Delphi	"	8
3	Ned	"	25	36	Sally	"	2
4	Nicholas	"	18	37	Edward	"	4
5	Jonas	"	16	38	Peggy	"	8
6	Jim	"	12	39	Isaac	"	23
7	Matilda	"	10	40	Cloe	"	37
8	Chapman	"	8	41	Orrs	"	20
9	Moses	"	22	42	Katy	"	60
10	Gargar	"	23	43	Kitty	"	21
11	Lucinda	"	5	44	Child	"	2
12	Armstead	"	3	45	Nancy	"	9
13	Binah	"	3	46	Richmond	"	23
14	Tom	"	1	47	Phebe	"	100
15	Cato	"	2	48	Lucy	"	5
16	Baby	"	1	49	Grandison	"	4
17	Daniel	"	37	50	Jackson	"	2
18	Rosanna	"	32				
19	Willis	"	21				
20	Peter	"	12				
21	Dice	"	8				
22	Fany	"	19				
23	Hannah	"	3				
24	Daniel	"	1				
25	Billy	"	35				
26	Jane	"	30				
27	Mack	"	10				
28	Sawney	"	8				
29	Moses	"	6				
30	Suckey	"	4				
31	Pegg	"	2				
32	John	"	1				
33	Caty	"	0				

Recovering the Story of Slavery in Clemson History

During my first semester at Clemson, I joined several professors in the Department of English, including Susanna Ashton, Cameron Bushnell, Angela Naimou, Kimberly Manganelli, and Michael LeMahieu, who sought to examine these men in all their complexities. We included tours of Fort Hill in our literature courses. We requested that the guides provide information about enslaved persons but quickly realized our students were receiving different information about enslaved African Americans from the docents. For example, during a tour for my students, our guide mentioned in passing that an inventory of enslaved persons, included in the deed for the sale of the plantation in 1854 by Floride Calhoun to her son Andrew, was kept in the Clemson Libraries' Special Collections & Archives. Shortly thereafter, I visited the archive and sifted through boxes in the Thomas Green Clemson papers. As I pulled out the folder with the "Deed to Real & Personal Estate," I carefully turned the pages of the deed handwritten on parchment paper for "Mrs. Floride Calhoun & Cornelia M. Calhoun & Andrew P. Calhoun," looking for the names.[17]

The deed for this business transaction included a history, map, and description of the 1,102-acre tract of land that comprised the Fort Hill Plantation. Also, presented in paragraph form, were details about the property being sold, beginning with the enslaved people—who were identified by name—followed by details about the tools, livestock, furniture, and other plantation assets. As my eyes moved to the next page, I saw the schedule for fifty enslaved persons. I ran my finger down the list, softly calling out their names and ages. The youngest was Caty, whose age was listed as zero; the oldest was one-hundred-year-old Phebe. Since she was born about 1754, could Phebe have been brought to the colonies from West Africa on a slave ship? The majority of enslaved people listed were women and children.

I also examined the inventory of enslaved persons that was completed for a valuation of the Fort Hill Plantation on April 26, 1865, about two weeks after the Civil War ended. Andrew P. Calhoun had died on March 16, 1865; and his mother initiated foreclosure proceedings against the Fort Hill estate shortly thereafter because Andrew had not paid the mortgage. The first page enumerated the most valuable property: twelve skilled enslaved laborers—house servants, a cook, gardener, coachman, miller, and blacksmith—worth from $800 to $1,500 each, followed by a list of livestock and buggies worth from $2.50 to $500 each. Enslaved people were still considered the most valuable commodity on the plantation. The inventory also included 127 enslaved field hands, organized as families, some of whom (like Sawney Sr. and his family) had been included in the 1854 deed. Others were from A. P. Calhoun's Cuba Plantation in Alabama.[18] I would soon learn that two enslaved persons, Polydore and Mennemin, who were not listed in either inventory, were owned by John C. and Floride Calhoun and are believed to be first-generation Africans.[19]

Now that I knew their names, I vowed to share them with the world.

I had first experienced the exhilaration of tracing a name thought lost to history in the winter of 2005, as I carefully cradled a slender blue-green bottle in my hands, slowly running my fingers over the inscription, "Mrs. H. E. Wilson—Hair Dressing." A few months earlier, as a graduate research assistant for English professor P. Gabrielle Foreman while completing my PhD at the University of Maryland, I had begun my research for a new edition of Wilson's *Our Nig; or, Sketches from the Life of a Free Black* (1859) by simply typing "Mrs. H. E. Wilson" into Google's search engine. My investigation led me to several bottle collector websites and numerous newspaper articles containing convincing evidence that Wilson had lived much longer and had been more successful than scholars formerly believed. Foreman entrusted me with this secret that would challenge the assumptions that scholars had made about the lives and literature of northern free Blacks in antebellum America until the book was published in 2009.

But my curiosity about African American biography had developed many years before I joined Foreman's research project. I am a family historian, the gatherer and guardian of memories and mementos. I grew up listening to my daddy recount childhood experiences and my paternal grandfather, Benjamin A. Robinson Sr., recite poems he had written or memorized, often around the dinner table. I also heard stories when I visited family members in the South and North—as I watched my daddy patch holes in the magazine-papered walls of the two-room home of my maternal grandmother, Amy Scott Williams, in Aiken, South Carolina; as I played hopscotch with my cousins on

Laflin Street near my Uncle Ben and Auntie Nancy Robinson's apartment building on the South Side of Chicago; and as I cleaned dirt from vats of vegetables—such as collard greens, raw peanuts, and shelled peas—my uncle John R. Harris harvested from his farm in southeast Georgia. I wanted to know the names of the two wives of my maternal grandfather, Robert Lee Williams Sr., (whom he'd outlived before marrying my grandmother) and their eight children—my aunts and uncles and second cousins, who were old enough to be my grandparents and parents, respectively. I was eager to learn more about my relatives in the black-and-white portraits that Othermother, my paternal grandmother Thelma Annette Earle Robinson, kept tucked in the top dresser drawer in the guest bedroom of her home in Columbia, South Carolina.

After my mother's death in 1987, my daddy designated me as the new keeper of the family's photograph and memorabilia collection that dates back into the late nineteenth century. My brothers often tease me, insisting that I imagine family stories to accompany the pictures. In 1999, I coordinated the creation of a quilt to commemorate my family's South Carolina roots for Othermother's ninetieth birthday, a patchwork of photographs of weddings and social events, of hand-embroidered notes and images, and of primary documents like a marriage license. More recently, I have begun to painstakingly piece together my maternal family history in Bamberg County and Aiken County, South Carolina, sifting through public documents, such as census, tax, and property records, to determine how my ancestors came to live in the Palmetto state and why they lingered long in a land that was such an unwelcoming place for people of African descent.

My first opportunity to conduct academic research regarding place and the biographies of Black people arose during a British Literature summer study tour in England in 1997, as I prepared for graduate school. The persistent presence of paintings featuring well-dressed African "servants" in museums and palaces compelled me to discover their stories and better understand their experiences. Three years later, I returned to England, inspired by my Caribbean literature professor's recollections of her research in the United Kingdom's National Archives. After securing funding for a one-week research trip, I was soon leafing through oversized texts, running my fingers along detailed accounts of slave rebellions and punishments in nineteenth-century Jamaica, preserved in elegant script on parchment. I stumbled upon the story of Kitty Hylton, whom editor Thomas Pringle mentions in a footnote in Mary Prince's *History* (1831). Hylton's master, Rev. Mr. G. W. Bridges, savagely struck and kicked her and then ordered her brutally whipped because she had not followed his instructions to cook a turkey by the time he arrived home for dinner.[20] As I documented Hylton's valiant efforts to hold her master accountable for his cruelty by filing a complaint with the local magistrate that slowly made its way to the floor of parliament, I gained a better understanding of how the isolation of the West Indies and distance from the British justice system exacerbated the abuse of enslaved Black women.

My desire to know the identities and stories of enslaved people of African descent peering out of portraits, laboring on Caribbean islands, and peopling my own family tree fueled my curiosity about the enslaved persons who had labored on the Fort Hill Plantation. Within a few months of arriving at Clemson University, I began devoting about half my research time to searching for stories about enslaved African Americans who had lived and labored on Fort Hill. Little did I know that my simple quest to learn more about enslaved people in my university's past would lead to the recovery and calling of the names of more than one thousand African Americans in the history of Clemson prior to desegregation in 1963: enslaved persons, sharecroppers, convict laborers, wage workers, cooperative extension employees, and musicians.

Hush, oh, hush, somebody's calling my name.

Section One

yank, v.
To pull with a sudden vigorous movement;
to jerk or twitch vigorously.

yank, n.2 and adj.
Yankee.

yank, n.1
A sudden vigorous pull, a jerk.

OXFORD ENGLISH DICTIONARY

Call: Of String and Mammy

RHONDDA ROBINSON THOMAS

She slept with a string around her wrist
which ran to the bedside of her mistress.
If Mrs. Clemson wished her for anything
during the night,
she pulled the string awakening Susan. . . .
[My brother's] choicest fruit is packed
with the "Mammy" brand label
in memory of and honoring
our loved and revered
"Mammy, Aunt Susan."
"AUNT SUSAN RICHARDSON," MYRTLE HERLONG, MAY 24, 1958

The myth of the faithful slave lingers because so many white Americans
have wished to live in a world in which African Americans are not angry
over past and present injustices, a world in which white people were
and are not complicit, in which the injustices themselves—of slavery,
Jim Crow, and ongoing structural racism—seem not to exist at all.
The mammy figure affirmed their wishes.
CLINGING TO MAMMY: THE FAITHFUL SLAVE IN TWENTIETH-CENTURY
AMERICA, MICKI MCELYA

Yank.

She felt the pull of a string.

The elderly Black woman recalled the feeling of being suddenly
roused from a restless sleep by a yank on the string tied around her
wrist. Soon she would hear the voice of her mistress Anna Calhoun
Clemson, wife of Thomas Green Clemson and daughter of proslavery
American statesman John C. Calhoun and his wife Floride, direct-

ing her to care for white people's needs but never her own. Like many enslaved persons, Susan Richardson couldn't remember her birth date, but she never forgot she had been enslaved, following the condition of her mother Daphne Calhoun and her father Bill Lawrence, both owned by John C. and Floride Calhoun. Best guess is that Susan was born in the Pendleton District, South Carolina, sometime between 1825 and 1830. In 1838, when Anna Calhoun married Clemson in the parlor of the Calhoun family's Fort Hill plantation house, the young bride received Susan as a wedding gift—a lady's maid—from her parents. During the next decade, Susan cared for the Clemsons' children, John Calhoun and Floride, laboring alongside her mother, the children's wet nurse.

When Thomas Green Clemson purchased the one-thousand-acre Cane Brake Plantation in Saluda, South Carolina, in the Edgefield District in 1843, he and Anna forced Susan and her parents to live and work alongside thirty-seven other enslaved persons they purchased. But when the Clemsons relocated to Belgium from 1844–1851 during Thomas Green Clemson's stint as a US diplomat, they left Susan and her family in South Carolina. After the Clemsons returned to the United States, they sold Cane Brake along with their enslaved persons, including Susan and her parents and siblings. By this time, Susan is believed to have married an enslaved man named Billy Richardson, with whom she had at least six children. Only the name of one son, Tucker Richardson, is currently known. Susan later attended the Red Bank Baptist Church in Saluda, where church records identify her as "Susan Clemson."[1]

After Emancipation, Susan Richardson and her family stayed in the Saluda area, where she and her children were employed by the Herlongs, a prominent and wealthy white family. Her children worked for railroad and sawmill businessman Vastine Jehu "VJ" Herlong, while she labored as "mammy" for three generations of Herlong children: those born to Mrs. Samuel Thomas Edwards, VJ Herlong's mother-in-law; to Edwards's daughter Myra and her husband VJ Herlong; and to Edwards's granddaughter, Mrs. Ernest Mathis. At some point in her post–Civil War quasi-free life, Susan Richardson shared some of her experiences in slavery with VJ and Myra Herlong's daughter Myrtle, one of the children she'd help raise. Myrtle recalled,

I wish I could remember more of what she told me. She went bathing in a creek or branch when a young girl living near Clemson. She told me that later she slept in a small room adjoining that of her mistress. She slept with a string around her wrist which ran to the bedside of her mistress. If Mrs. Clemson wished her for anything during the night, she pulled the string awakening Susan. She remembered so well Mr. Calhoun would come down to see his much loved daughter.[2]

Susan Richardson's memories of slavery reflect extremes of pleasure and pain. The creek that Susan likely bathed in was called Sawney's Branch (named in honor of Sawney Calhoun Sr., John C. Calhoun's favorite enslaved person), which may have provided a simple enjoyment and an escape from labor on the heavily wooded and secluded Fort Hill estate. The recollection of John C. Calhoun's effusive affection for his beloved daughter Anna, who worked for him in Washington, DC, as a copyist prior to her marriage to Thomas Green Clemson, marks the absence of observations about Calhoun's interactions with his wife Floride or his other children, as well as Susan Richardson's interactions with her father, Bill Lawrence. Yet Susan Richardson's clearest memory of her experience as an enslaved young woman is an act by her mistress that dehumanized her to the level of a mule compelled to obey at the yank of a string rather than the calling of her name. Susan Richardson was treated like a mule a century before Nanny would lament in Zora Neale Hurston's *Their Eyes Were Watching God*, "De nigger woman is de mule uh de world so fur as Ah can see."[3]

Yank.

Myrtle Herlong's brother, Albert Sydney Herlong, later established A. S. Herlong & Company, a fruit-packing enterprise in Leesburg, Florida. He eventually created a "Mammy" brand orange in honor of the woman whom the Herlong siblings and cousins characterized as their "loved and revered 'Mammy, Aunt Susan,'" who—according to Myrtle Herlong—had been an "inspiration" to them.[4]

However, the dark-skinned, heavyset, thick-lipped, wide-grinning Mammy figure featured in the advertisements designed for Herlong's

An advertisement for Mammy fruit distributed by A. S. Herlong & Company in Leesburg, Florida. The fruit was named in honor and memory of the Herlong children's caregiver Susan Calhoun Clemson Richardson, whom they called "Mammy, Aunt Susan," date unknown.

choice fruit bears little resemblance to the descriptions of "Aunt Susan" that Myrtle Herlong provides in her recollections. She notes that "Susan was part Negro, part Indian as was easily discernable from the color of her skin and the texture and straightness of her hair.... She was always immaculately clean, and my mother always saw that she was well-dressed."[5]

Myrtle Herlong also asserts that Susan and her husband, Billy Richardson, "reared a family of six or seven children, all of whom were good, respectable Negroes."[6] Her comments reflect the skin tone, hair texture, and respectability politics that continued to haunt post-

Susan Richardson holding Byron Herlong, ca. 1895.
Courtesy of Department of Historic Properties, Clemson University.

Reconstruction Black Americans both from without and within their communities. By the turn of the twentieth century, Booker T. Washington had begun advocating the virtues of cleanliness and the dignity of vocation work for African Americans.[7]

The Mammy caricatures featured in the Herlong fruit company advertisements are rooted in images associated with the plantation era that "Aunt Susan" had come to represent: loyal Black women who devotedly cared for white people while neglecting their own and their families' needs. She epitomized the Mammy whom Micki McElya argues white folks would cling to in the twentieth century, Black women who were "not angry over past or present injustices" and were unable to see and understand their employers' complicity in "Jim Crow, and ongoing racial injustice."[8] Indeed, the Mammy figure on the Herlong fruit advertisement holds a half-peeled orange in her hand, suggesting that she may be prepping the food to feed a white child or to serve at a meal to a white family. The advertisement becomes a form of enslavement, remanding Susan to her role as a contented enslaved lady's maid to Anna Calhoun Clemson, waiting to be summoned to work during the night with the *yank* of a string. Conjuring up nostalgia for the romanticized plantation era, the Mammy figure became an effective marketing tool for a variety of domestic products ranging from pancake mix to laundry detergent. During the early twentieth century, A. S. Herlong & Company, one of the most profitable fruit-packing companies in America, sought to increase sales by utilizing a highly proven promotional strategy. Did the Herlong children "honor" their "Aunt Susan" with a portion of the profits from these choice fruits?

I suggest that Susan Richardson functioned as a type of magical Mammy in Myrtle Herlong's imagination. She toiled for more than a decade as an enslaved caregiver for the Calhoun and Clemson families during the antebellum period. She worked as a devoted mammy for three generations of white Herlong children during the post–Civil War era. She served as a conscientious mother, who reared her own children as "good, respectable Negroes" to earn the seal of approval of her "white folks" and employment in a wealthy white family's railroad business.[9] When she grew old and could no longer labor as a live-in caretaker for white children, Myrtle Herlong claims Susan Richardson could not imagine herself in any other role. However, it appears that Myrtle Herlong could envision her faithful Mammy only in the lead supporting role of a southern white woman's plantation fantasy in post-Emancipation America. She reported that one of Susan Richardson's sons, a contractor, had invited his mother to live with him when she became infirm, but she refused: "Having lived in the houses of her 'white folks' for so much of her life she would not live in the house of her own son."[10] Instead, Susan Richardson preferred living by herself in the house her son built for her next to his own. She lived there alone until her death around 1910. She was buried in Aiken, though her exact gravesite is still unknown.

Perhaps Susan Calhoun Clemson Richardson enjoyed living and sleeping alone in her own home free of enslavers, children, and string.

Yank.

Response: Black Lives Have Always Mattered

MICHAEL LEMAHIEU

Yank.

A string is pulled.

"The exercises were opened with 'Maryland, My Maryland' by the Clemson Band, which was fine." So wrote Frances K. Ligon, of Anderson, South Carolina, in her diary in January 1902. "After the exercises in the courthouse were over we went out to see the monument unveiled. Miss Nora Hubbard did this." That would be one Lenora Connors Hubbard, a schoolteacher and member of the Anderson Ladies' Memorial Association, who worked for over a decade to fund the monument. "She was the one of every person living who should have done it," wrote Hubbard's friend Ligon, "for she did more towards getting the monument than anybody else."[1]

We have no diary from Susan Richardson. There is no monument to her.

How, Saidiya Hartman asks, does one "tell the stories of those who had left no record of their lives and whose biography consisted of the terrible things said about them or done to them"?[2]

"What," Natasha Trethewey asks of Black soldiers who fought in the Civil War, "is monument to their legacy?"[3]

Yank.

The string breaks.

"Col. Hoyt made a short address before the string was pulled. Unfortunately, when Miss Nora pulled the string it broke."[4] For a minute or two longer, the monument remains covered—as if there is still a chance, as if it might never be unveiled.

Yank.

The veil is removed.

"But a man climbed up on top of it and pulled it down. Immediately afterwards the Clemson Band played the taps and then the crowd moved away. I enjoyed the Band especially and I think everybody else did too. Altogether the day was a *big* success and one never to be forgotten by a patriotic Andersonian."[5]

The white supremacy enshrined in these Confederate monuments, it bears emphasizing, was not a fringe element of Jim Crow society. It was a state-sanctioned and publicly celebrated element of the Southern political establishment. In a speech on the floor of the US Senate in 1900, former South Carolina governor and original Clemson University trustee Benjamin Tillman proposed to "justify"—his word—"the necessity for stuffing ballot boxes, for shooting negroes, and for using violence and fraud in taking charge of our State government in South Carolina."[6] In South Carolina, Tillman proudly boasted, white supremacy trumps representative democracy.

Fewer than two years after Senator Tillman's remarks, when the Confederate monument was unveiled in front of the Anderson County Courthouse—an easy morning's drive to Tillman's native Edgefield County or to Clemson College—its meaning would have been clear. In theory the monument commemorates the dead; in practice it enjoins the living to continue the fight.

Engraved on the plinth on the south side of the monument are lines written by Father Abram J. Ryan, one of a handful of claimants to the title Poet Laureate of the Confederacy:

The world shall yet decide,
    In truth's clear, far-off light,
That the soldiers who wore the gray, and died
    With Lee, were in the right.[7]

To Frances Ligon, such lines testify to the commitment of Anderson's "patriotic" citizens to never forget. To Susan Richardson, in the last years of her life, and to all African American citizens in the South, such courthouse monuments send an altogether different message: do not come here seeking justice.

By 1902, when the monument was unveiled, Susan Richardson had long left the Pendleton District, which was divided into three counties, namely Anderson, Oconee, and Pickens. Pickens county was the site of Clemson University, which was built on John C. Calhoun's and then his son-in-law Thomas Green Clemson's Fort Hill Plantation. That Susan Richardson was emancipated off that plantation—never again to be tied to her mistress, never again to be yanked awake in the middle of the night—is a fact the Anderson County Confederate Monument laments.

As Frances Ligon notes in her diary, the unveiling of the monument began with the Clemson College band performing "Maryland, My Maryland." The song sets the words of an 1861 poem of the same title to the tune of "O, Tannenbaum." The poem was written by one James Ryder Randall, a native Marylander and Confederate sympathizer, who grew furious at the sight of Union troops marching through Baltimore on their way to the nation's capital:

Avenge the patriotic gore
That flecked the streets of Baltimore,
And be the battle queen of yore,
Maryland! my Maryland![8]

Edmund Wilson's monumental book, *Patriotic Gore: Studies in the Literature of the American Civil War,* takes its title from the song.

"Maryland, My Maryland" was adopted by its namesake as the official state song in 1939, and in the last eighty years there have been multiple efforts to undo that decision. The song refers to President Lincoln as "the despot" and "the tyrant." It roundly denounces "Northern scum."[9]

It was a song known well by Susan Richardson's mistresses.

In late 1861 or early 1862, Clemson family friend and noted American sculptor Henry Kirke Brown visited Anna Calhoun Clemson and her twenty-year-old daughter Floride while they were staying at the Clemson estate in Bladensburg, Maryland. Writing to his wife on January 12, 1862, Brown confessed discomfort in speaking to the two women about current events: "I was pained to hear them talk about the question of the day; there seemed rather more vehemence than delicacy in some of their remarks."[10] It's odd that Brown was surprised to hear vehemence about "the question of the day" in the remarks of the daughter and granddaughter of the man who declared in 1837, on the floor of the US Senate, that chattel slavery was "instead of an evil, a good—a positive good."[11]

Brown tried his best to be polite, but he couldn't stand it.

I allowed myself to drift into sympathy with [Floride] when she sang, "Maryland My Maryland" till I was almost appalled at the monstrous gulf which lay between us on this subject, which is testing the foundation of our national existence. . . . All she can see in this struggle is a desire to crush the South without cause. She thinks nobody at the North has any other plan save the abolitionists, whom she suspects more than any political party. . . . Neither herself or her mother will read anything but on their side.[12]

Floride wouldn't have had much patience for abolitionists, or "blind fanatics," as her grandfather called them.[13]

One of Henry Kirke Brown's most famous works is the bronze statue of Abraham Lincoln in New York City's Union Square, which was dedicated in 1870.

Another of his significant works is the bronze statue of Philip Kearny, New Jersey–born Civil War major general, which was installed in the US Capitol's Statuary Hall at the behest of the New Jersey legislature in 1880.

"Maryland, My Maryland" was a proslavery anthem sung by Susan's owners.

Yank.

James Ryder Randall wrote "Maryland, My Maryland" in Augusta, Georgia, his adopted home, where he was buried after he died in 1908 and where he is honored on the Four Southern Poets Monument. Another of the four is Father Abram Ryan.

Augusta is a mere twenty miles away from Aiken, South Carolina, where Susan Richardson died some two years later, around 1910. We do not know the location of Susan's grave.

Consider the lives we can connect through a song. From James Ryder Randall, who wrote it, to Father Abram Ryan, with whom he's honored. From Floride Clemson, who sang it, to her mother Anna Calhoun Clemson, who pulled that string. From John C. Calhoun to Thomas Green Clemson to Benjamin Tillman, for whom buildings, streets, universities, and towns are named. From even Frances Ligon and Lenora Hubbard, who enjoyed hearing the Clemson College band play it, four decades after Floride Clemson sang it.

One thread overlaps with another uncovering an interwoven tapestry of Confederate sympathy and memory—plantation houses, monuments, and Confederate flags.

Yank.

One need not pull too hard on any one of those threads to discover what binds them together.

Yank.

For Susan Richardson, those houses, monuments, and flags functioned as symbols of enslavement, oppression, and violence. They continue to function that way.

"If slavery persists as an issue in the political life of black America," Hartman writes, "it is not because of an antiquarian obsession with bygone days or the burden of a too-long memory, but because black lives are still imperiled and devalued by a racial calculus and a political arithmetic that were entrenched centuries ago."[14]

And if we call Susan Richardson's name, neither is it "because of an antiquarian obsession with bygone days." It is certainly not because of "the burden of a too-long memory."

Call My Name seeks to call those names and recall those lives that have been largely forgotten. At times that work is a matter of looking for different people in different places. At others it is a matter of looking differently in the usual places. The letter from Henry Kirke Brown to his wife is not in a private collection; it is in the Library of Congress. And, at still other times, it is a matter of grappling with Hartman's question of how to "tell the stories of those who . . . left no record of their lives": how to tell a story when one doesn't even know the dates of birth and death, when all one has is a name and recollections filtered through the memory of a woman who can only see a mammy-mother?

And it is, above all, a matter of thinking the experience of Black lives valuable enough to be sought out, recovered, and reflected upon. It's a matter of taking the time and the care to ask who is on the other end of the string.

Yank.

CHAPTER 1

The Calling

I Will Testify

◇◇◇

nobody mentioned slaves
and yet the curious tools
shine with your fingerprints.
nobody mentioned slaves
 but somebody did this work
who had no guide, no stone,
who moulders under rock.

tell me your names,
tell me your bashful names
and i will testify.
"At the cemetery, walnut grove plantation, south carolina, 1989"
LUCILLE CLIFTON[1]

. . . do hereby bargain, sell and in plain and open market deliver unto said
Andrew P. Calhoun the following Slaves fifty in number [viz.] Old Sawney,
Tilla, Ned, Nicholas, Jonas, Jim, Matilda, Chapman, Moses, Jargar,
Lucinda, Armstead, Binah, Tom, Cato, Baby, Daniel, Rosanna, Willis, Peter,
Dice, Fanny, Hannah, Daniel, Billy, Jane, Mack, Sawney Jr., Moses, Sucky,
Peggy, John, Caty, Mary, Delphin, Sally, Edward, Peggy, Isaac, Cloe, Orr,
Katy, Kitty & child, Nancy, Richmond, Phebe, Lucy, Grandison, Jackson.
Their ages and description more particularly set forth in a schedule here-
unto annexed.

Also all the plantation tools and implements, Stock of Horses & Mules &
Cattle, Cow provisions & provender, Household and Kitchen furniture . . .
DEED FOR THE SALE OF THE FORT HILL PLANTATION BY FLORIDE
CALHOUN AND CORNELIA M. CALHOUN TO ANDREW P. CALHOUN,
MAY 15, 1854

10565 | Wade Foster | Laborer | 13 | Male | Colored | S.C. | 5.8 3/4
Central Correctional Institution (S.C.), Central Register of Prisoners,
June 7, 1883–June 6, 1892. Prisoners 6146—10927

THE CLERK at the front desk of the Pendleton District Commission was my last hope.

"Can you recommend a text by a local African American writer?" I asked as I turned to leave the building.

"Have you considered *A Nickel and a Prayer*?" she responded.

Shortly after relocating to Upstate South Carolina in late summer 2007, I attempted to acclimate myself to my new academic community by investigating the history and culture of African Americans in the cities and towns surrounding Clemson University, namely Clemson, Central, Pendleton, and Seneca. For several days, I had been searching for a book by a local author that I could teach in my African American literature course during my first semester at the university. While sifting through the *Black Heritage in the Upper Piedmont of South Carolina Project* collection records tucked in manila folders in a metal file cabinet in the Pendleton District Commission office, I came across transcripts of interviews with local African American residents and newspaper clippings about community events. I also found oral histories recorded on cassette tapes that were stuffed in a box on the counter. I skimmed the catalog of recordings but did not find anything appropriate for my class that fall.

The desk clerk had suggested the autobiography of Pendleton-born African American social activist Jane Edna Harris Hunter. I knew nothing about Hunter or her life narrative. I soon learned the text was out of print, but two copies were listed in the catalog of Clemson University's Robert Muldrow Cooper Library. One was "missing." The other was available in Special Collections, but the book was so frail the archivists wouldn't allow me to see it. Instead, they scanned a copy of the text for my students. I purchased online a used, autographed copy for myself for about twenty-five dollars.

Hunter, the daughter of formerly enslaved parents, was born in 1882 on Woodburn Farm, a historic plantation located on Clemson University land. She grew up in Pendleton, attending school and working at Clemson as a chambermaid in a hotel located on campus and babysitter for a professor's children. After she completed high school at Ferguson and Williams Academy, a boarding school for African American students in Abbeville, South Carolina, her mother forced her to marry Edward Hunter, a man thirty years her senior. Before her first wedding anniversary, Jane Hunter permanently left her husband. During the next few years, she completed coursework at the Cannon Street Hospital and Training Institute for Nurses in Charleston, South Carolina, and the Training School for Nurses at Hampton, Virginia. Seeking a new adventure, she migrated with friends to Cleveland, Ohio, where she founded the Phillis Wheatley Association in 1911. In her autobiography *A Nickel and a Prayer*, Hunter includes additional details about her family's connections to Clemson: her mother Harriet had worked as laundress for professors and a cook for the Calhouns; her father Edward had been employed as a hod carrier (construction worker) for the crew who erected the university's earliest buildings.[2] Soon I was spearheading a Creative Inquiry (CI) project, *Discovery and Recovery: Preserving the Literary Heritage of Black South Carolinians*, to offer undergraduate students opportunities to conduct research for a variety of projects, including scholarly editions of out-of-print books, theatrical productions, oral history interviews, and photography exhibits.[3]

My first twelve-member CI undergraduate team completed research for an edited and annotated edition of *A Nickel and a Prayer*. Our work included analyzing scholarship, writing travel grants, preparing a book proposal that was accepted for the Regenerations: African American Literature and Culture series at the West Virginia University Press, conducting archival research in Cleveland, Pendleton, and Charleston, visiting historical sites, and writing text for the new edition. Our success compelled me to create a second project, *African Americans and Clemson University: Land, Literature, and Legacy*, a one and one-half year collaboration with Clemson geographer Lance Howard and historian Abel Bartley that I hoped to begin in the fall of 2008. I planned to mentor a CI team who would conduct research for biographies of African Americans at Fort Hill. I soon learned that many other Clemson employees and local residents had initiated similar endeavors with mixed success. Due to the challenges of recovering documentary evidence to piece together these life stories, my own efforts faced the same ebb and flow that often characterizes efforts to investigate the history of African Americans.

During those early months of my initial research efforts, the Hunter family's connections to the university stoked my interest in exploring the relationship between Clemson and the local African American community—just as the Clemson Area African American Museum (CAAAM) was initiating plans for opening a new facility. The museum was to be located in the building that once housed the segregated Calhoun Elementary School for African American children. After the Civil War, many freed men, freed women, and children, who had labored on the Fort Hill Plantation, settled nearby in an area that was incorporated as the town of Calhoun in 1892 and renamed Clemson in 1943. Other African Americans migrated to Upstate South Carolina to work at Clemson College. They established neighborhoods, schools, churches, businesses, and social venues in their segregated communities. In 2001, when then Clemson mayor Larry Abernathy initiated a plan for the city to purchase the building that would include a room to display local African American history, Black Clemson residents explored ways they could document and present their stories.

I soon joined the meetings and discovered more about the rich African American history of the local community and its interconnectivity to the development of Clemson University. At that time, few opportunities were available for Clemson faculty and staff to collaborate with community members to create a public narrative reflective of our shared history. By the end of my second year at Clemson, however, my work with the museum trustees ended abruptly after my department chair, concerned about the amount of time I was devoting to the launch of the new museum, requested that I resign from the planning committee and focus on fulfilling tenure requirements. The planning committee continued working, opening the CAAAM in 2010 with an exhibit that explored the development of twenty-one African American churches in communities in and around the city of Clemson.

While working with the CAAAM planning team, I learned about the Pendleton Foundation for Black History and Culture (PFBHC), a local organization that has been documenting the African American experience in their community for more than thirty years. When Clemson University was founded in 1889, Pendleton was the nearest town to the higher education institution. In 2003, graduate students from the Clemson School of Architecture's Studio South had collaborated with the PFBHC to revitalize Keese Barn, which had served as a community store-diner-antique shop and gathering spot for African Americans in the late nineteenth and early twentieth centuries. The PFBHC had purchased the structure in 1980 six years after its owner, Ben Keese, died. The goal of the project was to reconstruct a community space for all Pendleton residents that would also commemorate southern African American culture of the early 1900s and include a "Memorial

Block" made of materials from the original Keese Barn. "Both architecture students and the people of Pendleton are able to offer their knowledge and learn from each other in this joint effort to better a community—a true collaboration," explained Maggie Wilkins in "Architecture Project to Revitalize African-American Landmark."[4] After the architectural team discovered that the building was not structurally sound, however, the only portion of the project that came to fruition was a modernist type of "Memorial Block" that includes materials from the original building but does not reflect African American cultural traditions. The design for the memorial sorely disappointed many members of Pendleton's Black community.

Twelve years later, another African American community institution, the Bertha Lee Strickland Cultural Museum (BLSCM) in Seneca, South Carolina, was established to document and display the rich history of African Americans in nearby Oconee County. The town of Clemson was once a part of Seneca and Oconee counties, and many of Clemson's African American employees have lived and still reside there. The museum features exhibitions about local history such as *Places in Time*, which examined three of Oconee County's oldest African American landmarks, and national history such as *Colored Soldiers*, which highlighted the role of African Americans in the military from the Revolutionary War to the present.[5]

While community leaders sought innovative strategies to preserve and share the region's rich African American heritage, several Clemson professors initiated projects to increase understanding of the university's public history. In 2006, Clemson English professor Susanna Ashton published an essay in *College English* in which she critiqued the institution's lack of engagement with the history of Calhoun's Fort Hill Plantation in the establishment of the university. In "Texts of Our Institutional Lives: Don't You Mean 'Slaves,' Not 'Servants'?: Literary and Institutional Texts for an Interdisciplinary Classroom," Ashton asserts, "Our university sits on what was a huge plantation property and was founded, indeed, upon the spoils of forced labor. Few students, faculty, staff, or members of the community at large have any idea of this fact, despite the fact that in the very center of our campus is Fort Hill—the home built by John C. Calhoun's slaves."[6] Like Clifton, they were intrigued with the history of a place where "nobody mentioned slaves," the people who had built the plantation house, who had served its white occupants, and who had received no acknowledgment of their labor.[7]

Ashton offered an analysis of the university's official history that focused exclusively on the Calhouns and Clemsons through her "Representations of Slavery" interdisciplinary seminar for Calhoun Honors College students.

After studying the history of slavery and nineteenth-century American culture, Ashton and her students examined the Fort Hill plantation house as a text, utilizing Jennifer L. Eichstedt and Stephen Small's *Representations of Slavery: Race and Ideology in Southern Plantation Museums* as a guide for evaluating how the history of slavery was presented on the site and in the tour. At the end of the course, Ashton's students offered recommendations on how Clemson could improve visitors' experiences at Fort Hill. They suggested "making more brochures Web-accessible, including African American tour guides, reprinting the one brochure that deals with the slave presence and that is currently out of print, and devoting more tour time simply to recounting the ways in which a plantation was worked."[8] The students also proposed providing a map of the plantation, emphasizing the humanity of enslaved persons, creating an integrated narrative about enslaved people and their owners that includes the names of more enslaved persons, providing printed brochures and copies of primary documents, and erecting commemorative markers where granite stones from the Fort Hill slave quarters were repurposed as foundation stones for campus buildings. Ashton shared the students' suggestions with Clemson's administrators.[9]

By the time I arrived on campus one year later, none of the recommendations had been implemented. However, in 2011, Clemson approved the installation of a South Carolina National Heritage Corridor marker that features the following inscription: "Documenting the African-American experience at Fort Hill is an ongoing research project of the Department of Historic Properties at Clemson University."[10] The final inscription for the signage, approved by the South Carolina National Heritage Corridor, included few details about enslaved African Americans who had labored on the Fort Hill Plantation, however, and did not identify any of them by name. It also failed to mention the Black sharecroppers, domestics, and others who had labored on the plantation after the Civil War ended.

As I continued searching for the records of enslaved people who worked on the Calhouns' Fort Hill Plantation, I stumbled across four "Articles of Agreement between Thos. Green Clemson, of the one part, & the undersigned freed men & women of the other part" in Clemson's Special Collections & Archives.[11] I felt as though I was working backward chronologically, from the end of Reconstruction toward the antebellum period. I had wondered if anyone labored on Fort Hill after the Civil War ended. In "African American Status and Identity in a Postbellum Community: An Analysis of the Manuscript Census Returns," Clemson University history professor Orville Vernon Burton asserts that, after the Civil War, "[t]he goal of the white community was cheap labor dependent on landowners for jobs. The crucial issue was control: who would control the labor, the laborer or the landowner."[12] Thomas Green Clemson sought to maintain control of the Fort Hill Plantation, which, after her brother Andrew's death in 1865, now belonged to his wife Anna Calhoun Clemson, John C. Calhoun's daughter. Like the freed men and women who were emancipated throughout other parts of the South, those who lived in the South Carolina Upstate preferred owning land or engaging in tenant farming rather than sharecropping. Nevertheless, Thomas Clemson, like many other "[p]lantation owners, preferring to re-enslave the African American workers, were willing to seek a more attainable option: agreeing to pay wages or a share of the crop for labor."[13] Between 1867 and 1874, at least forty-four formerly enslaved persons made X marks as their signatures between their first and last names on at least four Articles of Agreement with Thomas Green Clemson and his agent. In so doing, they locked themselves into a labor system that offered housing on Fort Hill (likely the former quarters for enslaved persons) and a share of and payment for the crops they planted and harvested. All but four of the laborers were men. Five signed at least two of the annual agreements. Additionally, sixteen unnamed children, identified as boys or "half-hands," were listed alongside the adult laborers.[14]

As I examined the Articles of Agreement, it became increasingly clear that sharecropping for the freed men and women contracted to work on the Fort Hill Plantation mimicked slavery. In Thomas Clemson's post–Civil War plantation system, laborers were called to work from sunrise to sunset by the sound of the horn and were assigned the same tasks previously expected of the enslaved workforce. For every two days lost by absence or by refusal or neglect of a daily task or labor, workers forfeited fifty cents of their wages. They were required to care for all tools and pay for any that were damaged. They received as pay a one-third share of crops and five of every one hundred bushels of grain they harvested but were forbidden from selling any agricultural products. They could not leave the property without Thomas Clemson's permission. In return, Clemson and his agent promised

in which shall be entered all advances made
by him, and fines & forfeitures for lost time or
any cause, which book shall be received as
evidence in same manner as Merchants books
are now received in courts of Justice, and shall
have a right to deduct from the share of each laborer all his, or her fines, or forfeitures, also all
advances made to them subject to the decisions
of the authorities having jurisdiction of the same.

XVII.   It is understood that each company shall care for
and attend to the stock they work and if not fed
punctually at the time designated (Sundays not excep
ted) the company so offending shall forfeit the sum
of fifty cents for each offence to be deducted from
the share of the crop coming to said company.

January 5th 1874

William X Johnson
his
mark

John X Harkill
His
mark

Moses X Sherman
His
mark

Frank X Vance
His
mark

Pinckney X Cunningham
His
mark

David X English
His
mark

James X Jackson
X
mark

Nicolas X Jackson
his
mark

Samuel X Dangerfield
his
mark

Witness

John C. Harris

The final page of the labor contract between Thomas G. Clemson and freed men and women who affixed X marks for their signatures indicating their agreement to work as sharecroppers on the Fort Hill Plantation during that year, 1874. Courtesy of Clemson University Libraries' Special Collections & Archives.

to treat the contract workers with "justice and kindness." In case of dis-
agreements between Clemson and the freed men and women, however, the
agent's daily log was the only evidence accepted by legal authorities.[15]

The story of African American sharecroppers on the Fort Hill Plantation
is perhaps the most neglected history about African Americans at Clemson
University. Not only are they not mentioned in campus tours, but details
about their lives and labors are omitted from the early chapters of the first
volume of the latest version of the institution's official history, recently
retired Clemson university historian Jerome Reel's *The High Seminary: A
History of the Clemson Agricultural College of South Carolina, 1889–1964*, which
locates the genesis of Clemson history in the Cherokee era prior to the
American Revolution. In the spring of 2016, the University finally erected a
South Carolina historical marker for the Seneca River Basin, the last sliver
of undeveloped land on campus, which was once the site of the Cherokee
town of Isunigu and the fields where three groups of African Americans—
enslaved persons, sharecroppers, and convict laborers—once toiled, individuals whose labor was essential for the establishment of the university.
Yet the sharecroppers were not acknowledged on the marker for this historic site. Instead, recognition of their labor is included on one of the new
Clemson University historical markers that was installed near the plantation house in the center of campus in 2018.

Little did I understand how central Black labor was to the development
of Clemson University even after Reconstruction ended. During my first
semester at the university, I was told that an African American convict
crew had helped to build Clemson in the late 1800s. But it appeared nobody
had searched hard and long enough to find records about them. Clemson's
archives include details about the labor and related expenses for the state
convicts its trustees leased in to help build their college. This information is
tucked away in the institution's earliest records, mostly the trustees' business correspondence, meeting minutes, accounting ledgers, and annual
reports to the penitentiary and the "SC General" Assembly. But the names
of the laborers who had been forced to clear the land, build a dike, plant
and harvest crops, make millions of red bricks, and erect buildings and
houses for a land-grant college for white males in Upstate South Carolina
were unknown. The circumstances that led to their arrests, convictions, and
assignments to the Clemson convict labor crew in the late nineteenth and
early twentieth centuries were unspecified.

For nearly three years, I searched for some trace of the convicts who built Clemson. I had written the South Carolina Department of Corrections (SCDC), hoping they had established an archive or knew what had happened to the documents. I soon learned the SCDC did not keep historical criminal records. I also scoured Clemson trustees' earliest annual reports and correspondence. But their notes focused on facts: how many convicts they leased, how much money they spent for the convicts' care, how many structures the convicts built. But no names or ages. Just references that reflected the fact that these South Carolina convicts had been subjected to involuntary servitude, permissible by the Thirteenth Amendment because they had been convicted of crimes.[16] Clemson archivists initially directed me to Reel's *The High Seminary*, where he mentions convict laborers about twenty times in the chapter that relates the university's founding.[17] But I needed to know their names, to discover the circumstances that led them to be subjected to post-Reconstruction slavery. Each man was somebody's son, brother, husband, uncle, or neighbor. After listening to stories about the challenges the men in my family had faced growing up during the Jim Crow era in South Carolina, I had no doubt that life for these men had become even more difficult after they were classified as convicts.

Just as I was about to give up my search, a Clemson archivist suggested that I contact the South Carolina Department of Archives and History (SCDAH). After learning I could make a query via email, I sent a request on October 8, 2013, asking for information regarding convicts contracted to Clemson between 1890 and 1899, the date of the last petition for convicts, submitted to the state legislature by Clemson trustees, that I had discovered thus far. The next morning, I received a response from SCDAH archivist Marion C. Chandler:

The South Carolina Department of Archives and History does have the list of prisoners contracted out to Clemson College between 1893 and 1899. The lists include the prisoners name, prison number, date sent to Clemson, what happened to him (discharged from Clemson, returned to Columbia, send to Rock Hill [Winthrop?] or died). The most important item on this list is the prisoner's number. With the prisoner's number you will have easy access to the record of the prisoner. The Central Registers of prisoners are arranged by prisoner number and they give a great deal of information about each prisoner. That information includes age, race, occupation, physical description, where born, crime, where and when convicted.[18]

A few days later, I carefully opened the large white mailing envelope from the SCDAH and pulled out copies of pages filled with prison numbers, names, and notes neatly penned in elegant script about convicts who had been assigned to work at Clemson during the last decade of the nineteenth century. I whispered the first name and notes on the list, "9828, Carolina Richardson, Escaped Jul 13/90." Some had resisted. Halfway down the page, "9377, Pink Floyd." I smiled at the name that would later be linked with a popular English rock band. While scanning that page of the register listing the first thirty-six convicts assigned to Clemson in May and June 1890, I formulated questions. I noted eight had escaped—from the worksite or from the penitentiary? Seven were returned—to the penitentiary or somewhere else? Eight were discharged—from Clemson or from the penitentiary? Most names had no notations—why not? Did they work at Clemson or not? I soon learned that the majority of the public records regarding convict labor and the building of Clemson University had been sitting in the state archive and county courthouses for more than a century.

I slipped down to my colleague Angela Naimou's office, located on the same floor of Strode Tower. "I found them," I whispered, holding out the registers of convicts for her to see.

About ten days later, I drove two hours from Clemson to the SCDAH in Columbia to examine the registers of convicts and the descriptive rolls that contained demographic and court details about them. I quickly realized the archivist had underestimated the number of convicts who were assigned to the Clemson College work detail. As I turned the pages of the registers, I discovered the state penitentiary had assigned convicts to the college through 1915, not 1899. The total number was nearly seven hundred, far more than the fifty I had expected to find. I also learned that the penitentiary operated large farms where hundreds of convicts were forced to work like enslaved field hands, planting and harvesting crops for the state.

Locating the lists of convict registers was the easiest part of the process of recovering their penitentiary records. The registers were organized by the year the convicts were assigned to Clemson; the court records were organized by county. Although the state archive housed most of the court records, some counties had kept their records. Other records had been destroyed by fires, were lost, or were missing. I started by recording details about convicts from some of the counties closest to Clemson, namely Anderson, Greenville, Oconee, Pickens, and Spartanburg. Using the prison number for each person listed in the register, I searched the descriptive rolls recorded in oversized brown ledgers that included demographic details, sentencing information, release/parole/pardon dates, escape/recapture notes, and descriptions of distinct body features such as burn scars, missing teeth, or large moles. Some scholars I had consulted suggested that many of the Black men would have been arrested for loitering, simply minding their own business while standing on a street corner or walking down a road. But most of the convicts assigned to Clemson's work details were convicted of some form of larceny, often of stealing food, clothes, or livestock. A few were white. Most were under the age of twenty-five.

But one was a teenager.

Wade Foster's name appeared on the seventh page of the registers for convicts assigned to Clemson College on August 1, 1891. Notes indicate he was released from the work detail on January 4, 1892. I found him in the descriptive roll using his prison number, 10565. As I ran my finger across the page, I added his occupation, laborer, to my Excel sheet. Then I moved to the next column for age, stopped, and stared at the finely penned number. I whipped out my iPhone, snapped a picture of the page, and then swiped my fingers across the screen to enlarge the image: 13.

Wade Foster was a thirteen-year-old, black-haired, black-eyed, black skinned, four foot, eight-and-three-quarters-inch boy when he was committed to the state penitentiary. He'd been sentenced to six months at hard labor after being convicted of housebreaking in the daytime in Spartanburg, South Carolina—stealing six dollars' worth (about $173 in 2019 currency) of boy's clothing, a toy drum, and a pillowcase from his neighbor's home. *Thirteen.* Like the Thirteenth Amendment that made his incarceration possible through its provision for involuntary servitude "as a punishment for crime whereof the party shall have been duly convicted."[19] *Thirteenth.* Like the documentary produced by Ana DuVernay that locates the roots of mass incarceration in Wade Foster's lifetime. A thirteen-year-old boy from my hometown had helped build the university that hired me to teach early African American literature. About two years earlier when I had asked Clemson University's then president, James Barker, to authorize a new study of the institution's history, he had refused but encouraged me to pursue my

The section of South Carolina's Central Register of Prisoners where the name of thirteen-year-old Wade Foster, one of the convicts leased by Clemson trustees, was inscribed, 1891. Photo by the author.

research interests. How would I break the news of this unexpected discovery to the Clemson community and the public?

On April 17, 2014, the *Greenville News* published a front-page feature story titled "Research Honors the Lives of Convicts Who Built Clemson" about the labor of Wade Foster and other members of the predominately African American state convict crew leased by Clemson Trustees, which at the time had included Governor "Pitchfork Ben" Tillman. The story began, "He was 13." [20] My research inquiry had become a public history project.

My department chair informed the university's public affairs office about the story shortly before its release. I shared news of the article's publication with a group of friends at Clemson, including Leon Wiles, then Chief Diversity Officer. Wiles described my work as "interesting research . . . Sheds new light on the history of Clemson College and Ben Tillman. The real history of Clemson needs to be shared with Clemson students and faculty. Perhaps this year's [retrospective] on slavery and the academy will bring this information to light for the campus community."[21]

I responded,

> I believe it's time the university initiates this conversation. I've been at Clemson nearly seven years and the conversation seems no more important to the institution today than it did when I arrived. I am hopeful that the article, my research, as well as the *Race and the University* initiative that the College of AAH is sponsoring during the coming year will enable the University community to openly discuss this real history. It's the only path to wholeness.[22]

Clemson employees, local residents, members of my church, and strangers clipped the article from the newspaper and mailed or brought it to me. Only one anonymous detractor mailed me a typo-laden typed letter asserting that I should be devoting my energies to assisting young Black men who spoke Black English and wore sagging pants instead of digging up information about the predominately Black convict crew who built Clemson.

My approach to documenting and sharing Clemson history was markedly different from Barker's decision to adopt an uncritical, yet multicultural approach to the university's history in his essay titled "The Sacred Soil of Bowman Field." Clemson's Bowman Field stretches out like a green shag carpet in front of several of the oldest buildings on campus.[23] Named for Randolph T. V. Bowman, former Clemson instructor and assistant football coach, the grassy ground is a popular, cherished gathering spot, where members of the Clemson community have congregated to stage military parades, watch athletic events, create Homecoming floats, build Habitat for Humanity houses, celebrate First Friday festivals, and attend outdoor concerts.

In his essay, which is featured in the coffee table book titled *Clemson: There's Something in These Hills* by Clemson alumni Trent Allen and Kevin Bray, Barker lauds the contributions of Cherokees and a Jewish-American solider to Clemson history. He also describes the Fort Hill Plantation as a "farm" and African Americans who had labored there as sharecroppers and slaves as "farm workers." He opines,

This piece of ground has seen many lives and uses. Even before there was a Clemson University, this piece of earth was the home of the Cherokee Indians who gave us a system of government so clear that it helped shape the U.S. government we enjoy today. They also named our mountains "The Great Blue Hills of God."

This piece of earth, or nearby, marked the place where the first American died defending our country in the Revolutionary War, a Jewish soldier named Francis Salvador. This piece of earth was part of the farm of John C. Calhoun and Thomas Green Clemson. It produced crops of corn and cotton that supported the farm. . . .

Three Congressional Medal of Honor winners have marched on this field. When you walk on Bowman Field, you walk in their footsteps as well as the footsteps of Cherokees, the Jewish American hero, the African American farm workers, the athletic teams, the Clemson Cadet Corps and many ROTC units across the generations.[24]

Barker's revisionist approach obscures the complex history of genocide, removal, and labor that enabled the development of Bowman Field, however. By characterizing Calhoun and Thomas Clemson as farmers, Barker diminishes their roles as enslavers on a plantation and omits the labor of enslaved field hands, who planted and harvested corn and cotton the earth produced. By describing African Americans as "farm workers," he negates the oppressive conditions under which enslaved persons, sharecroppers, convicts, as well as wage laborers worked. By linking the history of Native Americans to the founding of America and the making of the Upstate region, he suggests a collaborative relationship that likely never existed: the colonists burned the Cherokees' town and killed most of its residents, and the federal government forced them to cede most of their land to white South Carolinians in violation of the treaties they'd signed.[25]

While Barker's version of Clemson history whitewashed the university's complicated spatiality of race and ethnicity, the autographed photo of Duke Ellington that Allen and Bray featured in the book hinted at a more complex narrative of race relations in the institution's early history. The editors did not include a citation for the photograph and could not remember where they had found the image when I inquired about its source. I eventually traced the photograph to a scrapbook Clemson alumnus George

Bennett had donated to Clemson University Libraries' Special Collections & Archives. While a Clemson student during the 1950s, Bennett was president of the Central Dance Association (CDA) that successfully negotiated a contract to bring Ellington and his orchestra to campus for three performances in March of 1955, just one year after the US Supreme Court *Brown v. Board of Education* ruling desegregated America's public schools. The CDA had begun booking African American musicians to perform at Clemson in the 1930s, carefully selecting respectable artists who would be acceptable to their southern, conservative white audience. Clemson cadets were eager to be entertained by talented and successful African American musicians but were unwilling to attend classes with Black students, enroll in courses taught by Black professors, or respect the leadership of Black administrators and trustees.

Barker, Allen and Bray, and Reel adopted similar approaches to Clemson's African American history: they avoided critical engagement with tangible historical artifacts, such as a plantation house that is the bull's eye of campus or a black-and-white photograph of a prominent Black musician inserted in a coffee table book filled with beautiful images mostly of white people, offering elements of Black history without explanation or context. These authors invited members of the Clemson community to simply accept without question their version of the university's history. However, historian Megginson, a Calhoun, SC, native, made a concerted effort to research the African American experience at Clemson and in the Upstate South Carolina region. In 1982, with the support of the Pendleton District Historical and Recreational Commission, Clemson University, Seneca River Baptist Association, Tri-County Technical College, and the South Carolina Humanities Council, he launched the aforementioned *Black Heritage in the Upper Piedmont of South Carolina Project* to document the local history of African Americans in interviews, photographs, and other materials, such as dramatic orations, cemetery inventories, and a museum exhibition. The initiative focused on five areas: family ancestry, economic profiles, religious life, educational institutions, and social interactions. An advisory board and assistant directors organized a public forum, *Celebrating Black Heritage: The Importance, Difficulties, and Techniques of Preserving Black Culture*, provided oral history training workshops, met with members of the local African American community, recorded oral histories, collected historical artifacts, facilitated group discussions, shared research findings, and displayed the exhibition at sites throughout South Carolina. At the completion of the project in 1990, materials were donated to Clemson Libraries' Special Collections & Archives to make them accessible to the public; and copies of the recorded interviews were given to the Pendleton District Commission archives.[26] Megginson would eventually publish this history in a book titled *African American Life in South Carolina's Upper Piedmont, 1780–1900*.

Clemson's archivists built on Megginson's Black Heritage project through the creation of the *Documenting the African American Experience at Clemson* digital archive. The collection currently includes more than one thousand images of African Americans at Clemson University and in local and statewide communities, dating from the early 1800s to the present. Materials range from a plaster bust of William "Uncle Bill" Greenlee, who was employed as a servant for the Fort Hill Plantation, a driver for Clemson University founder Thomas Green Clemson, and an employee of the university for more than fifty years, to documents associated with Harvey Gantt's successful legal battle to gain admission to Clemson, as well as his enrollment and matriculation at the institution from 1963–1965. Archivists plan to enlist the assistance of the public to identify people in the photographs and to expand the online archive with audio files and video resources.[27]

As I learned more about the work that had been done to document the stories of African Americans in Clemson University and local history, I soon realized that a cohesive narrative linking the stories of African Americans at the university with those of African Americans who lived and still reside in the local communities that developed around the institution did not exist. And I knew that I would never be able to piece this history together by relying on traditional research and archival methodologies. During the summer of 2011, while participating in the National Endowment for the Humanities institute on *The Role of Place in African American Biography* at the Massachusetts College of Liberal Arts, I was introduced to research techniques that transformed my approach to documenting the lives of African Americans in early Clemson history. Each of the scholars who made presentations at the institute emphasized the necessity of utilizing both traditional and unconventional sources when documenting African American biography, such as manumission papers, census data, account books, birth, marriage, and death certificates, city directories, cemetery inventories, military records, and church records. I would later learn that Ebony Coletu characterizes this practice as biographic mediation: "any structured request for personal information that facilitates institutional decision-making about who gets what and why."[28] Seminar participants were encouraged to consider subjectivity; to study enslaved people, for example, rather than focus on the system of enslavement; to adopt a multidisciplinary or inter-disciplinary approach that might include literature, history, anthropology, sociology, history, or architecture; and to seek multiple perspectives, including life narratives, oral history, letters, petitions, diaries, legal documents, and accounting books.

I had my first opportunity to utilize some of the techniques I learned in the institute at Clemson when Leon Wiles asked Abel Bartley and me to develop a commemorative calendar to assist with planning the fiftieth anniversary celebration of desegregation to be held in 2013. In January of 1963, Harvey Gantt became the first African American student to enroll at Clemson, after winning a class-action lawsuit on appeal to the US Supreme Court. Bartley and I partnered with the Clemson Black Alumni Council (CBAC) to collect potential "facts and firsts," both the names of individuals we should consider honoring and milestone events we should highlight. As I reviewed the list of suggestions CBAC provided—ranging from the first official African American organization, the Student League for Black Identity (SLBI) founded by Titus Duren, Joe Grant, Charles A. Williams, and other Black students in 1968, to Clemson's first African American Studies Program established by Henry Lewis Suggs in 1994—I was struck by the fact that considerations of the significance of a half-century of integration at Clemson focused almost exclusively on the post-integration period. Only one alumnus, Clemson trustee Louis Lynn, suggested that we also recognize the contributions of African Americans in the university's early history, namely the first cooperative extension agent and the longest serving domestic or janitor.

We eventually added a "Pre-integration" feature in February of the commemorative calendar for the Black History Month celebration of "diversity, change, and progress." Bartley wrote the text that highlighted George Washington Carver's lectures at Clemson in 1923, as well as the labor of African American extension workers, dining hall employees, and custodial staff. But he did not mention the contributions of the enslaved people and sharecroppers who cultivated and maintained the Fort Hill Plantation during the antebellum and Reconstruction periods; the predominately African American state convict labor crew who helped to erect the university's earliest buildings; or the wage workers who were employed as construction hands and domestics prior to the opening of the college in 1893. And we did not highlight the importance of African American staff and community members to Gantt's success at Clemson. During an interview in 1986, Harvey Gantt acknowledges the central presence and role of African American dining hall workers in his transition to Clemson:

> Then I walked into the dining room, and here I'm expecting to see this sea of white faces, and literally all over the dining room are black people. Admittedly, in a subservient role or workers in the dining hall. I felt very comfortable. I walked through the line and I got the biggest piece of apple pie because these folks were handing it out to me. They were saying, "hey, we are glad you're here. Boy, we're going to take care of you." So, all of a sudden my world was a different one. It was, "hey, you're not alone at all. You're the only student but, my gosh, look around you. You're going to be taken care of because you're back home in the South." . . . That was the initial support.[29]

Being in the South meant that Gantt and other African American students encountered visible reminders of slavery and its legacies as they walked past Calhoun's Fort Hill plantation house and buildings like Hardin Hall named for Confederate veterans. But they also interacted with African American wage workers, among whom were descendants of enslaved persons who had labored on Fort Hill. Many of these Clemson employees lived in nearby communities, where they welcomed Gantt and other African American students into their churches and around their dinner tables.

During the desegregation commemoration, I also taught an honors seminar, Renaissance at Clemson, that gave students the opportunity to examine Harvey Gantt and Clemson University founder Thomas Green Clemson as renaissance men. Both men completed scientific studies for their careers, while cultivating a keen interest and engagement in the arts. Students were required to develop a project for the course about either man or about a subject related to their lives and legacy. One student, Kali Kupp, created a website: *The African American Experience at Clemson*. While acknowledging that Clemson University had not denied the existence of negative events regarding African Americans in its history, she contends that "this full story has not been infused into the public history of the university. A Renaissance needs to occur, a renewal of knowledge about the full history of the land of Clemson University and the complicated journey of African Americans that has led to an integrated campus today."[30] To help visitors to the site understand this "complicated journey," Kupp included a timeline of significant events in African American history at Clemson, essays about African Americans at Clemson who have made important contributions to the university—including convict laborers, extension workers, and George Washington Carver—and reflections on the complexities of desegregation and its legacy and campus memorials. She also discussed Thomas Clemson's advocacy of slavery, roles as an enslaver and overseer and as an employer of sharecroppers and African American servants.[31] Kupp's research convinced me that Clemson students could play a vital role in ensuring that the history of African Americans becomes a central thread in the university's public history.

In developing her website, Kupp referenced the Thomas Green Clemson biography that had been published in celebration of the centennial anniversary of his birthday, July 1, 1807. I had hoped that the book would offer a critical lens on the university's founder. The contributors largely extolled Clemson as a renaissance man, however, while downplaying his roles as an overseer, slaveholder, and Confederate officer. I wondered how they would examine a letter Thomas Clemson had written to William Wilson Corcoran, his investment banker in 1878, asking him to make a financial contribution for his new college. Clemson also expressed some anxieties about potential state interference in the management of the institution. Three contributors to the biography quoted extensively from the letter, in which Thomas Clemson shared his vision for the creation of "an institution for teaching the Sciences and art, theoretical & practical, & thus raise the people of the state from ignorance & demoralization to prosperity[,] the hope of the well born."[32] His chief concerns revolved around raising enough capital for an educational venture that would help South Carolinians recover from the devastation of the Civil War, but he also worried about the influence a predominately Black state legislature could have on his public higher education institution. Clemson explained, "The project for the time would be untrammeled as a private enterprise, whereas the contrary might occur if in the hands of the Legislature representing two different races."[33]

In each instance when the contributors to the Clemson biography referenced this letter, however, they omitted the aforementioned sentence. Yet the sentence provides critical insights into Thomas Clemson's stipulation in his will that seven self-perpetuating trustees and six legislature-appointed trustees comprise the governing body for his new agricultural college. The history of South Carolina College (SCC) likely led to his concern about the potential impact an African American–controlled state legislature might have on the institution. SCC closed during the Civil War due to low enrollment after current and potential students began enlisting in the Confederate Army. During Reconstruction, the majority Black Republican General Assembly reopened the college, renamed it the University of South Carolina (USC), elected African American trustees, and advocated for the admission of African American students. After white conservative Democrats regained control of the statehouse in 1877, which ended Reconstruction, they closed USC and reopened the institution in 1880 with white faculty, trustees, and male students.[34]

During USC's transitional period, Thomas Clemson corresponded with Corcoran, expressing concern that African Americans could regain control of the state legislature since South Carolina had a majority Black population. In order to protect his new college from the influence of a majority Black state government in the future, Thomas Clemson gave his college's seven lifetime trustees a majority voting bloc. The first lifetime trustees he selected were all interested in agriculture, but they were also former slaveholders and Confederate veterans, effectively ensuring that they and their successors could thwart the intentions of an African American–controlled State Assembly should one arise and attempt to integrate Thomas Clemson's college and its board.

The trustees and the General Assembly kept Clemson College segregated until 1963, when they were legally forced to desegregate due to a federal mandate for the integration of America's public schools. Until relatively recently, Clemson trustees were fairly disengaged from discussions about Clemson's public history, except to approve recommendations made by the University Advisory Committee on Naming Land and Facilities or similar entities. In 1946, for example, they authorized a massive initiative to rename campus buildings, previously referred to by numbers, in honor of influential white male founders such as Clemson trustee Benjamin Tillman and former college president Enoch W. Sikes.[35] Trustees have also endorsed inscriptions for campus, state, and federal historical markers and applications for buildings to be recognized as national historic landmarks.

During the 2014–15 academic year, however, when members of the Clemson community—including staff, students, the Faculty Senate, the Undergraduate Student Government, and the Graduate Student Government—began calling for the renaming of Tillman Hall, then board of trustees chairman David Wilkins stressed in a statement to the *Greenville News*, "While we respect the many differing opinions of our graduates, our students, our faculty and staff regarding this matter, the Clemson University Board does not intend to change the names of buildings on campus, including Tillman Hall."[36] Wilkins viewed the proposed change as a "symbolic gesture" and suggested that the university could implement more substantive initiatives to represent its commitment to diversity.[37] Although the trustees avoided engaging the campus community in discussions about commemoration and campus history, several members of the Clemson community continued to participate in debates about the politics of naming and renaming buildings on campus throughout the spring 2015 semester. I also intensified my efforts to research, document, and share the stories of African American life, labor, and love in Clemson University and local community history.

But I needed more names.

I will testify.

Section Two

Through improvisation, jazz teaches you about yourself.
WYNTON MARSALIS

Call: Love, Duke Ellington

RHONDDA ROBINSON THOMAS

Jazz!

During the Jim Crow era, both Black folk and white folk loved *Jazz!*

In 1955, Duke Ellington took the A train from New York for his gig at Clemson College, while his orchestra and manager rode the bus. When the president of the student-run Central Dance Association (CDA), George Bennett, who had booked the Duke for three performances that weekend, arrived at the train depot in Clemson, South Carolina, with his friend Bob Talton, they found the Duke surrounded by Black Pullman porters vying for the opportunity to shake hands and have their photograph taken with the internationally renowned musician. Bennett had welcomed the opportunity to bring the Duke and his orchestra for the annual Spring Military Ball, recalling the musician was a "legend. There has never been any musician on this campus with the prestige that Duke Ellington had." The booking fee was three thousand dollars (about twenty-nine thousand dollars in 2019 currency).[1]

As early as 1938, CDA business manager Tom Stanley had contacted Mills Artists, Inc., a booking agency in New York City, about bringing the Duke to Clemson for a two-night performance. At that time, the cost was $1,800.[2] The following year, Bob Bundy of Charles Shribman Orchestras in New York recommended the Duke as one of twelve musicians—Black, white, and Hispanic—to perform at the CDA's November and December dances.[3] Bundy followed up with an offer to schedule Ellington for a dance in February 1939.[4] By the time Bennett became involved with booking musicians for concerts, he would travel to New York City and meet with agents to secure commitments for America's top musicians at five major dances each year—Rat Hop, Homecoming, Mid-Winter Ball, Military Dance, and Junior-Senior Dance. Dances were the major social event at the all-male military college. Young women traveled from all over South Carolina to dance with their dates, though often most of them came from the all-female Winthrop College in Rock Hill, South Carolina. The bands would play for a black-tie dance on Friday night, a concert on Saturday afternoon, and an informal dance on Saturday night.

When Bennett had talked with Al Celley, the Duke's manager, while making arrangements for the performance, he had learned there were three white members in the orchestra, Celley himself, the bus driver, and Dave Black, the drummer. Celley was concerned about the arrangements that would be made to provide overnight accommodations for the Black band members, including the Duke. Jim Crow segregation was still enforced in the South, affecting even an internationally acclaimed musician like Duke Ellington. Bennett suggested the Clemson House on campus, but Celley didn't think that would work. Instead, he recommended a colored tourist home for the band in Greenville he'd found in *The Green Book*.[5] The next challenge was finding a place for the Duke and his band to eat on Saturday. Clemson College, located in rural Upstate South Carolina, had very few restaurant options for any of its residents. Bennett contacted Dan Gentry, owner of Dan's Sandwich Shop, who readily agreed to make and serve a meal for the orchestra in a private room in his eatery.

Jazz!

White folks improvised a way around segregation all for the love of *Jazz!*

There was wide acceptance of Black entertainers by white American audiences during the Jim Crow era. By the end of the Great Depression, Clemson students expected the CDA to bring top-name entertainers— both Black and white—to campus for social events. When the CDA had booked Jimmie Lunceford, in 1939, Tom Stanley, the organization's business manager, in a letter to Harold F. Oxley, Lunceford's manager, explained how racism in the South affected his ability to book Black bands to play at Clemson:

As you probably know, we are always a bit shaky about having
colored bands down here because of the feeling that exist[s] in
the South. A feeling that came about long before you or I had any
say-so or opinion. I [sic] is my belief that the student body will
give LUNCEFORD a hearty welcome, because even though it is a
colored band, it is one of the best, and that in my opinion is the
thing that counts. [O]n many occasions I have dropped countless
nickels in a "slot" to hear one of LUNCEFORD's recording[s] when
there were many others to choose from.[6]

The CDA student leaders frequented concerts by Black artists
throughout the state. Indeed, music performed by big bands like
the Duke and his orchestra was the soundtrack of their lives—until
Elvis Presley popularized Rock & Roll in the 1950s. Besides, the CDA
provided entertainment not only for Clemson students but for the
local white community as well. Some white musicians performed at
venues in the city of Clemson, a few of the CDA's former members
recall. However, many Black musicians played on the Chitlin' Circuit at
Littlejohn's Grill, a club-restaurant-hotel owned by African American
entrepreneurs Horace and Gertrude Littlejohn. Some musicians like
Harry Belafonte refused to perform at Clemson during the 1950s when
the college was segregated, choosing rather to play at Littlejohn's Grill.[7]
   Although Clemson administrators allowed students to book Black
musicians to perform at social events on campus and hired Blacks as
farm hands, cooks, domestics, as well as for other service-oriented or
manual labor jobs, they would not admit Black students or hire Black
faculty. As early as 1948, African Americans sought admission to Clemson. When brothers Spencer M. Bracey and Edward Bracey applied to
the college that year, then Clemson president R. F. Poole denied their
request, indicating applicants exceeded available slots. The students
were attending a land-grant institution, the historically Black South
Carolina State Agricultural and Mechanical College, where they were
pursuing degrees in agricultural engineering; and South Carolina followed a policy of providing separate but equal higher education facilities for Black and white students. "As long as this policy is maintained,"
Poole declared, "the Board of Trustees of this institution does not feel
that it has the right to consider the application of a Negro student for

admission to a white institution."[8] By 1955, the US Supreme Court had ruled segregation in public schools unconstitutional in the *Brown v. Board of Education* case; however, South Carolina still resisted the integration of its colleges and universities, though some Clemson students like Harry Bolick had begun to quietly advocate for integration.[9] And Clemson still welcomed prominent Black musicians like the Duke to perform on campus.

Ellington may have also been easier to book for a concert at Clemson in 1955 due to his waning popularity. His new records weren't selling very well after he changed music companies. Press coverage of his music and performances had diminished. His standing in polls by critics and readers of influential music publications had dropped. By the summer of 1955, the Duke would be forced to accept offers for his orchestra to provide accompaniment for ice skating shows in order to make ends meet. Cultural historian Harvey G. Cohen characterizes this period as the Duke's "nadir."[10]

Despite the dip in the Duke's popularity, the CDA built up excitement for the concert series by publishing notices in the *Tiger*, Clemson's student newspaper, in February and March 1955. Student journalists described the Duke as the leader of a "widely heralded orchestra," whom critics had characterized as "America's foremost composer"; and they provided details about his rise to fame that confirmed his critical commendation.[11] The Duke had begun playing with his band on Broadway in the 1920s. He handpicked musicians and vocalists to create a special sound—complex, beautiful jazz rhythms that appealed to a broad audience. During the Harlem Renaissance, the Duke became more popular through the release of compositions such as "It Don't Mean a Thing If It Ain't Got That Swing," "Sophisticated Lady," and "Prelude to a Kiss," often performed at the Cotton Club in Harlem. Tickets for the Friday night dance at Clemson cost $3.50; for the Saturday afternoon concert, 50 cents; and for the Saturday night event, $4.00.[12] The cadets could use a portion of their yearly allowance provided by the college to pay for their military uniforms to purchase tickets.

Jazz!

White students improvised so they would not miss the Duke's *Jazz!*

The Duke arrived in Greenville about six hours before the evening concert. After Bennett and Talton took him for a ride around town in Talton's convertible, they dropped him off at Clemson College's Schilletter Dining Hall, where the evening concert was being held, and introduced him to the head chef at the college, an African American named Mr. Littlejohn. The Duke talked with and played the piano for the predominately African American dining hall staff, who cooked soul food dishes for him.[13]

Members of the Clemson College community were thrilled by the Duke's performance. Faculty were more acquainted with his music than the students and vied for opportunities to be chaperones at the weekend event. The cadets had earned bragging rights for securing one of the best musicians for their annual military dance. Bennett took the Duke to the CDA's office where the musician regaled the students with stories of his travels and performances. And then he and his band played for a room packed with white cadets in military dress escorting their white dates donned in fancy floor- or tea-length evening gowns.[14]

Later that evening when Bennett was dancing with his mother, whom he invited to all the dances, she asked the Duke if he knew the popular song "Melody of Love" by Billy Vaughn.[15]

He responded, "I don't believe I know it. Can you hum some of it for me?"

She hummed a few bars. He liked the melody.

During the first performance at the concert on Saturday afternoon, the Duke announced he had a special selection for George Bennett's mother. He performed the song for which he had composed a full orchestra arrangement based on the few notes she'd hummed the previous night.

Jazz!

The Duke improvised on the spot to create *Jazz!*

Before the final performance, the Duke and his orchestra were treated to a steak dinner at Dan's. The owner had nicely decorated the room, filled it with tables draped with white tablecloths and laden with plates of steaks so large they were hanging off the sides and French fries piled high, along with salad, cake, and sweet tea. The musicians enjoyed their meal so much they were late for the last dance in Tillman Hall. Throughout the weekend, Clemson students, chaperones, and their guests were treated to the band's standard numbers, including "Take the A Train" and "Black Satin." After the performances ended and Bennett went out to the bus to see the orchestra off, he shook their hands as they boarded the bus. All of them agreed: "This is the best engagement we've ever had in the South."[16]

The CDA nearly broke even on the Duke Ellington Orchestra concert series. They earned $3,301.25, but expenses were $3,428.44, leading to a loss of $127.19.[17]

During the weekend, the CDA received autographed photographs from two members of the orchestra, reflecting the respectability politics that influenced the CDA's process for selecting Black musicians to perform at Clemson. In the first photograph, trumpet player Cat Anderson, wearing a tweed jacket, dress shirt, and tie and holding his trumpet, smiles as he gazes directly at the camera. He wrote, "The Best to the C.D.A. 'Cat' Anderson." In the second photograph, Duke Ellington, in a houndstooth jacket, dress shirt, and striped tie is positioned leaning left, head tilted, with a piano keyboard in the background. He is smiling and looking away from the camera toward the right. Here is his photograph inscription:

> To My Friends of the C.D.A. Thanx—good luck
> LOVE
> Duke Ellington.[18]

In an interview with *Ebony* magazine, Wynton Marsalis asserted, "Through improvisation, jazz teaches you about yourself."[19] You learn how to hold yourself together while interacting with others. You always remember the main tune but are continually compelled to perform the song differently. The Duke learned to deftly navigate the color line, America's longstanding refrain, so he could keep playing *Jazz*—in the Jim Crow South and around the world.

Jazz!

Black folk and white folk improvised for the love of *Jazz!*

Duke Ellington sent this autographed photograph of himself to the Central Dance Association after his orchestra performed at Clemson, 1955.

Response: "World-Famous" Duke Ellington, the Central Dance Association, and the *Tiger*

BRENDAN MCNEELY

Jazz is the genre of "world-famous" bands, huge spotlights, and national acclaim.

In 1963, eight years after Edward Kennedy "Duke" Ellington's performance at Clemson College, Sonny Morris, a Clemson senior, contended in an article published in the student newspaper the *Tiger* that he "would like to see a few new white bands and performers. Clemson is against integration but the majority of our entertainers are colored."[1] In that same issue of the newspaper, editors included a front-page story about Black musicians—Brook Benton, Dakota Staton, Shep and the Limelites, and The Impressions—that praised their musical talent.[2] The student-run CDA had booked the musicians to perform at the annual winter dance. How can the opinions of some Clemson students be reconciled with the glossy versions of these musicians that were presented on the *Tiger's* front page?

Those glossy headlines were printed in the same newspaper that three years earlier had published a special feature section with a full-page spread that proclaimed, "The South Shall Rise Again!," in honor of the Confederacy on the centennial of South Carolina's secession from the Union.[3] The CDA invited Black artists to perform on campus, but its leaders also sponsored blackface skits for Homecoming celebrations. The Black musicians performed at an institution that continued to fly the Confederate flag and play "Dixie" at university-sponsored events until 1972.[4] What can be made of Black musicians' experiences in this kind of atmosphere?

Clemson's acceptance of groups like Ellington's orchestra and The Impressions was conditional. Clemson students, faculty, and administrators were willing to invite, even welcome, Black performers—drawing on the long and complicated practice and legacies of Black musicians performing for white audiences throughout American history—so long as those performers remained in their segregated place. Their experience was a constant reminder of the gross racial inequalities that existed and, in many cases, still exist today in South Carolina.

Jazz is "[s]omething that one regards as hard to describe or understand. . . . Chiefly depreciative."[5]

While the high praise heaped on Ellington in issues of the *Tiger* seems to contradict Clemson's treatment of him with regard to meals and lodging, that praise is actually indicative of the ideology behind segregation. Ellington was not allowed to stay overnight on campus or in downtown Clemson. In fact, he had to stay in segregated lodging almost an hour's drive away in Greenville. The *Tiger* newspaper articles published about him, celebrating his musical talent, seem to express the CDA's desire for the student body's approval of their invitation to a Black musician. In the years following the 1954 *Brown v. Board of Education* Supreme Court decision, there was an ongoing debate in the *Tiger*'s editorials regarding the performers that Clemson brought to campus, and it seems the CDA felt reluctant to invite Black musicians due to fears of negative student reactions.[6]

These fears of student reactions also explain the CDA's refusal to invite Ellington in 1938. Ellington's agent Norman Campbell reached out to Tom Stanley, the CDA's business manager, to inquire about having the Duke perform at Clemson. Stanley's refusal leaves no doubt to the CDA's reasoning at the time:

> I happen to know just how famous the 'DUKE' is. . . . I don't mind telling you that the 'DUKE' is one of the few colored bands that I would even consider having down here. I'm afraid that it will

be impossible for us to get together on this orchestra, because it would be impossible for us to offer you the price that I think you would want.[7]

While Stanley's remarks are framed as budgetary concerns, it is clear that he sees a problem with inviting African American musicians to play at Clemson. Stanley adds that "we don't know just what the reaction of the students would be to this band," summing up the CDA's fears of how students' responses would affect dance attendance.[8] However, these fears seem not to have prevented the CDA from inviting other African American musicians in the sixteen years between Jimmie Lunceford's 1939 concert and the Duke's 1955 performance. While scheduling conflicts might partially explain the delay, the Duke's band also experienced a marked dip in popularity in the 1940s and 1950s with the rise of popular artists like Frank Sinatra, likely reducing the financial investment required to invite the band. Thus, when examining the tremendous hype that the *Tiger* articles generated in anticipation of the Duke's visit, the adulation may stem more from a fear of student backlash at the decision to invite an African American performer whose popularity was waning and less from a recognition of the Duke's talent. The articles praising Ellington serve merely as a cover for the financial incentives and concerns about student complaints that animated the CDA.

Jazz *is the music of the modern Civil Rights Movement.*

The Duke's performance at Clemson, which occurred just prior to the fall semester of 1955 when the higher education institution became coeducational, predates its eventual integration by eight years. In 1963, Harvey Bernard Gantt became the first African American student to enroll at Clemson; and the same newspaper that heralded the arrival of the Duke and countless others as paragons of musical genius published editorials by Clemson students excoriating Gantt for challenging the southern status quo. This complete reversal of treatment and coverage explains the deeper ideology behind the CDA's adulations of Ellington: the student body accepted African Americans as musical performers or wage workers on campus, but only so long as they stayed in their place.

Many Clemson students' reactions to an African American student reveal that the CDA's welcoming of Ellington in 1955 was not an embrace of a more hospitable stance toward African Americans but rather a further outworking of the racist ideology that inspired them to cling to segregation for almost a decade after the *Brown v. Board of Education* decision. Some Clemson students' condemnation of Gantt reveals the superficiality of their praise of Ellington. The simplistic narrative presented by the *Tiger* articles presents a palatable version of the artist, in much the same way that the "Integration with Dignity" narrative Clemson has adopted glosses over the difficulties of Gantt's experience.[9]

Jazz was once controversial, then conventional.

In 1978, four years after the Duke died, his son Mercer Ellington brought the orchestra back to Clemson. While not the world-shattering force it once was, under Mercer's leadership the musical group was still producing albums at a remarkable pace, even winning a Grammy in 1988. Instead of receiving front-page treatment in the *Tiger* like his father, Mercer's performance was advertised in a series of short articles published on the Student Union's page that presented only the details of the concert itself, leaving little room for the admiration heaped on the Duke in the 1955 front-page articles.[10] Jazz was no longer the headline-grabbing, controversial genre it had once been; however, in a sense, the CDA had succeeded in making the genre so acceptable to Clemson audiences that even the name Ellington failed to generate much buzz in the student newspaper. Upon their arrival at Clemson, Mercer and the band were slated to play in Tillman Auditorium, named after SC governor, US Senator, Clemson trustee, and self-avowed white supremacist Benjamin R. Tillman—a reminder of Clemson founders' ideologies about race that would never have permitted enrolling African American students and hiring African American faculty, administrators, and staff.

Jazz is a genre of appropriation.

The stories of the African American musicians who performed at Clemson prior to integration reveal an attitude toward African American culture that has existed for over a century: the desire to appropriate Black art for white consumption, with blatant disregard for the struggles and hardships, joys and successes experienced by the people who create the art. As James Weldon Johnson observed nearly a century ago, "[T]here has been a steady tendency to divorce Ragtime from the Negro; in fact, to take from him the credit of having originated it."[11] This philosophy of appropriation, of divorcing art and music from their originators, bears itself out in the CDA's concert programs, especially before integration. By praising the quality of music while simultaneously accepting the oppressing and othering of those who created it, the editors of the *Tiger,* the leaders of the CDA, and the Clemson student body at large all participated in this form of appropriation. The student who complained that Clemson had failed to invite enough white performers was participating in this kind of appropriation—drowning out the voices of Black performers by forcing them to be palatable and appropriating their work.

Jazz *is an embrace of uncertainty—improvisation.*

When studying these musicians, it's easy to get drawn into the glossy depictions of them on the front page. After all, Duke Ellington was a brilliant and significant musician. However, meaningful discussion about the experiences of these musicians must move beyond merely fond remembrance of their music or performances and encompass a broader understanding of their own lived experiences and the conditions that informed the white community's acceptance of them.

How does one approach these glossy narratives within the context of discrimination and marginalization that lies behind them? Can the Duke's lived experience—and the experiences of the members of his orchestra—be recovered or accounted for when there exists no evidence of his visit beyond these pristine headlines except the nostalgic memories of white Clemson consumers of Black culture?

Jazz *is a world of contradictions—of glossy façades hiding darker realities.*

CHAPTER 2

The Project

Call My Name

◇◇◇

we are The Tigers,
built on a legacy of slavery, sharecropping and convict labor,
by slave owners, supremacists and segregationists,

but come to the campus of Clemson University,
and you'd hardly be able to tell it from looking around.

And it's a shame.

We'd be a beautiful Tiger . . .

if only

we could
see our stripes.
A.D. CARSON, "SEE THE STRIPES"

Mr. Wannamaker, Chairman of the Coast Experiment Station,
requested that they be given ten (10) convicts to work on the
Coast Experiment Station.
Moved, by Mr. Sease, that the request be adopted.
Motion Adopted.
BOARD OF TRUSTEES MINUTES, JULY 14–16, 1908
CLEMSON UNIVERSITY, CLEMSON, SC

Her maiden name was Wannamaker. Lucretia Wannamaker.
And she had a sister who insisted on being called "Miss Wannamaker."
REGINALD HAMPTON, MY SECOND COUSIN

I was immediately annoyed.

As I sought to learn more about African Americans in Clemson history, I began to wonder how the stories of enslaved persons were being told at other historic sites associated with prominent American enslaver politicians. While touring George Washington's Mount Vernon in the spring of 2013, I kept hearing docents referring to "servants," a euphemism for enslaved African Americans, which irritated me. During the tour, a different docent provides details about each section of the house as visitors walk through. When the second guide began to introduce us to the foyer, he informed us that guests visiting the Washingtons would have been greeted by a butler who would have welcomed them into the home and escorted them to a designated room. I'm thinking to myself that the butler must have been enslaved. At the end of this segment of the tour, the guide asked if anyone had a question.

"Sir," I asked, "was the butler an enslaved African American?"

"Yes," he answered, "his name was Lee and his wife Lucy worked as the cook." I was even more frustrated after discovering that the guide knew the butler's name and some details about his family, but he didn't call the butler's name during the tour. An enslaved man was simply the butler. Mount Vernon docents privileged his role over his humanity.

The docents' refusal to call the enslaved African Americans' names continued throughout the house, except in the guest room area, where the guide who led Mount Vernon's African American heritage tour was stationed. She provided details about the duties of enslaved persons tasked with ensuring the comfort of the Washingtons' guests. Each time a docent inquired if there were any questions, I asked about enslaved Africans and received lots of information about them.

I had arrived at Mount Vernon via public transportation, the Metro train and then a bus. As I entered the bus, I looked up at the older white driver, who looked back at me and then turned away without acknowledging my presence. I took a seat a few rows behind him and slipped into observation mode. As three white young adults boarded the bus, he greeted them warmly. When an African American woman stepped aboard, he said nothing. When two Hispanic women boarded, however, he asked each if they would like one of the Spanish newspapers he had available. I continued observing as we embarked on our twenty-minute ride to Mount Vernon. At one point, he called the three young adult white riders to the front of the bus and talked with them about the Mount Vernon experience, giving them pointers on what to see and where to find the best priced souvenirs. As we drew near the site, he yelled back for them to move to the left side of the bus for the best views of the Potomac River and pointed out the place where they would catch the bus for the return trip to the Metro train station. As we reached the Mount Vernon stop to disembark, I waited to leave the bus after the young folk. After I got off the bus, the driver noticed me standing with the white passengers.

"Oh," he exclaimed, "I didn't know you were coming here. Come back here. I have something for you." Why had an elderly white man assumed that a middle-aged African American woman would not be interested in visiting Mount Vernon, "[l]ocated on the banks of the Potomac near the wharf, the four-acre Pioneer Farm site explores George Washington's role as visionary farmer," where I could "[s]ee 18th-century plantation life through . . . beautiful gardens and grounds" and "[v]isit the Museum and Education Center and view a fascinating array of Mount Vernon artifacts," according to its website?[1]

When I stepped back on the bus, the driver handed me a copy of the bus schedule. I had already researched the route and noted the times for departures and arrivals. I smiled. Awkwardly.

In 2013, I, too, am sometimes invisible. Still.

When I returned to Clemson, I shared my experience with my African American literature students, fifteen white, one Black. I reminded them that I am Dr. Thomas in the classroom on our campus, but when I step into the larger world, some people see me only as a middle-aged African American woman, which prompts some of them to ignore me. The Invisible Woman. Perhaps my own invisibility compels me to help make Clemson Black history visible and viable.

Building a Professional Network and Finding the Archives

By this time, I had begun making presentations at academic conferences about my research, even as I continued to explore Clemson's archives. Early on, before I knew much of anything about the history of African Americans in Clemson history, I had joined two colleagues, Abel Bartley, historian, and Lance Howard, geographer, on a panel for the Slavery and the University

Conference at Emory University in 2011. During the presentation, I mused aloud regarding Susan's status as an enslaved woman due to her having both the Calhoun and Clemson names. But Susan was only one of more than one hundred persons of African descent who had been enslaved on the Fort Hill Plantation. Surely some of their descendants were still alive. When I initially contacted the Department of Historic Properties to request that they connect me with descendants, I was asked to write a brief paragraph about my research that they would give to anyone interested in talking with me. As I waited, I kept returning to Clemson University Libraries' Special Collections & Archives, searching for clues about African Americans in the university's history.

Recovering the convict records in the state archive made me feel confident enough to accept an invitation—from a professor who had learned about my work at the Emory conference—to present on a panel featuring papers about Slavery and Institutions of Higher Education at the 2013 American Society for Legal History (ASLH) Conference in Miami. We would examine case studies regarding the legal historical relationship between slavery and Clemson, Princeton, and Hampden-Sydney College. Historian Craig Wilder, then at the Massachusetts Institute of Technology, agreed to be our commentator.

Just after we learned our panel proposal had been accepted in July 2013, George Zimmerman was acquitted in his trial for the murder of Trayvon Martin. Activists contemplated calling for a boycott of businesses in Florida due to the state's "Stand Your Ground" laws. ASLH decided to proceed with the conference as scheduled due to the differing opinions of its members regarding cancellation, the prohibitive cost of rescheduling the event, and the loss of opportunities for scholars to present their work and expand their networks. However, they also organized a forum where conference attendees could discuss the aftermath of the trial.

I don't remember if the forum was held, but I do remember being very nervous as I looked on a sea of unfamiliar, mostly white legal scholars as I presented my paper, "From John C. Calhoun's Fort Hill Plantation to Clemson College: The Legalities of the Legacy of Slavery and the University of Upstate South Carolina." As I began to read my paper, I heard the pace of my voice quicken, which caused me to ad lib too much. My intention was to examine how South Carolina's legal system created oppressive conditions of bondage and exploitation for three groups of African Americans—enslaved persons, sharecroppers, and convict laborers—whose labor was essential for Clemson University's creation and development. Wilder's comments about my paper, which he sent to be read as he was unable to attend the conference, reflect the essence of my argument:

> Rhonda [sic] Thomas'[s] treatment of Fort Hill Plantation and Clemson College is a provocative analysis that follows the lived history of a plot of land that began as part of Cherokee country, long operated as a plantation, and was ultimately procured as a site for a college. The essay establishes the ways in which convict lease laws allowed continuities in the use and application of black labor long after the Civil War. Her work forces us to engage a disquieting reality: even after the end of slavery, colleges continued to access and exploit unfree black labor. The old Jim Crow was the articulation of a legal and institutional network that continued to bind the rise and growth of higher education in America to the hyper-exploitation of black bodies and in the shadows of Native destruction.[2]

While our panel coordinator believed our presentations were well received, my experience convinced me that I was more interested in telling stories about people, how laws constantly shaped and shifted their lives, than examining the legalities of slavery and its legacies.

Soon I was refocusing my attention on fulfilling the requirements for tenure. My department chair had advised me not to allow myself to be defined by my Clemson history research. He reminded me that I had been hired to teach and research early African American literature.

But I believed I could successfully research both topics, which are complementary.

I didn't follow my chair's advice.

At least not immediately.

Clemson University Community Explores
Race and the University

During the spring of 2014 following my presentation at ASLH, I was invited to be the fiftieth speaker for Clemson's RCID (Rhetorics, Communication, and Information Design) Research Forum. The main visual for my talk, "Slaves, Sharecroppers, and Convicts: Recovering the Story and Legacy of Slavery and the Making of Clemson University," was a timeline with Clemson's public narrative outlined on top and its African American stories hovering just below the line of demarcation between the institution's proud history and its painful past. I had begun to better understand Clemson's enormous indebtedness to Black labor for its existence, particularly its dependence on forced and leased labor. When my talk ended, a young African American man introduced himself as A.D. Carson, a PhD student in the RCID program. I had heard he was a spoken-word poet, and he informed me that he was writing a poem that might be suitable for the new *Race and the University* series our college was launching that fall.

The concept for *Race and the University* emerged from a series of conversations by the College of Architecture, Arts and Humanities' (CAAH) Arts and Humanities Faculty Council, of which I was a member. The genesis of the program resulted from our simple desire to create a book club for our colleagues. We selected Wilder's *Ebony and Ivy: Race, Slavery, and the Troubled History of America's Universities* as our first text and planned a discussion. As our conversations with then CAAH dean Rick Goodstein about the event continued, however, we expanded the idea to a semester and then to a year-long program that would encourage and facilitate conversations about race and the university starting with Clemson's own history—beginning with the Cherokee era followed by the antebellum period, Reconstruction era, and finally the Jim Crow years. Goodstein invited Diane Perpich, director of the Women's Leadership degree program, and me to cochair the planning team and authorized funding for the series. We believed the time had come for Clemson to have frank, open, public conversations about race and to implement some long overdue changes to make the university's public narrative more reflective of its complex history; our intent was to help make Clemson a more inclusive, welcoming place for people of all races, particularly people of color.

That fall, we quickly realized the need for the *Race and the University* initiative after the Clemson Undergraduate Student Government (CUSG) president gave a very inaccurate version of the university's history during the orientation for first-year students. At that time, prior to the start of classes each academic year, incoming students were required to participate in the "Kick-Off Clemson" program during their first week on campus, which included activities and programs that reflect the university's core values of integrity, honesty, and respect and were designed to ease the new students' transition into university life. At the large public forum, the CUSG president claimed that as soon as the laws changed, which would have been the 1954 *Brown v. Board of Education* US Supreme Court ruling that mandated desegregation of America's public schools, Clemson "integrated in a heartbeat." But desegregation didn't happen at Clemson until 1963, nearly a decade after the *Brown* case—and then only by court order because Gantt filed a class-action lawsuit when the institution repeatedly blocked his efforts to enroll.

Gantt's activism and enrollment paved the way for other African American students at Clemson like A.D. Carson to advocate for change. Through follow-up emails and conversations, Carson shared more details about the poem, himself, his work, and his adjustment to life in the South. He had come to Clemson from Illinois—the Land of Lincoln—where he had lived and worked before deciding to pursue graduate studies at a university built on Calhoun's Fort Hill Plantation: a higher education institution that also honors founding fathers who had owned, advocated the killing of, or otherwise oppressed African Americans. Carson arrived at Clemson and enrolled in his History of Rhetorics course just as Hollywood was releasing and promoting two significant films about race, *Fruitvale Station* and *12 Years a Slave*. He soon began producing a mixtape track of spoken word poems and rap songs about his Clemson experiences and impressions, before turning his attention to crafting a piece that critically examines the symbolism of the university's tiger mascot and Solid Orange Friday school spirit initiative. (On Fridays, members of the Clemson community are encouraged to wear orange, one of the school colors.)[3] After meeting and talking with Carson, I assured him that Clemson needed his voice and perspective.

By the spring of 2014, Carson was ready to launch the *See The Stripes* campaign. He crafted an official statement that describes the impetus for the initiative:

See The Stripes is a campaign to help raise awareness within the general student population about commonly overlooked contributions to Clemson University's history. The Tiger, Clemson University's mascot, as represented by the university's "Solid Orange" campaign, is both incomplete and inaccurate, as is a history that does not acknowledge both the positive and negative.

The central idea of *See The Stripes* is an acknowledgement that The Tiger has stripes, which are an integral part of its existence and survival. While The Tiger could be seen as "Solid Orange," a solid orange tiger could not survive without its stripes. Similarly, Clemson University's history has its dark parts that should be acknowledged— particularly the histories of laborers who contributed significantly to its development: slaves, sharecroppers, and convict laborers.

As the stripes on The Tiger complete the picture of the university's mascot, acknowledging the stripes on the uniforms of convict laborers, the strips of land worked by the sharecroppers, and the slaves, who bore stripes on their backs, help provide a necessary, more complete view of the history of Clemson University.[4]

The statement critiques the "Solid Orange" campaign and calls on Clemson to adopt initiatives that reflect its complete history. Instead of wearing orange shirts, Carson encouraged members of the Clemson community to wear black shirts imprinted with "SEE THE STRIPES" in orange ink on Solid Orange Fridays and thereby become the visible embodiment of the campaign slogan. In the spring 2014 semester we ordered T-shirts that arrived before classes ended. We distributed and began wearing them immediately—on Solid Orange Friday, the last day of the semester.

The *See The Stripes* campaign resonated with me. My history as a sixth-generation South Carolinian, descendant of enslaved persons and slaveholders, is interwoven in the tiger's dark stripes—the markings that transform an orange creature into a beautifully unique yet dangerous big cat.

Linking the Transatlantic Slave Trade to
Clemson University History

Between making conference presentations, assisting with the launch of the *Race and the University* series, and listening as Carson composed his "See The Stripes" poem, I continued visiting sites associated with slavery. I traveled to Colonial Williamsburg, situated down the river from the place where "20 some odd negroes" eventually became chattel. I traveled to Monticello, where American founding father Thomas Jefferson enjoyed the independence he'd maintained was essential for citizens in a democratic republic while he fathered as least six children with Sally Hemings, all of whom were enslaved from birth until his death. But my visit to Elmina Castle and Cape Coast Castle in Ghana, where captives became slaves, was transformative.

I must admit that part of the allure of going on a mission trip to build a school in Ghana was the slave castle tours at the end of our ten-day work obligation. As I neared the end of my journey on a plane from Frankfurt, Germany, to Accra, I was surprised to find myself surrounded by European and white American travelers. Why had I expected the journey to be a Black thing? When we flew into Accra under the cover of night, the city popped into view like a multicolored jewel sparkling in a sea of blackness. We disembark, and I wonder what sights will greet me in the terminal. As we walk along the corridor, I see a long line of African peoples standing three- to four-deep in a roped-off area, waiting for arriving passengers. They stare at me; I stare back at them. I am wondering if they think I am Ghanaian. I am thinking about African Americans who travel to Ghana expecting the locals to welcome them like long-lost family members. I am a brown-skinned woman whose wide nose and dreadlocked hair mark my body as being of African descent, and so I do not stand out immediately. But I am a South Carolinian, Western. I know that the moment I speak, my American accent will betray me.

The sights and sounds of Ghana soon demand my attention. I meet my host and other members of the group, and we head for the car. Men hustling for dollars in the parking lot keep offering to carry our luggage. As we drive out of town and stop at the first traffic light, a young boy comes up and stands at the car window, eyes looking imploringly at us for a handout. We pull away. When we stop at the next light, we are surrounded by girls carrying baskets on their heads filled with homemade treats for sale. Continuing our drive to the countryside, we see people standing along the pot-holed roads; occasionally there's a streetlight. There are construction projects in various stages of development: Ghanaians purchase land and then build structures as they secure funds to complete the projects, a process that can stretch out years, though the end result is debt-free living. The paved multilane city roads narrow to a two-lane highway, and we soon begin stopping at a series of checkpoints where men collect tolls. I wonder how far we are from the slave castles.

Later when we visit a large local open market, I am the only Black woman with a group of white volunteers, who are all wearing the same Maranatha Volunteers International maroon T-shirts. I hear a man yelling, "My sister, my sister!" I look over to see a brother dressed in a white head wrap, shirt, and pants. He catches my eye. "Yes, you. Come here!" I smile but don't move.

I turn and catch a local woman's eye; "You look Ghanaian," she says.

"I'm from the United States," I reply.

As my group makes our way through the market, the vendors scan the line of folks and often stop and stare at me. I return the gaze. Do they see a hint of themselves in brown-skinned me? Suddenly, the confluence of food smells—seafood (live crabs and dead smoked fish, including one curled up like a snake); produce (especially cassava, greens, and ripe red tomatoes); grains (mostly rice and millet); and dried beans (including black-eyed peas and pinto)—is mingling with the stench from piles of trash and exhaust fumes. Wall-to-wall people include women with babies tied on their backs and school children in uniform tapping me on the arm and waving "hello" as they slip by. Vending stalls are offering everything from livestock (four different types of chicken killed to order) to synthetic hair (straight or curly, brown or black) to vehicles (cars, taxis, trucks, vans, motorbikes). My senses are overwhelmed even as I feel exhilarated to be in the majority, surrounded by African people, feeling connected to them across the Atlantic, across generations to where the story of Africans at Clemson begins.

I am pulled into the swirl of the African Diaspora. But I still need to get to the slave castles.

I'm standing near the beach, staring out over the expansive Atlantic Ocean. "This is where it all began," I whisper as I think about the harrowing Middle Passage.

Soon we were walking up to the entrance of the Cape Coast Castle. The Portuguese had built the commercial wooden fort in 1555. Nearly a century later, the Swedes took over and enlarged the structure. Within a decade, the fort passed hands again to the Danes, who transformed the wooden fort into a castle of stone. By 1700, the fort had been owned by the Dutch and a Fetu chief before being taken over by the British and increasingly utilized for the transatlantic slave trade. Thousands of Africans were shoved into windowless dark, dank dungeons, where I stood, horrified by the guide's description of men stacked floor to ceiling and women pressed tightly side by side, during the months-long wait for the ships that would transport them to bondage in the Americas. And one day the captives would be purchased and would exit through the oversized wooden door of no return.

We also visited the Elmina Castle, entering by walking across a bridge over the empty moat that surrounded the structure. The Portuguese built the white-washed structure in 1492 as a safe harbor for ships associated with trading in West Africa. When the Dutch took over the castle in 1637, they transformed it into a major hub for the transatlantic slave trade. As I walked in the steps of the African captives, standing once more in the dark, dank dungeons where they were held, seeing the prisons cells for those who resisted and the iron gate that functioned as the door of no return, I better understood the diasporic nature of Call My Name: the story of Black peoples that began, not on John C. Calhoun's Fort Hill Plantation, but on the west coast of Africa.

African captives from both the Elmina and Cape Coast castles waded through troubled waters of the Atlantic that transformed them into enslaved persons, climbed into small boats that transported them to the slave ships, then descended into the holds where they were packed like sardines for a harrowing voyage designed only for the strongest to survive— men and women like Polydore and Mennemin, who ended up laboring and dying on the Fort Hill Plantation in Upstate South Carolina thousands of miles from home.

My trip to Seville, Spain, in the fall of 2017 further complicated my understanding of slavery and my desire to better understand its impact on my life and research as well as on Clemson history. One day I sneaked off from the Association for the Study of the Worldwide African Diaspora conference to visit Alcázar, the royal castle in Seville. As I stood in the opulent Hall of the

Ambassadors, where King Ferdinand II of Aragon and Queen Isabella I of Castile received Christopher Columbus after his voyages to the Americas, I sensed the profound disconnect that enabled rulers to condone such explorations, effectively setting in motion a series of events that would culminate in the expansion of the transatlantic slave trade. Did those royals—seated on their thrones positioned directly under a gold-encrusted dome in a room designed to present them as the center of a universe in which subjects were born only to serve them—think about the African captives who were forced to make the journey from captivity in the slave camp to labor on the Caribbean's deadly sugar cane fields? Did they hear the cries of slave traders, governed neither by the church nor by the crown, selling the Africans they herded along the cobblestoned streets of Seville into the liminal space of the walkway that wrapped around the Cathedral of Saint Mary of the Sea? Could they imagine enslaved Africans being transported to the Carolina colony, where some would eventually work on a plantation owned by a politician whose ideologies would help lead to a civil war that was fought to preserve an economy dependent on the right to own enslaved persons? Though Columbus eventually returned to Spain in chains, he was given an honored burial place in the cathedral, a crypt perched prominently on the shoulders of four men who represent Spain's conquests. We don't know where most of the persons who were enslaved and died on the Fort Hill Plantation are buried. We aren't even sure of their names.

As I traversed the transatlantic slave route, I wondered if we would ever be able to trace the lineage of enslaved people on Calhoun's Fort Hill Plantation back to Africa. I wondered if bringing Clemson students to study in Ghana or Spain would enable them to expand their understanding of how slavery in the antebellum South Carolina Upcountry was interconnected with the transatlantic slave trade. I wondered if such an experience could enable them to finally see the stripes.

See The Stripes Campaign Shifts Clemson's Public Narrative

By early summer of 2014, Carson had revised the words to his poem and added music. He dropped by my office several times to talk about his work-in-progress. When I read the poem for the first time, I felt as if Carson had found the words we all needed to describe the troublesome experience of working at a South Carolina university that refuses to acknowledge its full history: a higher education institution that has yet to admit that its existence is predicated on the exploitation of Black laborers—enslaved, employed, and incarcerated primarily by enslavers, supremacists, and segregationists.

"Can I have a minute to compose myself?" My voice choked as tears welled up in my eyes.

But I was also concerned. Carson opened his poem with an image of Clemson's football team running down the hill of Memorial "Death Valley" Stadium:

> I had no idea the sprint down The Hill, which Brent Musburger famously referred to as "The most exciting 25 seconds in college football" has been, since the tradition started, the football program—the coaches, the staff, the athletes—running down a hill that has a plantation house standing at its summit. The "Most Exciting 25 Seconds In College Football" is literally the Clemson Football Program running downhill, away from the university's slaveholding past and a relic standing as a symbol of it, onto the field that generates significant amounts of money for the school and a large part of its reputation.[5]

Carson was making an explicit correlation between the enslavement of African Americans during the early American period and the exploitation of African American athletes during the modern era. Scholars, sportscasters, and athletes have all made similar arguments, but I knew loyal Tiger fans would be upset by the harsh critique of a football program that Coach Dabo Swinney and his staff were transforming into an Atlantic Coast Conference powerhouse.[6]

Nevertheless, we persisted.

By early July, we had begun planning the See The Stripes Poetry, Music, and Dance Fest that would serve as the kickoff event for the Race and the University series. By mid-July we finalized copy for the See The Stripes postcards that would be distributed that fall and ordered wristbands. I had also returned to the SC state archive to request more court and penitentiary records for convicts assigned to Clemson College, including Wesley Bolling, a twenty-four-year-old farmer from Greenville County, South Carolina, who had received a pardon in 1891 from Governor Tillman. Bolling had been convicted of manslaughter for the murder of a Black man he believed was seducing his wife. Shortly after Bolling was sentenced to two years of hard labor in the state penitentiary, the white jurors who had served at his trial successfully petitioned Tillman for a pardon, asserting that they would have done the same thing under the same circumstances. White jurors supported a pardon associated with Black-on-Black crime. Had Bolling killed a white man, however, he may have received a life sentence or been lynched. Tillman's willingness to pardon African American convicts initially surprised me until an archivist at the SC archives informed me that governors dispensed pardons like candy during the late nineteenth and early twentieth centuries.[7]

Carson officially launched the campaign on Sunday, August 17, 2014, three days before the fall semester began. His poem not only ignited a discussion about how Clemson shared its history on campus but coverage of the campaign led to national and international discussions about race and the university. The *Daily Kos* published an article titled "Clemson Student Exposes Historic Racism at University with Provocative Video," which elicited positive comments.[8] When *Campus Reform* published "Campaign Compares Clemson Athletics to Slavery, Accuses University of 'Whitewashing' History," however, it included a quote from Clemson political science professor J. David Woodard, who falsely characterized Carson's work as "fascism." Woodard asserted, "It's looking at things only through racial lenses and not seeing anything else when in fact there is no racism associated with this."[9] *Campus Reform* claimed they reached out to Carson for a response, but he was never contacted by the organization about the article. Within a year, Carson would write an opinion piece for the *Guardian* asserting, "My South Carolina university is whitewashing its complex racial history."[10] Soon, he was receiving disturbing emails. I advised him to send them directly to Kimberly Poole, an associate dean in the Office of Advocacy and Success, Division of Student Affairs, who handled such issues for Clemson students by providing resources and support.

A few months after the launch of *See The Stripes*, a Clemson alumnus whom I had met with a few months earlier to discuss my research on African Americans in the university's history called to express serious concerns about Carson's work.

"Rhondda, tell me you don't have anything to do with this," he pleaded.

"What are your concerns?" I inquired.

Members of Clemson's chapter of the Delta Sigma Theta Sorority, Inc. performing a step show at the *See the Stripes Dance, Poetry, and Music Fest,* the kick-off program for the *Race and the University: A Campus Conversation* initiative, 2014. Photo by the author.

The alumnus said some Clemson staff were worried about the negative depiction of the Fort Hill tours in *See The Stripes*.

"Was anything in the poem untrue?" I asked.

He couldn't identify any inaccuracies. But he assured me there was consternation regarding the exposure of the deliberate omission of the "controversial" practice of slavery in the tours of John C. Calhoun's "home" (as directional signs near Clemson characterize the historic Fort Hill plantation house). Although I was able to allay this caller's fears by assuring him that Carson's poem was sparking much needed conversations about how Clemson engaged with its history, various people continued to express concerns about the potential negative impact of *See The Stripes* on the University's reputation. They kept criticizing Carson's representation of Clemson history but could not deny its truth.

Yet a large crowd had turned out for the *See The Stripes* event in September 2014, which kicked off the *Race and the University* initiative, where Carson shared the spoken word video version of the poem.

As we continued providing opportunities for the campus community to engage with the university's history through the *Race and the University* initiative, we had mixed success. Only a handful of people attended the Clemson Brickmaking Project program held in the two-hundred-seat Lee Hall auditorium about a month later. Before the program, James Bostic Jr., the first African American to earn a PhD from Clemson and a former Clemson trustee, and I had stopped by the Fort Hill plantation house, where we had hoped to witness the installation of a new exhibit on antebellum clothing for enslaved persons and enslavers, curated by Clemson theater professor Kendra Johnson and her Creative Inquiry undergraduate team. By the time we arrived, however, the displays featuring plantation clothing were already in place—a weather-distressed shirt and pants for an enslaved male field hand positioned in the reconstructed detached kitchen; a calico dress that enslaved lady's maid Susan Calhoun Clemson would have worn situated in the bedroom where her enslavers, the Clemsons, slept; and an ivory silk dress styled for Anna Calhoun Clemson installed in the parlor where she married Clemson University founder Thomas Green Clemson.

Bostic and I had met a few weeks earlier to discuss several of my college's humanities initiatives. Two days after that meeting, Bostic sent me an email informing me that he had enjoyed the meeting and was considering whether he would allow me to write a story about his familial ties to the university and his family's experiences at Clemson. I eventually learned that his great-grandfather, Hillard Evans Pegues, a descendant of French Huguenot immigrant Claudius Pegues, had completed a two-year agriculture program from Clemson Agricultural College in 1899–1900. Three other Pegues brothers attended Clemson: Olin Marcellus, who was in the first class ever to graduate from Clemson, earned a bachelor's degree in engineering in December 1896; Elbert Sanders, who completed a two-year agriculture program at Clemson with his brother, Hillard Evans in 1899–1900; and Sarius Olivia, who graduated from Clemson with a bachelor's degree in agronomy in 1910. After graduation, Hillard returned home to rural life in Kollock (renamed Wallace in the 1950s), South Carolina, where his wealthy father, Rufus M. Pegues, owned fifteen thousand acres of land. After his father's death, Hillard, a lifelong bachelor, managed a successful farm on land he had inherited from his father. He also fathered a child, Lula Kollock Douglas (1905–1975), with Marsha Kollock Douglas, an African American woman who had worked as a housekeeper for the Pegues family. Two other Pegues brothers also fathered children with African American women. As Lula grew up, she was accepted by the Pegueses and included in family activities and events. Like her mother, she worked as a housekeeper for the Pegues family from age fourteen until her death in 1975. She eventually married Jesse Bostic, with whom she had fourteen children, seven of whom survived to adulthood. The eldest son was James E. Bostic Sr., who married Lula Mae James. When the time came for their son James Jr.—who, as a high school student in Marlboro County, South Carolina, had an afterschool job as a bookkeeper for the Pegues family farm—to attend college in 1965, both the white and Black members of his extended family were glad he could attend Clemson College, which had been desegregated in January 1963. Cousin Rufus M. Pegues, son of Sarius Olivia Pegues, paid the tuition and fees for James Bostic Jr.'s undergraduate education. Although Clemson University did not recognize Bostic Jr. as a legacy student while he completed his bachelor's degree in textile chemistry in 1969 and doctorate degree in chemistry in 1972, his relatives are proud of his familial connection to some of Clemson's first white graduates. In 2016, Clemson University awarded Bostic the Clemson Medallion, its highest public honor.[11]

While Bostic and I were at Fort Hill, I had hoped he might have the opportunity talk briefly with Clemson's Historic Properties director Will Hiott about incorporating more details of enslaved African Americans into the Fort Hill plantation house tours, but the conversation didn't happen. As we were leaving the exhibit, I invited Bostic to attend the Clemson brick program.

Bostic joined about five other attendees in the cavernous lecture hall, listening intently as I gave my first public presentation about the incarcerated men and boys who built Clemson. At the time, I did not know how often or how long Clemson trustees had leased incarcerated laborers. I had very little information about the conditions under which the prisoners had worked. But I knew many had escaped during the early years because they worked in a remote area. I knew most were under the age of thirty and had been convicted of some form of larceny, often for goods worth twenty-five dollars or less. I knew the convicts had made millions of red bricks for the earliest buildings on campus, four of which are still standing:

Hardin Hall, Trustee House, Sikes Hall, and Tillman Hall. Two other presenters followed me. Denis Bronson, director of Clemson's National Brick Research Center, provided insights about the many different types of bricks that are used for campus buildings; and then Clemson geography professor Lance Howard and Clemson facilities project manager Rick Owens discussed historic and contemporary brick-making techniques. The program flowed smoothly, and everyone participated in a lively discussion that followed the presentations. Our only regret was that our audience was very small.

Clemson Alumnus Invests in the Project

During our walk back toward the center of campus, Bostic suddenly stopped and said, "I'm going to give you some money for your project. I'll call you in a few days."

"Thank you," I stammered, surprised by the unexpected offer of financial support for my research. *That's so sweet*, I thought to myself. *It would be great to have a small grant to help defray my research travel expenses this spring*. As a junior humanities professor, my sole frame of reference was the two-thousand- to three-thousand-dollar stipends I'd received to attend NEH summer institutes or to conduct archival research for other projects.

A few weeks later, Bostic called with an update on his funding proposal: "I'm going to give you fifty thousand dollars and ask the provost to match my gift, which means you'll have a hundred thousand dollars for your research," he informed me.

I was excited but concerned. I tried to find words that tempered my joy about his gift with my apprehensions about the probability of administrative support.

"Will you still give me fifty thousand dollars if the provost refuses?" I inquired. Bostic responded with a laugh, assuring me that the provost would provide the funding.

My fears were not unfounded. My first and only encounter with a Clemson administrator about endorsing a university history project had ended with then president Barker refusing to accept my proposal. When I had inquired about the process for making the request, I was advised to consult with Leon Wiles, Clemson's first chief diversity officer, who eventually presented my idea to the administrative council, as I was not allowed to attend the meeting. When Wiles informed the council of my proposal for President Barker to simply authorize a new study of Clemson history to determine if anything had been overlooked or undervalued, no one responded. Reportedly, some people began squirming uncomfortably in their seats. Finally, the president advised Wiles to tell me that I could research any topic I wished, but the university would not launch a new history initiative. I later learned that Clemson's historian was researching and writing a new comprehensive two-volume history of the institution, *The High Seminary*, that would be published by Clemson University Digital Press. I could only guess that Clemson administrators believed a new history project was already under way.

By the time Bostic offered a contribution for my project, however, Clemson had a new president, James Clements, who had hired a new provost, Robert Jones. I was cautiously optimistic about the prospects of university support for my research.

A few days later Bostic called with a second update. "It's a done deal. You've got your money," he exclaimed. It's difficult to describe the swirl of emotions that this unexpected, generous gift evoked—joy, relief, and gratitude. When I found my voice again, I thanked Bostic for his and his wife Edith's generosity and slowly began to realize how this gift and grant would significantly change my ability to move my work from a dream deferred by a lack of resources to a research project that could profoundly enrich Clemson history. Within two years, Provost Jones and Bostic pledged to match their original donations, with Jones increasing the second grant to $60,000.

Bostic not only offered financial support, he also arranged for me to have access to campus resources that greatly enhanced my research, including securing the assistance of Clemson project manager Marjorie Campbell. But when he invited me to join him, Barker, and Reel to discuss my research in December 2014, I hesitated. I had not spoken directly with Barker since he had refused to authorize a new campus history project. However, I had sent him an email of appreciation in August 2013 after he publicly affirmed that Harvey Gantt resorted to filing a lawsuit to gain admission to Clemson in 1963 and that Gantt was the most dignified person throughout the nearly three-year ordeal. That fall, Gantt had been the featured speaker for the convocation in honor of the fiftieth anniversary of integration. To allay my reluctance, Bostic assured me that a conversation with Barker was essential to healing the rift between us and advancing my work. I reluctantly agreed.

We were to meet and talk in the Lee Hall III, the new state-of-the-art building in the School of Architecture, where Barker was teaching, and share lunch at a restaurant in the Madren Conference Center, a beautiful red-brick building complex situated on the university's John E. Walker Sr. Golf Course overlooking Lake Hartwell. The initial site of our meeting seemed particularly apropos, as Barker had described the academic space as "the building that teaches."[12] The building was constructed on the site where the quarters for enslaved persons who had labored for the Calhouns and Clemsons on the Fort Hill Plantation had stood. When I arrived in the bright white conference room, only Bostic and Barker were seated around a large table. An uneasy silence enveloped us, punctuated by small talk initiated by Bostic. *Where was Dr. Reel?* I wondered. I felt more comfortable conversing with him since we chatted amicably from time to time in the reading room of Clemson Libraries' Special Collections & Archives.

We soon learned that Reel was running late and would join us for lunch. Bostic then turned to me and said, "Dr. Thomas, why don't you share a bit of your background and how you became interested in documenting African American history at Clemson with President Barker."

I took a deep breath and began with a declaration, "I'd never heard of Clemson until 2007 when I applied for a postdoc position in the English department." I went on to explain that my grandparents had completed only a few years of elementary school. My parents were legally barred from attending Clemson in the 1950s during the Jim Crow era, so they earned teaching degrees from Allen University, a historically Black higher education institution in Columbia, South Carolina. Thus, I had not grown up hearing stories about or visiting Clemson like many of my white students and colleagues. The startled look on Barker's face conveyed his surprise that a sixth-generation South Carolinian would not have known of Clemson's existence until the early twenty-first century. I shared with him my shock at learning—on my first day at work—that Clemson was built on Calhoun's Fort Hill Plantation and that the rich history of African Americans associated with the university was virtually untapped and unacknowledged publicly.

We continued our conversation over lunch in the Madren Center restaurant. I heard Reel's distinctive voice before I saw him. The maître d' escorted us into the private dining room. As if they were celebrities, my charming lunch companions shared greetings with familiar folks who were dining or working in the establishment. In the ensuing discussion, I realized Reel didn't know as much about African Americans' contributions to the university as I thought he did and that Barker and I had missed the opportunity to develop a friendship years earlier while he was Clemson president. After lunch we headed to the cemetery to find the chain-link fence that marked the probable location of the burial ground for enslaved persons who had labored at Fort Hill and convicted laborers who had died while building Clemson. Although we drove around the cemetery several times, we could not locate the graveyard for enslaved persons and convict laborers.

A few months after my meeting with Bostic, Reel, and Barker, I received an email from Barker informing me that he had been thinking about our conversation and inviting me to collaborate on a project with his architecture students. He had assigned his second-year class a semester-long project focused on Cemetery Hill, where the African American burial ground is located. He asked me to make a presentation to them about my research, provide resources for their project, and attend the final day of class when the students would present their work. I agreed and soon found myself standing alongside university historian Reel, juxtaposing the history of enslavement, sharecropping, and convict labor at Clemson with his silver-lining approach to relating the institution's complex history. That methodology for sharing university history was rarely questioned until the early twenty-first century.

As I prepared to work with the architecture students, I returned to Cemetery Hill and slowly drove around the perimeter of the cemetery, searching for the fenced-off area that marked the location of the burial ground for enslaved persons and convict laborers. Just as I rounded the final curve before reaching the exit, I spied a black chain-link fence. After parking and walking closer, I noticed that the area sloped down the hill in the direction of the old Seneca River and was positioned on the lowest rung of the site where the Calhoun family plot was located. Were the remains of the enslaved intentionally buried toward the water in keeping with beliefs that the souls of Black folk returned to Africa via waterways? Yet the positioning of the graves mirrored the location of housing on the Fort Hill Plantation, with the Calhoun's house sitting atop the hill and quarters for both enslaved house servants and field hands always located downslope, separate and unequal.

Clemson Student Activists Demand Transparency about Campus History

While I began to engage more with Clemson faculty and alumni, I continued to support student activism on campus. Just a few weeks earlier, I had participated in a die-in on Bowman Field to protest the killing of Michael Brown by a white police officer and the failure of a grand jury to indict the white police officer who caused Eric Garner's death. On July 17, 2014, on a sidewalk in the New York borough of Staten Island, Garner, gasping, "I can't breathe," had died in a police choke hold. The first die-ins are believed to have been started by activists in 1970 to protest environmental pollution, but they have also been utilized by antiabortion, gun control, and antiwar activists.[13] I had learned of the die-in from my colleague Angela Naimou, who asked if I was participating. I must admit that rainy weather made me hesitate. But I pushed past my discomfort and was soon standing in front of Old Main waiting for the protest to start around 5:00 P.M. on December 4, 2014.

I initially thought this was my first protest, but then I remembered leading my own "revolt" in the eighth grade, when the principal of my school forbade my rumbustious eighth-grade class from taking a trip to celebrate our graduation from middle school. My brothers Donald, Carlton, and I had enrolled in Berean Junior Academy, a private, parochial, segregated Seventh-day Adventist school, after our parents relocated our family from Blakely, Georgia, to Atlanta. My sister Monika was still a toddler. That was just before the segregated public schools in Early County, Georgia, were finally slated to integrate in 1970. As my daddy, who taught mathematics at Washington High School for Black students, and his colleagues contemplated the changes the merger would bring about, including the possibility of some of them losing their jobs or seniority, they decided to meet with white school administrators and collectively address their concerns. During the meeting, however, daddy reported that he was the only one who spoke up, which led to him being offered an administrative position in the new integrated Early County High School. Instead, he and my mother accepted new jobs at Berean Academy. I joined the fifth-grade class of mostly boys, which quickly earned a reputation for reducing teachers to tears and running off substitutes. By the time we were eighth graders, our principal did not believe we had earned the privilege of publicly representing our school, which was so highly respected that then US Congressman Andrew Young had enrolled his children there one year. Instead of accepting the principal's pronouncement, we planned an independent class trip, with the support of our parents, selling candy and pickles to cover the costs of dinner at the Piccadilly Restaurant in the Greenbriar Mall and an outing to Six Flags Over Georgia to celebrate our achievements. We also purchased a trophy for our favorite teacher (my daddy), sneaked it into the church where our graduation ceremony took place, and surprised him—and school administrators, our class sponsor, teachers, and families—with a presentation just before the end of the program.

But on that cold, rainy December day at Clemson, I was following the lead of my students and standing in solidarity with the Garner family, whose patriarch was murdered by a white police officer on a New York sidewalk. When my colleague and I arrived, nobody seemed to know who was leading the protest. Maybe Clemson senior Wallace Mack, I wondered. About ten minutes later, Mack appeared, jumped up on a red brick pillar in front of the building, and provided instructions. We were to be peaceful and silent for this on-campus protest.

During the first documented protest organized by African American students at Clemson in 1969, sixty left campus, fearing for their safety as they faced an intense backlash regarding their request that Clemson discontinue displaying the Confederate battle flag and playing "Dixie" at official public campus events.[14] After Gantt desegregated Clemson in 1963, the university still allowed the playing of "Dixie" and the display of the Confederate battle flag at Clemson-sponsored programs. By the fall of 1969, Black students and their allies had begun requesting that both practices cease. White students and their supporters refused. Nearly all the Black students left campus in protest. After then Clemson president Robert Cook Edwards addressed their concerns, the students returned.[15] Within about a week, more than 3,300 white students, nearly half the student body, signed a petition insisting that the traditions continue.[16] Clemson student Sandy Edge, who helped organize the petition drive, explained, "Dixie and the flag at Clemson symbolize the spirit of the school. . . . The athletes had said the flag and Dixie had really helped them by instilling spirit in them which made them strive to do better."[17] By 1972, however, the administration agreed to discontinue these activities, along with the Country Gentleman mascot, whom some believe favored a southern planter whose roots stretched to the university's founding by a Confederate Army veteran and its establishment by Confederate veterans or sympathizers, who were hired as administrators and faculty and appointed as trustees.

Back on Bowman Field, Mack asked us to walk toward the crowd of Clemson students who were vainly attempting to break the world record for the longest chain of high-fives, but not gather too close or disrupt them. We walked silently, unnerved by the sight of police cars parked along Calhoun Drive, which led up to Old Main. I looked around to find myself surrounded by students, faculty, and staff. But I was particularly struck by the sight of a young student-mother with her baby strapped tightly to her chest.

As we reached our designated spot, some lay on the ground, including the mother and her baby; others, including me, held hands, providing a protective ring around our fellow protesters.

As Mack talked a bit more about the significance of the event, he invited us to chant, "I can't breathe" fifteen times in memory of the number of seconds Garner struggled for his life. Initially, I resisted. Being present seemed enough. But after a few moments, I realized that I could be fully engaged only by joining the chorus of voices. "I can't breathe," I whispered. But my voice grew stronger with each incantation of the phrase until it seemed I was articulating my own Clemson experience. The campus climate had become so stifling for members of underrepresented groups that I suddenly realized "I can't breathe" either. But nobody was choking me. I looked and acted as if all was well. Still, I was fighting for my life. I felt marginalized in an increasingly hostile academic environment. The dire reports about campus climate strengthened my sense that the oppressive atmosphere having a negative impact on underrepresented students was adversely affecting me, too.[18]

After the die-in, racist anonymous comments were discovered on Yik Yak, including "what are these tar babies doing on Bowman Field[?]" and "go back to Africa!"[19] In *The Tar Baby: A Global History*, Bryan Wagner asserts, "At least since the 1840s, 'tar baby' has been used as a grotesque term of abuse, and it continues to feel like an assault no matter the circumstances in which it is employed."[20] Graffiti also appeared on campus, including a curious juxtaposition of "#BlackLivesMatter" with "#STOPPLAYINGVICTIM." The comments conflated a racist term with the familiar refrain of white nationalists, who claim that America is not meant for Black people and that Black lives have never mattered here as much as theirs.

Two days after the die-in, photographs surfaced on social media of Clemson students dressed like gang members at an off-campus "Cripmas" party. In January 2007, students had hosted a similar gang-themed off-campus party they called "Living the Dream" the day before the Martin Luther King Jr. holiday. At least one student wore blackface. Others drank malt liquor. Then President Barker had said, "I was appalled, angered and disappointed when I learned that a group of Clemson students participated in activities at an off-campus party that appeared to mock and disparage African Americans. . . . Many people have been offended and deeply hurt."[21] Students met with administrators, demanded changes, and requested apologies. The student party-goers wrote a letter of apology for "any disrespect we have caused. We invited all races and types of peoples [to the party] and never meant any racial harm."[22] Barker believed more needed to be done. Similar student social events continued occurring, confirming his concerns.

Seven years later, evidence of another gang-themed party emerged online. This time, Clemson's Sigma Alpha Epsilon fraternity hosted the event. After seeing the pictures from the second party, upset students wrote messages in Christmas cards to President Clements, intending to deliver them to his campus home. Their plans were thwarted when Clements met them on Library Bridge in the center of campus with his daughter Grace and promised to address their concerns. In a follow-up email sent to the campus community, Clements said the event had raised more questions about the campus climate, then stated, "But the free expression of opinion must not cross the line and become harassment or intimidation, just as rallies and protest marches must not cross the line to lawlessness."[23] Student protesters and their allies believed Clements was issuing a similar warning both to Cripmas partygoers and peaceful protesters that obfuscated the distinctions between the two groups' intentions and methodologies. He promised to continue the conversation with student protesters in a series of forums during the spring 2015 semester. The university eventually suspended the fraternity's activities and placed the chapter on probation for two years. But student protesters demanded more actions to improve the campus climate.

My colleagues Chenjerai Kumanyika, Andrea Feeser, Todd May, and I devised a means to advocate for students: we planned a meeting followed by a candlelight vigil for faculty and staff seeking meaningful and tangible ways to be allies for students who had been affected by racist incidents on campus. At the meeting, I recalled my introduction to Clemson and growing interest in and research about its complex history. I admitted to a fear of speaking up as an untenured Black faculty member, stemming from then Clemson president Barker's initial refusal to meet with me to discuss or endorse a new Clemson history project. But the #BlackLivesMatter movement was having an impact on me, too. I needed to breathe again. Applause filled the room as I ended my remarks.

By this time, so many people had packed the small meeting room that we moved to a larger auditorium, the one where the brickmaking program had occurred, to share the student activists' five demands for change:

1) build a new multicultural center;
2) secure more funding for organizations of students of color;
3) increase the number of people of color in faculty and administration;
4) change the names of offensively named buildings, for example, Tillman Hall; and
5) make diversity a key goal of Clemson University.

In 2010, under Barker's leadership, the university had prioritized diversity as one of the key components of its 2020 Roadmap, a ten-year strategic plan with the goal of enabling Clemson to be one of the nation's top twenty public universities and a Carnegie Tier One (R1) research institution. Two years later, the Division of Student Affairs conducted a campus climate survey that yielded conflicting results regarding diversity and inclusion. While some respondents believed Clemson offered opportunities for students to make friends and interact with people from diverse cultures, others thought the university emphasized diversity too much. Still others believed that certain student populations were "treated differently," leading to feelings of exclusion and alienation, and that the university's predominantly white student body created an unwelcoming environment for students from underrepresented groups. Some respondents even admitted they had considered leaving Clemson due to issues related to inclusion and equity.[24]

I, too, had considered leaving Clemson for similar reasons. The university offered little support for faculty of color to acclimate to a historically white higher education institution in the most conservative Republican area of South Carolina. Standing on Bowman Field, hands joined with others in solidarity with Clemson students whose consciousness had been raised about their own needs by the #BlackLivesMatter movement sweeping the country, I was willing to be an ally. Johnetta Elzie and DeRay McKesson later came to campus, joining Clemson graduate student A.D. Carson in a discussion of twenty-first-century activism in the social media age before the primarily Black audience that filled the Palmetto Ballroom in the University Union Building. We had been encouraged beforehand to include both allies (folks who would speak up and stand with us in our fight for diversity and inclusion) and accomplices (folks willing to take a bullet for us, to step between us and dangerous individuals or situations).[25]

Throughout my career in the academy, I had always striven to be an ally. When I had begun teaching nearly twenty-five years earlier at Columbia Union College (CUC, now Washington Adventist University) in Takoma Park, Maryland, as a thirty-something single professor, I was often mistaken for a student. I devoted time to not only perfecting my pedagogy but supporting students in an array of activities. I organized student committees to plan Black History Month events that expanded from a month to a year-long series of programs. As the sponsor of the Gospel Choir, traveling on buses and vans and sharing meals with the student singers, I sat proudly in performance sites ranging from country churches to Constitution Hall in Washington, DC, where the Daughters of the American Revolution had once denied Marian Anderson the opportunity to sing. At CUC, Black students had also experienced a consciousness-raising event when the demographics became increasingly Black, much to the consternation of its primarily white constituents. The students worked secretly, planning a protest in front of the main administration building. They were inspired, in part by Spike Lee's movie *Do the Right Thing*, to demand that the college embrace diversity and provide equitable financial assistance. As I worked late one afternoon in my office in Morrison Hall, I heard a knock on the door. Expecting to see a student, I instead found the provost asking if I knew anything about the protests Black students were engaged in that day. Although I was unaware of their actions, I was not surprised by this development. One of the student activists later explained that the protest coordinators decided not to inform me of their plans to protect me from accusations of complicity by administrators. Additionally, as coordinator of the journalism program, I held the precarious position of faculty sponsor of the student newspaper, the *Columbia Journal*, who encouraged student journalists to critically examine issues in a balanced and forthright manner. Without prior knowledge of the students' plans or the protests, I was better positioned to ensure unbiased coverage of campus unrest.

But the issues affecting Clemson students at a predominately white and conservative public higher education institution were informed in part by the global forces for change in the treatment and well-being of Black and brown peoples. I was now working at a university where only about 6.5 percent (rather than nearly 50 percent) of its students were Black. And their concerns were exacerbated by social media platforms, where photographs from a private off-campus Cripmas party, racist graffiti spray painted on campus, and offensive comments shared on platforms like Yik Yak could become international news with the click of a computer key, portending dangerous implications for Clemson students. After my colleagues and I conveyed our plans for the vigil to student activists, Clemson student Shaquille Fontenot created a poster designed for her peers that publicly proclaimed,

> Our Faculty Allies Present:
> A Candlelight Vigil.
> In Solidarity with Student Protesters.
> In Remembrance of Those Lost.
> We Stand With You
> #BlackClemsonMatters
> #weseeyouCU

I am walking with the group of faculty and staff on a route from Lee Hall to Library Bridge, where we will meet the students. As we reach the top of the hill on Fernow Street, retracing part of the path that enslaved persons would have taken between the Fort Hill plantation house and their granite stone barracks-like quarters near the plantation fields, we see Calhoun's flood-lit, white-pillared mansion with green shutters, which had been built mostly by enslaved laborers, glistening in the twilight on our left. We turn right at the corner and walk down the sidewalk that juts against Calhoun Drive alongside Trustee Park, which stretches out behind the red brick Trustee House, built by a predominately African American state convict crew in 1890 on the site where enslaved laborers had once tended the Calhouns' private vegetable garden. As we reach the top of the stairs that lead down to the bridge, we see the students waiting for us. And soon we are together, standing in solidarity, strengthening each other for the struggle.

When Clemson student activists returned to campus after the holiday break in January of 2015, they and their allies staged a #StudentBlackOut[26] march from Death Valley Stadium to Sikes Hall, the main administration building, to present seven grievances about current conditions and seven demands they believed would improve Clemson's campus climate:

> In adhering to Thomas Green Clemson's vision of "a high seminary of learning" and Clemson University's portrayal of its history of diversity starting with "integration with Dignity" in 1963, we concerned Clemson students present for your consideration grievances representative of Clemson University's failure to fulfill and uphold Mr. Clemson's vision and its own mission, particularly to educate "undergraduate and graduate students to think deeply about and engage in the social, scientific, economic and professional challenges of our time" and its foundation through "the generation, preservation, communication, and application of knowledge," nor has it upheld its commitment "to the personal growth of the individual and promotion of an environment of good decision making, healthy and ethical lifestyles, and tolerance and respect for others." We have also included, for your consideration, demands to address our grievances.

> Current list of student grievances:

> 1. We feel as though President Clements'[s] public statement re: The Crip'mas Party is woefully inadequate and insincere. Additionally, we feel Clemson students, particularly those members of underrepresented communities[,] were and are targets of insensitive, ignorant, alienating and (sometimes) criminal/predatory comments on social media (i.e., Yik Yak).
> 2. We feel that students from underrepresented groups have no place to meet and feel safe among other students who represent those groups (and allies).
> 3. We feel student government does not represent the student body as a whole financially. Due to a lack of representation from students

of a variety of backgrounds within predominant student leadership organizations, we feel that their requests for funding are overlooked when evaluated by those that allocate monies.

4. We feel that the percentage of faculty of color should, at least, be comparable to the percentage of students of color.

5. We feel there are several buildings that are named after individuals who were known for their prejudice against underrepresented groups and makes [sic] us feel disrespected, uncomfortable and not welcomed.

6. We feel many administrators and faculty could benefit from training to be better prepared to teach and engage with students from underrepresented groups.

7. We feel that Clemson does not embrace its students from underrepresented groups, which makes those students feel as though they are not part of the Clemson Family.

Current List of Student Demands

1. We want President Clements to *immediately* make a public statement from Clemson University—to students, alumni, faculty, staff, administration and media—denouncing both the Crip'mas Party and hateful statements from members of the Clemson Family via social media (Yik Yak, Facebook, Twitter). Additionally, we want a public commitment from the Clemson University Administration to prosecute criminally predatory behaviors and defamatory speech committed by members of the Clemson University community (including, but not limited to, those facilitated by usage of social media).

2. We want the construction of a multi-cultural center, a safe space for students from underrepresented groups.

3. We want more funding for organizations whose primary constituencies are of underrepresented groups (international students, students of color, LBGTQA community, etc.).

4. We want the percentage of people of color in faculty and administration increased.

5. We want the names of offensively named buildings, ex. Tillman Hall, changed.

6. We want incentivized diversity training for administrators and faculty.
7. We want "Diversity" included as a Clemson University core value, starting with a "diversity"/university history component added to the CU1000 course.[27]

As I stood with other faculty and staff in support of the students, I heard Almeda Jacks, vice president for student affairs, promise to provide an answer from the administration by the time the board of trustees would meet in February.

Expanding the Project's Network and Impact

By the end of February 2015, although student activists still had not received an answer to their demands from the administration as Jacks had promised, I continued to make progress in securing the support and funding I needed to expand my research. A month earlier, Bostic had recommended that we meet and talk with President Clements about my research. I hesitated as the memory of former Clemson president Barker's refusal to approve an investigative study of the university's history lingered. As I began introducing my project to President Clements, I wondered if he had any objections to my work. Although I knew he could not forbid me from researching Clemson history, I also realized he could make my work more difficult by refusing to support faculty or institutional efforts to share the institution's complete history. President Clements assured me of his interest in Clemson history and support of my work. I was cautiously optimistic that with his support, Clemson would move closer to sharing all of its history. Soon afterward, I provided Clements with a tour of some of the sites associated with African American history on campus.

Within six weeks of the tour, Clemson issued a news release heralding, "Professor to Use Grant to Document African Americans in Clemson History." I had begun informally calling my work *The Susan Project*, in honor of Susan Richardson, the enslaved woman who had been owned by both the Calhouns and the Clemsons on the Fort Hill Plantation. But the name suggested that the project was about Susan, not the hundreds of African Americans—free and enslaved people of African descent, sharecroppers, convict laborers, wage workers, musicians, and students, faculty, administrators, and staff who came to Clemson after desegregation in 1963—whose stories I was documenting and sharing.

By this time, I had joined the National Council on Public History (NCPH) and a proposal examining the theme "History on the Edge," which I had submitted for a talk at the organization's 2015 annual meeting in Nashville, Tennessee, was accepted. As my proposal described it, my paper would "explore the University's persistent refusal to include the story of slavery, currently characterized as too 'controversial' to talk openly about, in its public history and the efforts that are being made to rememory the story, as Toni Morrison suggests, in an effort to reconstruct the forgotten and erased narratives of African Americans who labored as slaves, sharecroppers, and leased convicts on Clemson soil." I hoped that public historians would appreciate that "my research aims to enrich the story of Fort Hill, one of America's 'national treasures,' by uncovering more of the complex narrative of an American house and a peculiar institution that is critical to understanding the relationship between the story and legacy of slavery and the history and mission of Clemson University."

I was apprehensive about presenting at a conference intended for historians. My first experience at a historians' conference at the University of North Carolina–Chapel Hill (UNC) a few years earlier had left me feeling like an outlier as a literary scholar who loves history. The respondent for my panel had offered a searing critique of my paper while lavishing praise on a presentation by a UNC history student, whose work was interesting but not groundbreaking. Later, the legal historians at the American Society for Legal History were cordial but left me feeling I needed to focus more on the laws and codes that governed the lives of Black folk rather than the people and stories that were associated with my Clemson project. I looked forward, however, to interacting with public historians. Everything I heard about them convinced me that they preferred collaborative, interdisciplinary work, and embraced storytelling as a vital tool for engaging with the public about the past. Indeed, my first NCPH conference convinced me that public historians are a welcoming group. When I arrived at the conference, I immediately felt as though I was among old friends.

I began my NCPH conference experience by attending the workshop "Giving Voice to the Long-Silenced Millions: Best Practices for Interpreting Slavery at Historic Sites and Museums," held at President Andrew Jackson's

Hermitage. The Fort Hill tours had not changed much in the nearly eight years I had been teaching at Clemson. And after my frustrating experience at Mount Vernon, I hoped to gain insights into telling stories about enslaved persons, especially on the geographical site of a prominent politician's plantation where my university had been built. The facilitators, Kristin Gallas from the Tracing Center on Histories and Legacies of Slavery, Nicole Moore from the City of Virginia Beach History Museums, and Marsha Mullin from The Hermitage, urged us to create conscientious interpretations that reflected comprehensive content, race and identity, institutional investment, community involvement, visitor experience and expectations, and staff training. Fort Hill tours needed to provide learning opportunities and facilitated conversations. Docents would need to function as teachers, utilizing storytelling to illustrate themes through detailed, factual historical accounts of different individuals, which visitors would find harder to ignore than abstract statements about slavery. Visitors would be encouraged to express and work through their resistance. The facilitators asked us to ponder answers to the following question: "What are some ways your institution can shift its messaging, in print, online, etc., to recreate a more inclusive narrative or impression of what your site is about? What might happen if the entire tour of your site was given from enslaved persons' perspectives?" I wondered, "Could that ever happen at Fort Hill?" How could I incorporate these recommendations into my own work? The workshop affirmed my belief that storytelling must be the central component of my project.

The practical tips offered in the workshop energized me as I prepared to make my presentation on the panel "Interpreting Race," where presenters would "analyze public interpretations of challenging aspects of African American history."[28] Two other scholars joined me: Lynn Rainville, an anthropologist from Sweet Briar College, which was also built on a plantation, discussing "Databases and Enslaved Families: Tracing the Roots of African-American Communities in Virginia," and Kurt Terry examining "The Perpetual Wound: Legacy, Memory, Meaning, and the Lynching of Jesse Washington," alongside my talk exploring "Plantation House or Historic Home? Remembering the 'Controversial' History of Masters Calhoun and Clemson's Fort Hill at Clemson University." Conference attendees filled every seat and lined the walls of the seminar room. They listened, engaged, and tweeted—including Monica L. Mercado's tweet, "How do your #public history projects interpret race? We have a lot to learn from Lynn Rainville and @profo7's place-based inquiries #ncph2015."[29] During the Q&A, a public historian asked about institutional support for my research and advised me not to allow Clemson to depend upon me to complete its public history work. Although I had secured support from the administration by this time, her query about my becoming the responsible agent for the recovery of the African American history narrative at Clemson was concerning. Why was my research needed when Clemson employed a university historian, who was writing a new two-volume official history of the institution; a Department of Historic Properties director; and Special Collections & Archives staff? Why was an English professor devoting half her research agenda to a public history project? Perhaps because I was willing to openly and consistently share what I was learning about African Americans in Clemson history. Perhaps because I was beginning to understand that conducting this research was becoming the most compelling reason for to me to stay at Clemson.

As the project grew, the next natural step was to incorporate an international component, so, upon the recommendation of a colleague, I pursued the opportunity to present at the Oxford Roundtable. Hosted at Harris Manchester College, one of the higher education institutions affiliated with the University of Oxford in England, the roundtable creates a multidisciplinary space in which scholars present papers on selected topics. My presentation, "Like Father, Like Daughter: The Impact of John C. Calhoun's 'Slavery as Positive Good' Ideology on Anna Calhoun Clemson, Mistress and Education Philanthropist," fit well with the theme of Women, Religion, and History. During the final dinner at the end of the conference, I arrived late and the only seat available was next to one of the event organizers. He began asking me more about my project. As I lamented the lack of support for a university-sponsored campus history project, he turned to me and said, "You should do it."

Unexpected Discoveries Shift the Trajectory of My Research

When I returned to South Carolina, I headed back to the state archives.

As I began scanning the pages of the descriptive roll for the prison numbers of convicts assigned to Clemson College, confirming their names, and then recording demographic details and court records, leased laborers became men. And more teenagers.

Until Prison Number 10930.
Name: Davis, Simon.
Occupation: Farmer
Age: That can't be a —

I grab my iPhone, snap a picture of the number noted in the "Age" column. Then I take two fingers and swipe them across the screen to enlarge the snapshot.

Heartbeat quickens. Breath shortens. Eyes mist.

Age: 12

I run my fingers across the page, tracing the record of Davis's stint in South Carolina's penal system.

Sex: Male
Color: Colored
Place of Nativity: Abbeville Co.
Height: 4' 11"
Offense: Burglary and larceny
Number: First offense
Remarks: Small scar right cheek both little fingers crooked.

Davis appeared before Judge J. B. Fraser in the Abbeville County Court of General Sessions in June 1892. The judge examined the evidence, found Davis guilty, and sentenced him to five years of hard labor in the state penitentiary, June 11, 1892–June 16, 1897.[30]

Davis's name appears in the Farm and Contract Register for Clemson College for convicts assigned to the college in 1894, which means he had likely turned thirteen by the time the penitentiary deemed him eligible for leasing by Clemson trustees. However, the space in the Notes column next to his name is empty. Details that could provide insights into whether or not he ever worked at Clemson were omitted. Yet his early release is a trend I've noticed as I've researched and documented the predominately African American convict labor crew who built Clemson College. Davis was discharged nearly six months early on January 16, 1897. Which means he was likely leased. Convicts who worked at Clemson frequently were awarded early release, perhaps in recognition of their forced labor for the state.[31]

A few weeks after I learned about Davis's inclusion on the list of convicts assigned to Clemson College, I traveled solo to the Abbeville Court House to search for the records of his court case. South Carolina is filled with beautiful two-lane back roads that connect cities and towns throughout the state. As I grew up in a family of long-haul drivers, I early learned to love road trips, especially after four summers of car adventures with my daddy at the wheel as he drove us from our home in Blakely, Georgia, to Stanford, California, where he was completing his master's degree in mathematics. For three summers in the late 1960s between my eighth and tenth years, my brothers Donald and Carlton and I excitedly mapped out different routes to the West Coast, enabling us to visit nearly every state west of the Mississippi and see many national treasures like Yellowstone's Old Faithful geyser, Yosemite's majestic redwoods, and the Grand Canyon's breathtaking expanses. But my current treks on my home state's country roads are always tinged with fear caused by regular sightings of Confederate battle flags imprinted on the tags of cars and trucks that follow me, sometimes a bit too close to my rear bumper, or implanted proudly in the front yards of houses ranging from metal trailers to brick mansions. If my car breaks down or I have an emergency, will I meet heritage or hate in the person who answers the door? Not knowing keeps me on edge, especially when I drive anxiously through dead zones where my cell phone connection drops for miles. Orange and white Clemson paw flags are welcome signposts of Clemson family ties that run deep across the state, offering a measure of assurance of safe havens.

The hour-long ride from Clemson to Abbeville proved to be mostly pleasant and uneventful, with only one sighting of a Confederate flag displayed prominently in the front yard of a home as I whizzed down Highway 28. When I parked in front of the Abbeville Courthouse, I looked up to see a large marble stone emblazoned with "JOHN C. CALHOUN" at the top. The inscription reads,

Near here, from 1807 to 1817, were
situated the law offices of
John C. Calhoun.
Born in the Long Canes District of Abbeville March 18, 1782.
Died, Washington D.C.
March 31, 1850.
Member of Congress

1811–1817

Secretary of War

1817–1825

Vice President of the United States

1825–1832

United States Senator

1832–1842, 1845–1850

Secretary of State

1844–1845

I have been bumping into Calhoun commemorations most of my life, starting with the name of the city of Calhoun, where my boarding high school, Georgia-Cumberland Academy (GCA), was located in the northern part of the Peach State. GCA was established in 1965 for white Seventh-day Adventist students and was integrated during the 1969–70 academic year by Daniel Parham. Ironically, this Georgia railroad town where the school was located—situated on former Cherokee land, renamed for the proslavery statesman after he died in 1850, and located on the site of a major Civil War battle in 1861–62—developed alongside Dixie Highway.[32] Indeed, memorials and monuments for Calhoun appear throughout America on the names of streets, squares, and schools.

I soon realized that Davis's criminal records were tucked in a rusty metal box perched high on a shelf that could be reached only by climbing a rickety iron ladder. When I checked in, the clerk of the Abbeville Court had informed me she would call an inmate who was working in the office that day to pull the files for me. Soon the inmate, a white man, walked in wearing a grey shirt and matching pants with a distinctive blue stripe that stretched down his leg from hip to ankle, marking him incarcerated, but also strangely reminiscent of Confederate soldiers' uniforms. The inmate was assigned to help me find the historic records for a twelve-year-old "Colored convict" who had also been leased by the state over one hundred years earlier.

Instead of asking the incarcerated man to assist me, however, the clerk decided she would brave the ladder and pull the files herself. The thick collection of records for Davis included an indictment, arrest warrant, recognizance papers, and testimonies. I carefully unfolded each document, laid them all on the table, and snapped a photo of each. Simon Davis, a twelve-year-old Black boy from Abbeville, was sentenced to five years of hard labor in the state penitentiary after being convicted of stealing a piece of jewelry.

A couple of days later, I was sitting in the Clemson University Broadcast Production studio, waiting to record a ninety-second sound bite for the Academic Minute about my research on convict labor and the building of Clemson University. The Academic Minute "features researchers from colleges and universities around the world, keeping listeners abreast of what's new and exciting in the academy and of all the ways academic research contributes to solving the world's toughest problems and to serving the public good."[33]

"Let's do a sound check, Rhondda," the engineer calls out as we prepare to begin.

I take a deep breath and begin reading a script I've read so many times the words flow easily, but with a greater sense of urgency than when I had rehearsed them before locating Davis's prison records: "Wade Foster was not the youngest convict laborer. Records list a boy of twelve among the prisoners who made bricks for campus buildings, cleared college land, and dug foundations and drainage dikes."

"Okay, Rhondda," I hear the engineer's voice calling me through the sound system and take a break.

The white freelance writer who wrote the script walks into the studio.

"Rhondda, it's good. But you sound strident," he insists.

I don't remember how I responded. But I was thinking, *It's because I am. I'm angry. A twelve-year-old boy is on the register of convicts assigned to build my university. I'm angry about that. Reading Simon's records has ignited my anger. I must tell his story.*

"And Rhondda, could you smile?" the white engineer pleaded. "It would help."

Help who? my thoughts were hurtling back toward 1892, trying to imagine what a "Colored boy" may have felt when he realized he was being sent to the penitentiary at hard labor for five years for stealing. Did he understand his sentence? *How can I tell the story of a twelve-year-old African American felon, whose name is on the list of convicts who built my university, with a smile and in a conversational tone?*

I begin again . . . starting with the story of Wade Foster, the teenager whose entry into the criminal justice system had compelled me to go against the advice of some Clemson colleagues, who had warned me that I could lose my job by publicly identifying the boy as one of the hundreds of convicts whom trustees leased to work at Clemson.

Wade Foster was thirteen when he helped to build a university he could never attend. His children could never attend. His grandchildren could never attend.

Foster was a criminal; a black boy caught stealing six dollars' worth of clothes from a white family. Sentenced to six months in prison, South Carolina gave Foster to Clemson University to serve his sentence as convict labor. South Carolina called convict labor "slaves of the state."

From 1899 until 1908, convict labor built Clemson University. Documents found so far list 557 convicts sent to Clemson. All but twenty-nine were African Americans.

Wade Foster was not the youngest convict laborer. Records list a boy of twelve among the prisoners who made bricks for campus buildings, cleared college land, and dug foundations and drainage dikes.

Convict labor—the stereotype robbed the men and boys of their individuality and their contributions to history.

Who were the convicts? What were their crimes? How long did they serve?

That the work of convicts was valued—though not their lives—helped to answer the questions. My research led me to the South Carolina state archive, which had ledgers and accounts of the convict labor business arrangement.

South Carolina was not the only state to use convicts as laborers, but it was the state that used them more than any other to build universities.

The aim is not to diminish Clemson's reputation but to enrich it, to give a complete accounting, to use the past to inform the present and future. The goal of this research is to have markers installed and for campus tours to include the convict labor story.

We cannot change our history, but we can use history to bring about change.

Records list a boy of twelve among the prisoners . . .

His name was Simon Davis. Born in Abbeville County, the birthplace of John C. Calhoun.

Convicted felon.

See The Stripes, Clemson. Show them to the world.

A few months after the release of my Academic Minute about convict labor and the establishment of Clemson, I was sitting at a desk in the Prindle Institute for Ethics at DePauw University scanning through 193 entries in an Excel spreadsheet, searching for information about incarcerated laborers in the notes my research assistant, Edith Dunlap, had culled from Clemson board of trustee minutes from 1890 to 1925. My proposal for examining the role of American universities in creating and supporting the prison industrial complex, using Clemson University as a case study, had been accepted for the "Hearing the Inarticulate: Ethics and Epistemology in the Archives," a ten-day seminar and retreat at DePauw. I had begun drafting biographical narratives about four African American members of the convict crew that built Clemson. The first was thirteen-year-old Foster, convicted of larceny and housebreaking in the daytime and sentenced to six months of hard labor in the state penitentiary. Next was eighteen-year-old Frank "Duck" Mason Jr., convicted of housebreaking and compound larceny and sentenced to twelve months of hard labor in the state penitentiary. Mason Jr. was pardoned after serving eight months due to intervention by his father's white Democratic friends, who sought to honor Frank Sr.'s loyalty to his master during the Civil War and to the predominately white Democratic Party after the war ended. The third was twenty-three-year-old laborer Samuel Smalls, convicted of raping a white prostitute named Bertie Brouthers, sentenced to life in the state penitentiary with hard labor, but pardoned after serving thirteen years. And finally, thirty-one-year-old African American George R. Shaw, convicted of malicious mischief, sentenced to six years of hard labor in the state penitentiary, sent to work at Clemson College three times.

After his release, Shaw settled in nearby Calhoun, South Carolina, where he married and had a family, became a successful landowner, bricklayer, and farmer, and joined the Abel Baptist Church, where he is buried in the church cemetery. As a sixth-generation South Carolinian and as a scholar conscious of my own privilege as a tenured faculty member in the academy but also sensitized by my own experiences as an African American female being silenced within marginalized groups, I believed that, by learning about the convicts' worlds and carefully conveying what I saw and learned, I could contribute to the development of meaningful ways to resurrect and reaffirm the voices of the silenced incarcerated men who had built Clemson.

But first I needed to better understand the reasons why Clemson trustees had decided to lease convicts to build their segregated college. I needed to discover if the trustees left any evidence of their attitudes toward, interactions with, care for, or use of the boys and men on the convict crew. Hence my deep dive into the notes from the Clemson trustee minutes.

George Richard Shaw, his children Hannah, Georgia, and Lewis, and his wife, Rozenia Brown-Shaw (left to right), date unknown. Photo courtesy of Rosa Grayden.

As I scanned the Excel sheet on my computer screen, an entry regarding the use of convicts near Charleston intrigued me. In July of 1908, "Mr. Wannamaker, Chairman of the Coast Experiment Station Committee, requested that they be given ten (10) convicts to work on the Coast Experiment Station."[34] I vaguely remembered reading several letters Wannamaker had written to Clemson president Walter Riggs about his work at the station while I conducted research in Clemson's Special Collections & Archives. But the Wannamaker name sounded more familiar. As I continued working through the research notes, I suddenly remembered why I recognized the Wannamaker name. A few months earlier, I had called my cousin Charles Earle to ask for my great-great-grandmother's maiden name as I knew her only by her married name, Lucretia Earle. Lucretia had raised my grandmother, Thelma Annette Earle Robinson, after her daughter Lavenia was struck and killed by lightning while holding my grandmother, an infant. My daddy had visited her home when he was a child and described her as being a white woman. My grandmother had given me several pictures of Lucretia, which confirmed the descriptions I'd received of her as a tall, white-skinned woman with straight hair down to her ankles. The 1920 census categorized her and her grandchildren as mulattoes, however. Charles directed me to his brother Reginald Hampton, who informed me that Lucretia's birth name was Wannamaker and that I could confirm this information through her death certificate, which was available on familysearch.com. I found the death certificate, which classifies her race as "Non-white," and entered the information into my family tree, including the names of her parents: her mother, Louisa Wannamaker, and her father, simply Wannamaker, as no first name for him was included. Hampton also told me that Lucretia had a sister, who insisted on being called "Miss Wannamaker."

I didn't think about Lucretia Wannamaker Earle again until a few minutes after I came across the name Wannamaker in those research notes for the Clemson board of trustee minutes. Was I related to Clemson lifetime trustee and experiment station manager John Edward Wannamaker? My grandmother had named her youngest son Edward. My parents affirmed the family tradition by giving their eldest child, a son, the middle name Edward.

I called Dunlap. "You're not going to believe this: I may be related to Clemson trustee John Wannamaker." She laughed. We both marveled at the intriguing possibility.

I send a text to my Clemson colleague Andrea Feeser:

I may have an interesting tie to Clemson history. I have just confirmed that my paternal great-great-grandmother's name is Lucretia Wannamaker. . . . Have also learned about a Mr. Wannamaker in archival records who was not only the supervisor for the construction of Clemson's experimental station in Summerville (late 1890s–early 1900s), but he was the first lifetime trustee and first chairman of Clemson's board of trustees. . . . I will likely hire a genealogist to help me resolve my mysterious ties to the Wannamakers.

She responds, "Remarkable."

In seeking to ensure that the names of hundreds of African Americans are dusted off and pulled out of the archives, I inadvertently helped to confirm my own ancestry.

When I return home, I am sleepless. In the middle of the night, I shake my husband awake. "I may be related to John E. Wannamaker. One of Clemson's first lifetime trustees," I tell him again.

He wakes up just enough to say, "Okay," rolls over, and goes back to sleep.

I couldn't breathe on campus. I couldn't sleep at home. But I kept searching for clues about African Americans in Clemson history.

Unsettling Clemson History: The Project Needs a Name

A few months earlier, I had made a presentation for the "Hallowed Grounds: Sites of African American Memory" Black History Month program for South Carolina's FBI–Columbia Division. At the end of the program, the audience gave me a standing ovation followed by closing remarks from the director, who said my work epitomized a quote he'd heard: "There are three deaths: the first is when the body ceases to function. The second is when the body is consigned to the grave. The third is that moment, sometime in the future, when your name is spoken for the last time."[35] Most African Americans in Clemson history—slaves, sharecroppers, and convicts—had experienced the first two deaths. All of them were threatened with the third. My project could help ensure their names were never forgotten.

By the spring of 2016, the C19 Conference, through its theme of "Unsettling," pulled the threads of my work together and catapulted me into another realm. My mentor and friend professor of English John Ernest organized the "19th-Century Black Lives Matter: Unsettling Interventions in African American Literary and Cultural Studies" panel and invited me to present a talk titled "Of Slaves, Sharecroppers, and Convict Laborers: Unsettling Clemson University's Public History." My dissertation advisor Carla Peterson was in the audience and invited me to make a presentation that fall at my alma mater for doctoral studies, the University of Maryland, as part of the Democracy Then and Now Series. The series was cosponsored by the Nineteenth-Century Americanists, directed by Robert

S. Levine, who had also served on my dissertation committee. UM students packed the room, and nearly all stayed until the end—surprising my hosts, who remarked that students slipped out before the end of most programs. During the Q&A, Levine asked me to tell the students a bit about John C. Calhoun, which surprised me. But then I realized many millennials know very little about the antebellum history and literature that undergird my work. As we neared the end of the program, my goddaughter, Lillian Tyler, asked the final question: "Why did you choose Call My Name as the title for your project?"

By this time, I knew I needed a new name for my research project. My work now encompassed six different groups, from free Africans to people of African descent experiencing enslavement, emancipation, and desegregation in America. My working title, The Susan Project, no longer seemed to fit. I desired a title associated with the identities of many different individuals, one that emphasized the humanity of persons who had been exploited and all but forgotten. I settled on Call My Name to evoke the call-and-response tradition associated with African American culture: I am calling the names of African Americans in early Clemson history and inviting an array of people to assist me in making their stories publicly accessible. The name evokes as well the various roll calls that occur in academic communities like Clemson. And it provides an antidote for the annoyance I felt at not hearing called the names of enslaved Africans who labored for George and Martha Washington on the Mount Vernon Plantation.

I have affirmed known names, found new names, and continue to search for the names of Black people in Clemson history. Calling their names, we can postpone indefinitely their third death. They will be remembered and talked about for many years to come.

Call my name, Clemson.

Section Three

Poor people, people of color—especially[—]are much more likely to be found in prison than in institutions of higher education.
ANGELA DAVIS

Call: The Twelve-Year-Old Felon

RHONDDA ROBINSON THOMAS

Shocked!

The boy is finally caught.

Three witnesses claimed the suspect struck on Saturday night, January 30, 1892, breaking into the home of Mrs. Margaret Martin in Mt. Carmel, South Carolina, and taking jewelry and a pocket book worth two dollars. Two dollars in 1892 was equivalent in purchasing power to $55.38 in 2019 currency. They agreed on the identity of the suspect, the same person one of the witnesses believed had been stealing from other people's homes for more than a year and committing even more serious crimes. But nobody had any proof. Until now.

Within forty-eight hours, somebody notified William Frith, Mt. Carmel's constable, of the theft. Frith swore before Judge T. L. Covin, trial justice for Abbeville County, South Carolina, that the suspect had confessed to breaking into Mrs. Martin's home and stealing goods, including a piece of jewelry the suspect had shown him. Based on this evidence, Frith requested and was granted an arrest warrant.

Frith and another witness, Mary Taggart, provided sworn testimony to Judge Covin. Frith maintained that Martin's home was "feloniously and burglariously broken open" by the suspect who took "jewelry and a pocket book the value of two dollars."[1] Taggart began her testimony by claiming that the suspect broke into her house the evening after he had burglarized Martin's home and then stole and ate some rations. She caught and kept the suspect in her home overnight, eliciting a confession. Both Frith and Taggart signed their witness statements with an X mark for a signature between their first and last names, which reflects illiteracy. Can we trust testimony from people who were unable to check its authenticity? Covin requested that Frith bring the suspect before him so that justice could be served, and he issued a recognizance to testify to Frith and Taggart, making them duty-bound to appear at the trial and repeat their statements about the suspect's connection to the robbery. Failure to do so would result in a levy of one hundred dollars against their property. They were also advised to "keep the peace of the state" toward the suspect. If they did not, the recognizance would be voided, there would be no evidence for the trial, and the suspect might be released.[2]

For nearly six months, Frith and Taggart kept their distance from the suspect, who became a defendant at the trial on June 16, 1892.

Judge J. B. Fraser facilitated the one-day trial at the Abbeville County Courthouse. R. H. Cochman, the jury's foreman, declared they found the defendant guilty of burglary and larceny in the nighttime. The indictment indicated that with "force and arms" the defendant took from "the dwelling house of one Margaret Martin there situate, feloniously and burglariously did break and enter with intent the goods and chattels of Margaret Martin in the said dwelling house, there and then being, then and there feloniously and burglariously to steal, take and carry away, against the form of the Statute in such case made and provided, and against the peace and dignity of the same State aforesaid."[3] During the late 1800s in South Carolina, the crime of theft was deemed to be more heinous when committed after sunset. Larceny committed against South Carolina residents posed a threat to the peace and safety of local communities. Judge Fraser sentenced the defendant to five years at hard labor in the state penitentiary in Columbia, South Carolina, which was ninety-two miles east of the defendant's hometown. By October 31, 1892, he had become one of nine hundred prisoners confined in the penitentiary and labor camps run by the state.[4]

Shocked!

A boy becomes a felon.

During the boy's first year at the state penitentiary, the superintendent supplied Clemson College with an average of eighty-one convicts per day, along with clothing and shoes. The penitentiary also paid $3,118.49 (about $89,850 in 2019 currency) for the cost associated with guards to control the prisoners. Similar allocations of prisoners and supplies were provided to the Industrial School for Girls [now Winthrop University] in Rock Hill, SC. The penitentiary superintendent described both as a "heavy drain on this institution."[5] The state and Clemson shared costs associated with convict leasing, but it appears penitentiary administrators did not believe the system was as profitable as they had anticipated it would be.

Nevertheless, in their annual report for 1892, Clemson trustees provided a glowing report of the convicts' work:

> We are pleased to be able to report that the small force of three or four carpenters and the convicts have during the year accomplished very satisfactory results. They have completed the kitchen, room for the boilers, placed the boilers, built smoke-stack and baking department, and the kitchen is now ready for use. They have completed the inside work of the Dormitory, except painting, and it is now ready to be occupied, and is capable of accommodating six hundred students, being perhaps the largest house in the State. They have completed the dining room, finished building the walls of the Chapel, put on the roof, put in the windows and floored it. They have completed the walls of the President's house and put the roof thereon. They have nearly completed the Infirmary and have built a brick house for Laundry, 40 by 50 feet. They have built another brick Professor's house and covered it in. They have built the tower to main building above the roof, and would have completed it but for want of necessary material we were not able to purchase, and are now flooring, ceiling and plastering the Main College Building, which work we hope to finish in about a month from this date unless the material therefor [sic] be exhausted. They have also made 900,000 brick [sic], sufficient probably to complete the buildings as planned by the Board.[6]

Incarcerated men and boys were the essential labor force for the establishment of Clemson College.

Shocked!

A teenaged felon helps build Clemson.

Within two years of the start of his incarceration, the boy's name appeared once on the 1894 register of convicts that the penitentiary superintendent W. A. Neal gave Clemson College trustees—including SC Governor and self-avowed white supremacist "Pitchfork Ben" Tillman—the authority to lease convicts to build their higher education institution. That register is the only record that has been recovered thus far about the prisoner's connection to forced labor at a segregated, land-grant higher education institution for white males in Jim Crow South Carolina. Because there are no notations by his name in the register, details regarding his participation on the workforce are unknown. But the boy may have been forced to help build a college he could never attend. He may have been a member of the incarcerated work force Clemson trustees leased to rebuild the Main Administration building that had been destroyed by a fire in 1893. That year, Clemson trustees claimed in their annual report, "The convict labor heretofore furnished by the State has proved invaluable both in the construction of buildings and the development of the farm."[7] Then they asked for at least thirty-three more state convicts the next year on the same terms. By that time, a stockade had been built for convicts, and classes had begun for white cadets.

Shocked!

The teenaged felon is rearrested—for stealing.

The convicted felon was discharged from the South Carolina state penitentiary on January 16, 1897.

When the felon, Simon Davis, an African American farmer, had first been confined in the state penitentiary on June 16, 1892, he was twelve years old. When he was assigned to the incarcerated workforce for Clemson College in 1894, he was likely thirteen or fourteen. When he was released from state penitentiary on January 16, 1897, he was probably sixteen or seventeen.

In a PBS interview about "Race in America," Angela Davis asserted, "Poor people, people of color—especially[—]are much more likely to be found in prison than in institutions of higher education."[8] More than a century after Simon's incarceration, poor Black young men were still disproportionately represented in the poverty to prison pipeline. Nearly of college age after serving five years in the state penitentiary, Simon was classified as a criminal rather than a high school senior. As a seventeen-year-old felon, his employment and educational options were severely limited.

Within a few months of his release, Simon had been arrested again and charged with stealing again. Witness James Wideman declared in a sworn statement that the boy "did break and enter into the dwelling house. . . . And then did steal and carry away therefrom 1 overcoat, 1 hat, 1 undershirt, 1 Top Shirt, 1 shot gun, 1 Pr Pants, 1 Pr drawers, one vest and one Pocket Book the personal property of said deponent and worth the sum of Twenty Dollars."[9] Like the two witnesses for the boy's trial five years earlier, Wideman affixed his X mark for a signature between his first and last names. Additional witnesses, Lizzie Brown and J. S. McQueens, affirmed Wideman's testimony. W. E. Cothran, magistrate for Abbeville County, instructed Constable J. M. Pounds to "apprehend the said Simon Davis and bring him before me to be dealt with according to the law."[10] Cothran later reported that Simon was arrested, "having stolen property in his possession—confessed his guilt to the first named witnesses with several others and was committed to jail to answer at Court of Sessions."[11]

The records for Davis's second trial have been lost.

His whereabouts thereafter are unknown.

Shocked!

History lost track of Davis.

We will keep searching until we discover what happened to Simon Davis.

Response: A Seat at the Table

THOMAS MARSHALL

As I walked into the historic Hardin Hall at Clemson University at around 12:19 P.M. on Wednesday, August 17, 2016, for my first college class, I made my way up the stairs to Philosophy 101. When I walked into room 233, I immediately noticed that I was the only Black student in my class.

I was shocked!

Thoughts of *Am I good enough? Do I belong here?* flitted through my mind. Being a first-generation college student did not help either. Consider the stats: being Black, male, and a first-generation college student at a predominantly white university does not always add up to graduation. I chose to take a seat in the very front of the classroom, knowing that once I selected this seat, it would be mine forever, at least metaphorically. This is something that Simon Davis, who likely helped build Hardin Hall, never could have imagined as he labored on the convict workforce for Clemson College in the late nineteenth century. My taking that front row seat was more than just a place in a classroom. It was a seat at the table.

When I initially applied to colleges, Clemson was not very high on my list. Nestled near the Blue Ridge Mountains in rural Pickens County in the most conservative part of Upstate South Carolina, the university's greatest claim to fame for me was its athletic prowess. I did not think about coming to the school. During my senior year of high school, after months of decision-making and trying to figure out my next steps, I decided to enroll in Clemson University the night before National Decision Day. Eventually I chose Clemson because it felt like home. After visiting my sister, who was already a student at the university, I just had a feeling. But the reason I was able to even have an opportunity to apply and live a successful life at Clemson is due to the labor of Simon Davis.

During the first semester of my sophomore year, I took my first African American heritage tour of campus. As I learned about this history, more specifically that a predominantly Black state convict crew built my school . . .

I was shocked!

Then I experienced a range of emotions—frustration, anger, and even guilt that I was fortunate enough to walk the halls of buildings and take classes while Black convicts sweating to build those buildings had to watch white students do that every day.

The late-nineteenth-century media may have painted Simon as a degenerate or someone who was not of good character, but I consider him to be a hero. The toughest part about Simon is that we do not have much information about him, but he is a known convict laborer who worked on building Clemson. We know he was from Abbeville, South Carolina, ironically John C. Calhoun's hometown. We know he was cited for "stealing" and was sentenced to five years of hard labor in the state penitentiary. We know Clemson trustees leased him like a slave to help build their new public college. We know his tasks likely included helping build the kitchen, making sure dormitories were ready for white male students, and even working on the brick walls of the first president's house. We know he labored at Clemson when he was between twelve and fourteen years old. We know he was accused of stealing again a few months after he was released from the penitentiary. But we don't know anything about his upbringing or his family. We don't know how he felt about being forced to build a college he knew neither he nor his friends could attend. We don't know what happened to him after he was released from prison.

A typical day for me on campus consists of going to classes, stopping by Starbucks for a snack, and going home to my residence hall, where I live and work with other students. Before moving into my room on campus, I did not have to paint its walls or wonder where the furniture would come from. I did not have to work long hours to ensure that the construction would be completed in time for classes to begin. When I go to the president's house, I have the honor of seeing President Clements and shaking his hand. I enjoy the pleasure of walking through the house's pristine rooms, not constructing its walls. At Clemson, I have the opportunity to do anything I set my mind to—because of boys like Simon Davis. I even have the chance to pursue leadership roles. But it is because of Simon that I am able to do all of these things. He was forced to help construct some of the oldest buildings on the campus that I call home.

When I arrived at Clemson, I was nervous, excited, and very, very scared to leave home for the first time. I was involved in many different activities and organizations in high school, and I wanted to make an impact at my college, too. I think making an impact is a very cliché thing that many students say that they want to do, but what does it truly mean? For someone who is Black at a predominantly white public higher education institution, making an impact is not easy. Clemson's student population is only 6.5 percent African American and over 80 percent white.

I am shocked!

I knew navigating systems and spaces that were built by the hands of convict laborers would be challenging. But I also believed Clemson University was a place where I could thrive. Indeed, my Clemson experience has been full of thriving through ups and downs, highs and lows. But my latest experience taught me that history can be made anywhere, even here where people like Simon Davis did not get a chance to attend school, though his impact is still felt today.

I have been involved in the Clemson Undergraduate Student Government my entire time at the university, and in the spring semester of 2019, I decided to run for vice president. This was not an easy decision, but one that I knew would challenge me and enable me to grow. My campaign was historic because my running mate was also a person of color, a Black female student named Diamond Brown. To my knowledge, we were the first all-minority ticket to ever run for student government office at Clemson. We sought leadership positions because we wanted to uplift others and create a campus culture where everyone felt welcomed and a part of student government. Our slogan and plan was to "Elevate." We wanted to elevate Clemson by raising the standards, empowering other students, while soaring to new heights. Unfortunately, we came up short and lost in the general election by only 120 votes.

I was shocked!

This outcome was initially disappointing, but then it hit me. Our loss was historic, not because our names were on the ticket. My involvement led me to something greater than I could imagine. Clemson gave me the platform and chance to conceive and share my ideas with the world, something that someone like Simon Davis never had the opportunity to do. My historic campaign was not about me or the words that I said or even my passion. It was about leaving a legacy. I think legacies are one of the most important things a person can do for someone. And to leave a historic one in the process is a tall task. I am not saying my Clemson experience has been all peaches and cream. I have had some rough times, faced inequalities, gone through the worst of growing pains, and much more. But I can say that being at Clemson has been the greatest time of my life, shaping and molding me into the man I am today.

The word opportunity always comes to mind when I think about the intersection of Simon Davis's story and my story. I think about the way Simon was forced to help build a college that he knew he would never have the chance to attend. As sad and unfair as it is, he still was a part of building a significant, influential higher education institution. Conversely, I was afforded the opportunities not only to enroll in Clemson but also to run for student government office. Although I lost, I was still given the greatest thing in return: growth. An ability to change. A chance to shake the status quo. And for that reason, I know the work of Simon Davis will not be in vain. The long hours that he spent building the university is why I walk this campus's sacred grounds. It is why I run for student government positions. And it is why I live.

I cannot thank Simon Davis enough for his sacrifice so I can have opportunities at Clemson University today. Simon's sacrifice not only enabled me to become a student and thrive at Clemson, his labor helped create a university that now hosts an annual Men of Color Summit, where young Black and Hispanic men are given the chance to prepare for enrollment at the university. The 2019 Summit was nothing short of amazing. Being able to work as a Tiger Alliance Ambassador and help lead and guide high school students around the conference was a joyful experience. This indescribable feeling stemmed from my being able to share insights with so many students, while guest speakers and professionals poured theirs into me. Long gone are the days of young Black and brown boys simply getting to college. We are now excelling in and out of the classroom and are the leaders at institutions that were not initially built for us. "What we do today will matter to people who are born after I die."

Clemson culture—shocked!

CHAPTER 3

The Challenge

Creating Collaborations

◇◇

And lately Isseys [*sic*] trying to burn us all up.
FLORIDE CALHOUN TO PATRICK CALHOUN, APRIL 3, 1843

I tell you it's gonna rain
it's gonna rain
you better get ready and bear this in mind
   God showed Noah the rainbow sign
   Won't be water but fire next time.
CHARLES JOHNSON, "IT'S GONNA RAIN"

They have names. . . . They're not just faceless people.
Wow, this is pretty amazing.
S. EPATHA MERKERSON

You've got to be kidding, I'm thinking, while I watch the white police officer unhook the latch on his gun holster as he approaches the driver's side of my rental car.

As I drove to Monticello, enjoying the quaint historic towns and bucolic back country roads of Orange County, Virginia, I spied the blaring blue lights of a police car in my rearview mirror just as I—in my large white SUV rental with tinted glass windows—was accelerating on the open road. I had forgotten I was driving in small town America, despite the warning I'd received from a friend; she had told me she had received three speeding tickets during her first six months in the state. The police officer hit the back of my vehicle with his hand, startling me, as he swaggered up to the driver's side door.

"I clocked you at fifty-seven in a thirty-five mile per hour zone," he begins.

"I thought I was outside of the city limits. I didn't see the speed sign," I respond.

"You didn't see the sign? You got some kind of emergency?"

"I am unfamiliar with this area. I have an appointment at Monticello and need to get there by 3:30."

"I need your driver's license and registration."

"Here's my license, but the car is rented."

"Who did you rent it from?"

"Enterprise, at the airport."

By this time, my thoughts have shifted toward Mike Brown and Eric Garner and Tamir Rice, who were all killed within seconds to minutes of their encounters with police. The officer takes my license and goes back to his squad car. As he slowly fills out the paperwork, I glance at him in my rearview mirror. I have no idea why this takes so long.

When he comes back to my car he announces, "I'm going to give you a ticket."

"You could give me a warning," I counter.

"I can't. I could have cited you for reckless driving, which would have meant jail time." After examining my license, the officer knows I'm from South Carolina and likely won't be able to come back and fight this charge on April 24, 2015, my court date.

"Don't you know what a speed sign looks like?" he quips.

I can feel myself growing angry, so I immediately stop engaging him. The last thing I want to be is a Black woman alone and dead on a bucolic back country Virginia road.

"How much will the ticket be?"

"It's six dollars for every mile over the limit. They will tell you when you call this number."

I am tempted to taunt him: *You can't do the math?* Instead, I take the ticket and drive away, slowly. I suddenly realize I may have been driving even faster if I had been playing my road music soundtrack. The vehicle's sound system had stopped syncing with my iPhone a few miles before I received the ticket. The situation could have turned out much worse.

A few weeks after returning to South Carolina, I pay the $200.72 speeding fine, which includes a four percent processing fee, online.

Seeking Insights and Inspiration from Historic Virginia

My willingness to drive on the back roads of Virginia to visit historic sites that could help me better understand how to tell the stories of people of African descent in slavery and freedom grew out of my desire to resolve a dilemma: How could my colleagues and I ensure that our students were receiving a balanced tour of the Fort Hill plantation house and all its occupants? One solution we considered was to secure grants to fund collaborations that would enable us to create our own tools for investigating Fort Hill history. In the fall of 2014, my Department of English colleague Gabriel Hankins, hired to help develop our digital humanities program, had joined me in writing an application for a National Endowment for the Humanities (NEH) grant to create a mobile app. The goal of *Re-placing Race at Fort Hill: Uncovering the Hidden Histories of Public Spaces with Mobile Technology* was to change the way the public experiences the complex racial history of America's historic plantations, beginning with Fort Hill. The app would reveal the places and share the stories associated with the enslaved African Americans who worked there, as well as the African American sharecroppers, convicts, domestics, and wage laborers who labored on the land upon which Clemson was built. We would collaborate with Clemson colleagues who specialized in mobile app design. Our intentions were ambitious. In future stages, Hankins and I hoped to extend the prototype through joint initiatives with major national historic sites such as Mount Vernon and Charleston's Drayton Hall, locations that had similar hidden histories of race and space. We wanted to replace the racial history of these historic spaces with concrete and visible details about the often overlooked lives of the enslaved and exploited men, women, and children who lived and worked at Fort Hill and at partner sites.

The NEH did not fund our mobile app project. However, rejection did not diminish my dream of collaborations with staff at plantations once owned by prominent American politicians.

Up to this point, the focus of my research and source of my collaborators had primarily been Clemson. But as I learned more about its history, I began to reach out to other slavery scholars, museum professionals, and community members who were conducting similar research; I was seeking ideas on how to engage my campus and local communities in discussions about enslavement and its legacies at my university. I was still interested in utilizing web technology to make the history and legacy of slavery at Fort Hill more accessible to the public. While seeking a database model for sharing these stories in early 2015, I came across *People of the Founding Era*, an online resource that provides biographical details primarily about the founding fathers and the people with whom they were connected. I contacted Sue Perdue, its director, who connected me with Kirt von Daacke and Kelley Deetz at the University of Virginia (UVA), where the higher education institution's president had recently established a commission on slavery and the university.[1] Deetz responded immediately and scheduled a series of meetings with a few members of the commission, community advisory board, UVA tours, and UVA students, who were planning to establish a memorial for enslaved laborers and who had produced the brochure "Slavery at the University of Virginia: Visitor's Guide." She also offered to introduce me to the coordinators of the Getting Word Project at Monticello and suggested that I add a tour of James Madison's Montpelier Plantation and a trip to the College of William and Mary to talk with Jody Allen, director of the Lemon Project.

During my first visit to and tour of UVA, I immediately sensed a strong connection to Jefferson that permeates the campus. His words are etched onto the landscape, his image is reflected in a statue, his aesthetics are imprinted in the design that makes the campus feel like an extension of his beloved Monticello. My tour with UVA student guides offered illuminating insights into the challenges of sharing the history of slavery and the university with the public. My guides were somewhat knowledgeable about the campus, but they kept interrupting each other to fill in details, such as the type of architecture used for the buildings in the Academical Village, the oldest part of campus, designed by Jefferson. One student guide seemed enamored with facts about the pavilions, providing minute details about the structures.

"Who built them?" I asked.

"Slaves," one guide answered. "But the University only owned three or four slaves."

"Where did the others come from?" I asked.

"They were hired."

"Did they live on campus?"

"Some lived in shacks behind the pavilions. We'll show them to you. But some [Black workers] were free."

"How were they freed? Did they earn their freedom?"

"Yes, they worked and earned freedom."

I was skeptical. Which enslaved persons, the few the university owned, or the others rented from nearby landowners? What were their names? When were they freed? What happened to them? These tours of historic sites of slavery almost always raise questions, mostly unanswered.

Next, we entered the stately red brick, two-story, white-columned Colonnade Club, UVA's first building, which includes a manicured garden in the back of the building. My guides pointed out the red brick walls that were built to conceal the unsightly slave quarters from passersby. UVA's Academical Village looked like Monticello with a similar spatial structure: enslaved persons laboring out of sight—on the lower level of the house or through concealed staircases at Monticello; behind brick walls at his college. At UVA, enslaved persons rose early to cook, clean, and prepare the students' clothes.

Earlier that day as I was driving from UVA to Monticello for a meeting with Aurelia Crawford, a member of the Getting Word African American Oral History Project staff, I thought about Jefferson's five-thousand-acre plantation, situated on hills overlooking his college in the valley, and the African peoples whose life experiences were shaped by the practice and legacies of slavery in both places. *How can we locate descendants of the enslaved who worked at Fort Hill?* I wondered. *Would they be willing to share their family stories?* Getting Word staff established the initiative in 1993 by collecting oral histories from descendants of Monticello's enslaved community throughout the United States. The Thomas Jefferson Foundation began to support their work after DNA research confirmed that Thomas Jefferson was likely the father of Sally Hemings's children.[2] After Getting Word created a public profile, even more people discovered they were descendants of Monticello's enslaved families.

Yet some docents at Monticello still seemed uncomfortable sharing the stories about slavery. As I took the main house tour, the docent kept apologizing for depressing us each time she mentioned slavery. She was sorry for having to tell us about the sexual dynamics of Jefferson and Hemings's relationship or the valet who continued to clean Monticello after Jefferson died. *Don't assume I'm depressed!* I wanted to shout. When I returned to Monticello in 2018 just before they opened the recently excavated room where Sally Hemings is believed to have lived, I took a Hemings Family tour to learn about the new discoveries regarding the Hemings family. The older, experienced tour guide characterized the sexual relationship between Jefferson and Hemings as a "liaison."

"Could it have been rape?" I asked.

"I prefer to use 'liaison' because rape makes people feel uncomfortable," he explained.

My behind-the-scenes visits to all these historic plantation sites, especially my experiences at Monticello, Mount Vernon, and Montpelier, have convinced me that most of the staff are trying to be forward thinking. But it seems that they trot out an inoffensive experience for the everyday visitors and quite another for visiting historians, scholars, and conference attendees. In Mount Vernon's archeological lab, I held bits of pipes, buttons, dishes, and a cufflink embellished with coral—artifacts staff have recovered in a dig onsite. As I talked with a graduate student from George Mason University, who directed the field school at Mount Vernon's slave cemetery, he explained how they had discovered graves on the sides of the hill that slope down toward a river, a site similar to location of the cemetery for enslaved persons on Calhoun's Fort Hill Plantation. As I examined the photographs of the graves, white indentations in the ground shaped like mummies, I ran my fingers across the two small images believed to be infants. The archeological team had surveyed only the first area of the site and expected to find more graves. They decided against unearthing the remains out of respect for the descendants and the local Black community's wishes. They encouraged me to develop a field school for Woodland Cemetery and the two sites adjacent to the Fort Hill plantation house, where enslaved persons are believed to have worked and lived, and to collaborate with South Carolina's historic preservation director in Columbia, who apparently is very interested in this type of work. Mt. Vernon's hybrid course model—community and traditional archeology and research—could work at Clemson. I also talked extensively with the staff member who, with the assistance of two student interns, was establishing a database that will enable them to document every mention of an enslaved person in an assortment of primary documents. The goal is to create minibiographies as well as to provide better insights into the lives, labors, and mobilities of enslaved Africans at Mount Vernon. Could we do something similar for Fort Hill, using the correspondence of the Calhouns, Clemsons, and their kith and kin networks?

Soon I am on the road again, driving around Richmond, Virginia, trying to find the historical marker on the site where Gabriel Prosser was hanged after his rebellion failed in 1800. Virginia's Department of Historic Resources cataloged the marker as "SA 66 Execution of Gabriel." The road dead-ended. I was about to give up. I decided to retrace my route, driving back across the bridge on US highway 250 a final time. As I looked directly ahead, I spied the historical marker on the right side of the very busy multilane highway. There was no place to pull over. *Who decided to install the marker in such an inaccessible space?* I wondered. *Do they really want people to see it? How many people have given up before they found the marker?* Not very accessible, just like the story of Gabriel's life and the history of African Americans at Clemson and in much of American history.

My trip to Richmond included a drive over to Washington and Lee University, which coincidentally occurred in March 2015 on the same day the chapel reopened after the Confederate battle flags were removed and placed in the institution's museum. The university is named for two slaveholding men, George Washington and Robert E. Lee, who both fought in wars, the American Revolution and the Civil War, respectively, to establish slaveholding nations. As I rounded the corner and caught my first glimpse of the tall, red brick, white-columned Colonnade—Washington Hall, Robinson Hall, Payne Hall, Newcomb Hall, and Tucker Hall, a National Historic Landmark situated in the center of campus like the Fort Hill plantation house at Clemson—I felt as if I was experiencing a *Back to the Future* transport, this time to Tara, the O'Hara's plantation, in *Gone with the Wind*.[3] *How do folks of color navigate this space?* I wondered.

My first stop was the chapel, known as the "Shrine of the South." Edward Valentine's life-size marble sculpture of Confederate general Robert E. Lee, installed in 1883, is prominently displayed in the pulpit area. Lee is presented in his Confederate general uniform, asleep on the battlefield. *Are official university events held in the chapel?* I wondered. I headed downstairs to the museum, stopping briefly by the crypt where Lee is buried. I cannot fathom why some people still revere the man who led an army that was willing to die for the right to continue enslaving people of African descent— including my ancestors.

While Washington and Lee University took steps to come to terms with its ties to Confederates, Clemson followed the lead of past trustees and administrators in obfuscating this aspect of its history. About the time Clemson's College of AAH rolled out the first year of its *Race and the University* initiative, the trustees resisted calls from student activists and their allies to rename Tillman Hall or endorse a reexamination of Clemson history. Conversely, Washington and Lee president Kenneth P. Ruscio created a working group composed of professors, an archivist, a student, a dean, and advancement staff to research African Americans' contributions to the institution from the antebellum period to the present. While this university heeded students' calls to address their concerns about their institution's Confederate history, Clemson continued to affirm the deliberate omission approach reflected in the characterization of its founder as a "Soldier" in the inscription on his statue, not a *Confederate* soldier. Some buildings at Clemson are named for Confederate veterans, like Hardin Hall, which honors the university's first chemistry professor, Confederate colonel Mark Hardin; but in historical markers recently erected on campus the university emphasizes the founders' service to the institution and the state of South Carolina, not to the Confederacy. On the Washington and Lee University website, its president lists African Americans at the institution as one of his primary issues and initiatives.[4] At that time, visitors to Clemson's website could not easily determine administrators' commitment to documenting and telling its story of African American life, labor, and legacies. Both institutions, whose founders include prominent slaveholders and white supremacists, struggle with how to share the history of slavery and its legacies in an era when campus and local communities are increasing demanding transparency, honesty, and accountability. But Washington and Lee chose a markedly different approach than Clemson in addressing its history, responding to student concerns, and publicly owning and seeking meaningful ways to address, document, and share its complicated history.

Although my travels to higher education institutions and historic plantations in the Virginia countryside, a place where enslaved persons like my maternal great-great-grandfather Robert Williams were sold and sent to labor in the Carolinas, convinced me that some of my greatest collaborators could be found at universities and house museums, I realized I also needed to initiate partnerships with members of communities near Clemson. As community members became more aware of my work, some contacted me to discuss my project. In July 2015, I received an email from Sheriff Rick Clark of Pickens County: "I have been interested in your work about the people who built the oldest buildings on Clemson. As a CU alum, Hort '00 & MPA '30, Tiger Brotherhood member, and a former CUPD [Clemson University Police Department] officer, I would like to talk with you about what you have learned and what your vision is for the future for this project. Could we meet sometime?"[5] We met and discussed our shared interest in documenting Clemson history. More recently, after I was awarded an NEH Common Heritage Grant, Clark emailed me a congratulatory note, in which he reiterated his desire that a memorial to African American laborers be installed near Tillman Hall.[6] Around the same time, Harold Cheatham, emeritus Clemson professor, asked me to facilitate two discussion sessions for a course on racism at the predominately white Fort Hill Presbyterian Church in the city of Clemson. Additionally, Clemson Area African American Museum (CAAAM) trustees Bessie and Robert Kemp invited me to attend their board meetings. Indeed, I was meeting and talking with many different community members, but I didn't feel as though I was gaining any traction for Call My Name. How could I move these conversations beyond curiosity about my work to actual engagement with it?

Finding Community Partners for Call My Name

One of my first collaborative efforts came from an unexpected source: the Kemps recommended that I talk with an elderly lady who was connected to the Fort Hill Plantation. The director of Clemson's Historic Properties had also mentioned her to me and promised to provide contact information but had not followed through. On Wednesday, January 20, 2016, as I drove north on Old Calhoun Highway away from Clemson toward Greenville, South Carolina, I was surprised when my GPS directed me to turn off the road about fifteen minutes from campus. Soon I arrived at a ranch-style brick home, where Eva Hester Martin, her husband John Martin, and her daughter Valerie Martin-Lee were waiting to talk with me. When I entered the family room, eighty-nine-year-old Eva Martin led me to a table covered with a lace tablecloth, where she had created a family tree photo collage featuring six generations of relatives, beginning with her grandmother Matilda "Mama Tildy" Brown, who had been enslaved on the Fort Hill Plantation, and ending with her great-grandchildren. She had strategically placed other documents around the photographs, including newspaper clippings about her mother, Anna Brown, copies of Fort Hill inventories of enslaved persons, the *African Americans at Fort Hill* brochure, along with family heirlooms, including a metal flat iron and thimble that had belonged to her mother. My

Celebrates
103rd Birthday

curiosity was piqued when I saw people in the photographs who appeared to be white or very light-skinned African Americans.

"Could you give me a few minutes?" I asked Eva Martin and her family as the realization settled within me that I was standing in the room with descendants of an enslaved African American family who had lived, labored, and loved on the Fort Hill Plantation. The site where Clemson University, my employer, was built. The place where I taught narratives by former enslaved persons in my early African American and American literature classes.

"I've been looking for you all for a long time," I explained to the Martin family. *I had been searching for descendants of persons enslaved at Fort Hill for eight years.* "And here you were, living just down the road from Clemson all along."

During subsequent interviews, Eva Martin shared a wealth of family stories, stretching back to the days when her ancestors were enslaved at Fort Hill and then experienced freedom in Upstate South Carolina. Her grandmother, Matilda, "Mama Tildy," often recounted the day "when freedom come" at the end of the Civil War: she was eight years old. She may have been born on Andrew Pickens Calhoun's Cuba Plantation in Alabama because her birthplace is listed as Alabama in the 1880 US census. Eva Martin's great-grandfather Sharper had chosen the surname Brown to replace the Calhoun name they had been given by their owners. Mama Tildy frequently talked about Sharper's intelligence and enjoyment of telling stories and reading to his grandchildren. Her daughter Anna, Eva Martin's mother, believed that her grandfather may have once lived in the South Carolina Low Country, where enslaved African laborers had perfected the process of cultivating rice, because he also knew how to grow the crop. Anna kept the new family name, Brown, rather than her father's last name, Williams, in honor of her grandparents, who had raised her.

As I learned more about Martin family history, I marveled that Clemson's Historic Properties staff knew that an ancestor of an enslaved person whom the Calhoun family had owned lived close to campus, yet it was one

Photo collage of Eva Hester Martin's extended family, beginning with her grandmother Matilda Brown, who was enslaved on the Fort Hill Plantation, and ending with her great-grandchildren, 2016. Photo by the author.

of my community partners who ensured that I met Eva Martin. The CAAAM trustees' willingness to help was timely, for Eva Martin and her husband were packing in preparation for a move to Atlanta. I was further perplexed by the delay in our meeting after Eva Martin informed me that she had come to campus, bringing the original copy of her grandmother Mama Tildy's photograph with her as evidence of her familial connection to Sharper and Caroline. I had seen the photograph of Mama Tildy in some publicity materials about African Americans at Fort Hill but never was informed that her granddaughter lived just a few miles down the road from Clemson.

Eva Martin's story not only helped me to flesh out the history of African Americans at Clemson, her complex family ancestry illuminated the complicated story of race relations in South Carolina, which solved the mystery of the white-skinned people in the family photographs. Her mother Anna entered into a common-law marriage with Thomas J. Hester, a white ferryman, whose family was so wealthy and influential they incorporated their own town named Hester, South Carolina. At least three of the Hester brothers entered into common-law marriages with Black women in the late nineteenth and early twentieth centuries when interracial marriages were outlawed in South Carolina. "The Hester brothers did whatever they wanted to do," Eva Martin explained.[7] Her father operated a ferry along the Savannah River while her mother took care of their home and ten children. Eva Martin was the youngest.

I introduced the Martin family's story of enslavement to freedom to the public on my project website (www.callmyname.org) by creating a kind of photograph essay: it featured a color picture of Eva Martin's mother, Anna, a member of the first freeborn generation of their family, tucked in between the black-and-white image of her grandmother, Mama Tildy, and the color print of Eva wearing her high school graduation cap and gown. After completing high school, Eva Martin earned a degree in chemistry from the Colored Normal Industrial Agricultural and Mechanical College of South Carolina (now South Carolina State University), married her sweetheart John Martin, and enjoyed a distinguished career as a medical laboratory technician in Chicago and Los Angeles before retiring and moving to Greenville in the early 1970s. Although her parents lived together as husband and wife, they were never acknowledged as a family unit by the state of South Carolina or in the US Census. The legacies of slavery in the Jim Crow South were also manifested when they died: Thomas Hester was buried in the white

Hester family cemetery in Calhoun Falls, South Carolina, in 1938. His common-law wife, Anna B. Brown, was buried in the Black Hester family plot in the Glovers African Methodist Episcopal Church cemetery a few miles down the road—in 1981, long after Jim Crow restrictions had ended.

A collaboration with StoryCorps and CAAAM enabled me to preserve and share the story of Eva Martin and other African Americans connected to Clemson University and the city of Clemson with an even larger audience. StoryCorps's mission is "to preserve and share humanity's stories in order to build connections between people and create a more just and compassionate world."[8] The organization offers everyday people opportunities to record conversations about their lives and impart generational wisdom. My intention was to emphasize the significant contributions of African Americans who labored on John C. Calhoun's Fort Hill Plantation and at Clemson University—and then to make the stories available to the public through StoryCorps's Griot Initiative, a collection of stories told by African Americans, which are archived at the Library of Congress. StoryCorps facilitators recorded forty-minute interviews by pairs of individuals ranging from Fort Hill descendants to current Clemson employees. After the interviews, participants received a broadcast quality audio recording and decided if their interview would be publicly released. Call My Name received permission to archive and share portions of the interviews in various formats, including online streaming, books, documentaries, exhibitions, and radio programs.

The interviews took place at the CAAAM, located in the Calhoun Elementary School, which had been established for Black children in the 1940s. Our interviewees included the following pairs:

1. Eva Hester Martin, 90, and her daughter Valerie Martin-Lee, 61, recalled stories about their ancestors' transition from slavery to freedom and Eva Martin's upbringing as the youngest daughter of a white father and Black mother who had entered into a common-law marriage in South Carolina during the Jim Crow era.
2. Patricia Fruster, 70, Clemson, South Carolina, resident, and her cousin Eric Young, 40, Clemson University alumnus, talked about their ancestors, Frances and Thomas Fruster, who had been enslaved by John C. Calhoun and his family on the Fort Hill Plantation.
3. Danny Cannon, 86, and his brother-in-law, David Green, 83, retired Clemson University wage workers, recollected the challenges

special needs of its community partners. I decided to enroll in a three-day workshop to help me determine if the organization would be a good fit for Call My Name.

The workshop exceeded my expectations. Five female participants of diverse ages, ethnicities, and background gathered in a converted warehouse space in Berkeley and faced the seemingly daunting task of creating a digital story in three days. We began by pitching our ideas. An undergraduate wondered how to compellingly share her lifelong commitment to community activism. An environmentalist grappled with how to convey her concern about climate change. Another participant sought to inspire members of her community to take the helm of a successful afterschool program for young people she had created. A professor from the Middle East wished to share recollections of her work as a feminist. Another professor wanted to give advice to her children about identity formation. And I decided to tell the story of how the Call My Name project came to be, both as university and family history. We affirmed and challenged each other as we distilled years of experiences into four- to five-minute clips. The success of our work, both individually and collectively, stemmed from a collaboration grounded in an authentic, open, and honest exchange of ideas.

My insistence on thoughtfully considering collaborations with StoryCenter and other organizations reflects my need to tread carefully with potential partnerships. The threads of Clemson history gleaned from narratives that have been shared with Call My Name thus far present a complex community history, revealing the stresses on a relationship between nearby towns and a university that is still haunted by the history and legacies of slavery and segregation. For example, while white Clemson students enjoyed the jazz of Duke Ellington in 1955 on campus, local Black residents were dancing to the soul music of James Brown at the Black-owned club-restaurant-hotel Littlejohn's Grill in town. After Clemson characterized Harvey Gantt's enrollment in the institution in 1963 as "integration with dignity," families in the local Black tight-knit community provided support and encouragement in spaces like the "Kool-Aid house" for the small group of trailblazing Black students, who were taking advantage of the opportunity made possible by Gantt's class-action lawsuit to earn a degree at Clemson. These included a legacy student, James Bostic Jr.—whose white great-great-grandfather was one of Clemson's first graduates. One fall semester, at least one white male student threw food at Bostic and other Black male students when they entered the dining hall nearly every day for the first three months of classes. When they complained to then Clemson president Robert C. Edwards, the administrator asked them to identify the perpetrator. After they identified their white tormentor, Edwards dismissed the student from Clemson the next day. While Clemson touted the legacy of Thomas Green Clemson and his vision for a "high seminary of learning" for the *white* sons of South Carolina, Black Clemson employees claimed a heritage of labor—notably by convicts and wage workers. Black labor enabled the fulfillment of Clemson's vision during the Jim Crow era when Black South Carolinians were legally barred from enrolling in or being hired for certain jobs at the university. While Clemson presented a carefully crafted history intended to encourage pride and the erasure of the painful parts of its history, Black folks proudly recalled the stories of their enslaved ancestors who labored on the Fort Hill Plantation, where Clemson was built. They also encouraged young people to keep searching for answers and opportunities, especially explorations that might lead them to see the Clemson tiger's stripes.

Community Outreach Connects Call My Name to More Local Descendant Families

Even as I sought collaborations with national organizations, working with local groups yielded its own rewards. My initial collaboration with the Clemson Area African American Museum (CAAAM) led to other initiatives with community partners and with professor Lee Morrisey, director of Clemson's Humanities Hub, an NEH Creating Humanities Communities matching grant. Clemson's Humanities Advancement Board provided matching funds for the project. We began attending local gatherings, holding monthly meetings, and planning events with members of the Call My Name Coalition—the Bertha Lee Strickland Cultural Museum (BLSCM) and the Lunney Museum in Seneca, South Carolina; the CAAAM; and the Pendleton Foundation for Black History and Culture (PFBHC)—in order to engage Black communities, connecting Clemson University history with local stories. In October 2018, Morrissey attended a community meeting organized by Jermaine Durham, a graduate student in Clemson's Department of City Planning and Real Estate Development, to discuss historic Black neighborhoods in the city of Clemson. Since I was unable to attend the gathering, Morrisey sent me updates via text message. He soon began texting me about a participant named Rosa. I asked if the person was Rosa Grayden. He confirmed her identity and then told me her family name was "Shawl." I wondered if he meant Shaw. George R. Shaw was one of the convict laborers who helped build Clemson. Carl Redd, Clemson libraries' archivist, had introduced me to Shaw when I first began conducting research for Call My Name, as some details about him were included in a local African American oral history project coordinated by historian W. J. Megginson, which was housed in Special Collections. I had also recovered property records from the Pickens County Deeds office for land Shaw had purchased in the city of Calhoun (later renamed Clemson) in the early 1900s.

The following day, I emailed Grayden, inquiring about the property her family once owned in the city of Clemson. She described the location, provided information about her parents and siblings, and indicated that her paternal grandparents' names were Robert and Rosena Shaw.

"This is amazing information. I'm going to call you soon. I need to talk with you about your grandfather, George Shaw," I replied.

"How do you know so much about my family?" Grayden later asked during our conversation in her office at Clemson, where she is employed as an administrative assistant.

"Rosa, I've been researching your family for years. I found some information about George Shaw and your relatives on ancestry.com. Your grandfather was one of the convict laborers who built Clemson," I explained. She looked surprised. No one in her family had shared this information about her grandfather.

"I wondered where I got my spunk," she finally replied.

I had just confirmed the identity of the first of the nearly seven hundred convicted laborers who had been assigned to help construct Clemson University—by being attentive to details a local resident had shared in a local community meeting.

Morrissey and I segued into sponsoring our own events and cosponsoring activities with the Call My Name Coalition to establish connections with local residents. The first event was a luncheon with special guest Richard Rothstein, author of *The Color of Law*, to which we also invited the city of Clemson council members, mayor, and sheriff, Clemson University city planning graduate students, and local residents. This gathering led to additional revelations about the Grayden family's contributions to both the building of Clemson University and the creation of businesses in the city of Clemson. The next event occurred in December of 2018 when the PFBHC revived its annual Kwanzaa Show, a variety show about African American history and culture, which—beginning in 2020—will include a storytelling booth for Call My Name. The CAAAM followed with a Black History Month Prayer breakfast in 2019, featuring presentations by Lee Gill, Clemson's chief diversity officer, and Bostic about their personal and Clemson experiences and the importance of town-gown initiatives that support the humanities. This event will be held annually with the goal of doubling attendance each year. The BLSCM continued hosting its annual Black History Month luncheons. The 2019 event featured guest speaker Berlethia Pitts, a professor, Seneca native, and Clemson alumna. These initial efforts with our community partners culminated in a major initiative, "Documenting Your Family Story," a two-day NEH-funded Common Heritage event in February 2020, where members of local African American communities brought 671 family heirlooms such as letters and photographs that were scanned at no charge. Participants were also given the option of donating their images to the Call My Name project.

Call My Name Coalition–sponsored events have proved to be an excellent source of community stories for the project. As she has done for the past two years, BLSCM director Shelby Henderson invited me to give an update on the Call My Name project at the BLSCM's 2019 Black History Month Luncheon. As I entered the meeting space, a few attendees informed me that they are following the project's Facebook page. When I rose to speak, referencing notes on my iPhone, I recalled how during the past week, Harvard University professor Henry Louis Gates Jr., with assistance from genetic genealogists, had given actor S. Epatha Merkerson a #FindingYourRoots journey, which introduced her to ancestors she never knew existed— enslaved persons sold by the Jesuits affiliated with Georgetown University.

"They have names . . . ," she exclaimed through tears when she saw the documents related to the sale of her family members. "They're not just faceless people. Wow, this is pretty amazing."[11]

I connected the national story to local history: "My Call My Name project is seeking to do the same thing for African Americans in Clemson University history—to give faceless people names," I explained. "First there were enslaved persons who labored on John C. Calhoun's plantation. And then there were sharecroppers, former slaves, who worked for Thomas Green Clemson, the University's founder, during Reconstruction. And then there was a predominately African American state convict crew who built Clemson."

My cell phone rang. I didn't recognize the local number. I tried to dismiss the call so my Apple watch wouldn't start ringing. But I hit the wrong button, answering the call instead. I hoped the person on the line wouldn't start talking. I quickly hung up. My phone locked. I tried to keep talking as I punched the code to unlock my phone and get back to my notes. I stumbled through introductions of the Black wage workers whom Clemson hired and Black musicians who performed at the institutions for white audiences during the Jim Crow era, as well as the Black students, faculty, and staff who came to Clemson after desegregation. I invited members of the audience to provide the names and job titles of African Americans who had worked at Clemson, deceased or living, through 1972, on the forms Morrissey was distributing.

Out of the corner of my eye, I saw a woman smiling intently at me, as if she had found something I was saying to be intriguing. I soon learned she was the featured speaker, Berlethia Pitts, chair of the Department of Languages and Liberal Studies at Fort Valley State University in Fort Valley, Georgia. During her remarks, Pitts focused on the necessity of seeing Black history as American history that should be shared year-round. She also asserted that telling stories about African Americans could be a means to connect people, both locally and nationally, and help them learn from the past. After the program, I wanted to speak with Pitts and acknowledge how her talk dovetailed so beautifully my work. When I walked up to her, hand outreached, she hugged me.

"I changed my talk last night," she exclaimed. "I was reading sections I just wrote last night. I didn't understand why until I heard your presentation. I was supposed to come behind you and affirm your work." While earning a master's degree in English at Clemson, she had helped create an African American Arts program, launched by featured speaker Nikki Giovanni. I had unknowingly been walking in the path of African American history and culture Pitts had created for others who, like me, would follow in her footsteps at Clemson.

After the luncheon ended, I stood at the door, hoping a few attendees would give me names of local African Americans connected to Clemson or their communities. I smiled at the folks exiting the auditorium, trying to catch someone's eye. A woman named Patricia Webb slipped a sheet into my hand with names and positions inscribed on every line:

Lovejoy Keels, supervisor in one of the dining halls
Tryphena McCaden, Schilletter dining hall
Olivia Talley, dry cleaner
Elias L. Kibler, Agriculture

"I need to tell you a story about him, my grandfather," she said as she pointed to Kibler's name and circled back inside the building. I scribbled "grandfather's story" beside his name and waited. Later when the auditorium was nearly empty, I met Webb's sister and together they shared fragments of recollections of a shattered dream of forty acres and a mule, a story that still evokes the pain of unrecoverable loss.

"My grandfather was a successful farmer. . . Clemson used to consult with him all the time . . . But they wanted his land. . . .One year, he had a bad crop and couldn't recover. . . . Clemson bought his land, over where the [Oconee County Regional] airport is now located," the sisters patched together the story, finishing each other's sentences.

Kibler was born in Anderson, South Carolina, in 1866, just one year after the Civil War ended. His parents, Samuel, a farmer, and Millie Kibler, a housekeeper, had been enslaved in the same place their American citizen-son was born. The 1880 census noted that ten-year-old Kibler's occupation was "Work on Farm"[12] in Fork, South Carolina. He was the eldest son of eight children, third-born, with two older sisters and five younger siblings, three sisters and two brothers. He could neither read nor write. In 1890, twenty-two-year-old Kibler married Dora M. Owens, and by 1900, he had moved his family to Seneca, South Carolina, become a farmer, and rented a home for his wife and their four children on a farm. He had also learned to read and write, having completed the fourth year of high school. Two men identified as servants, James Hood and Edgar Jenkins, also lived with the Kiblers and worked on the farm.[13] By 1910, Kibler owned his home and farm and his family had expanded from four to nine children.[14] Over the next thirty years, members of the Kibler's extended family moved in, with grandchildren listed among the residents counted in the census—all living on the farm that their grandfather owned and where his children assisted with management of the family business as farm hands.[15] By 1940, however, seventy-one-year-old Kibler had suffered a setback and was renting a home he had lived in since 1935 with his wife, a son, a daughter, and grandson. He was still farming, working sixty hours a week on his own account but seeking income from other sources as well.[16] He died in 1949 at the age of eighty-three and was buried in the Oak Grove Cemetery in Utica, South Carolina, with Dora, who died about eight months later in 1950, buried next to him.[17]

Clemson College's Early Engagement with African Americans: A Lecture by George Washington Carver

Although Clemson University was segregated until 1963, its staff still consulted Black farmers like Kibler for advice regarding agricultural practices. In 1923, college administrators invited George Washington Carver to give a lecture to about one thousand cadets. By this time Carver, who had been born into slavery during the Civil War in 1864 in Diamond, Missouri, just two years before Kibler was freeborn, had become an internationally renowned agricultural scientist. In an article titled "Prominent Negro Addresses Cadets" published in the *Tiger*, Clemson's student newspaper, a writer remarked, "For the first time in Clemson's history a negro spoke in the college chapel on Nov. 20. And the cadets enjoyed his lecture. He is probably one colored man out of a million who would have held the attention of the Clemson boys." Instead of offering a recap of the lecture, however, the writer inserted biographical material about Carver from "Who's Who in America."[18] Perhaps the writer felt the most important aspect of this event was Carver's presence on campus. In *The High Seminary*, Reel includes a brief overview of Carver's visit in a section titled "Clemson 'Integrated,'" which also notes the presence of Clemson's first non-Caucasian graduate Yukata Tsukiyama, a Japanese student who majored in textile engineering and was apparently quite proficient at playing ping pong.[19] Reel's characterization of an Asian student and African American scientist "integrating" Clemson obfuscates the fact that the land upon which the higher education institution was built has been an "integrated" space from the arrival of European colonists—on land inhabited by Cherokees—through the founding and development of Clemson College. African Americans who were laboring as

Botanist, scientist, inventor, and educator George Washington Carver with Clemson College cadet Kelly E. Traynham, 1933. Courtesy of Clemson University Libraries' Special Collections & Archives.

cooks, domestics, laundry workers, and farm hands for Clemson at the time of Carver's visit are invisible in Reel's *The High Seminary*, the university's official published history.

Furthermore, Carver engaged easily with Clemson college students and faculty because he had already begun the practice at other white higher education institutions. About ten years after this historic event at Clemson, two Clemson cadets, Kelly E. Traynham and Carroll Chipley, and chemistry professor Wallace Fridy visited Carver in his research laboratory at the Tuskegee Normal and Industrial Institute in Alabama to learn more about his work. The university became aware of their visit when Traynham's widow, Lib Traynham, donated three letters Carver had exchanged with cadets, along with several photographs they'd taken together. Carver wrote one of the letters to Wallace Fridy, who took a road trip with Carver as one of his "Blue Ridge Boys." Carver affectionately calls the cadets "my boys" and offers them advice on academic pursuits and social life.

Michael Kohl, director of Clemson Libraries' Special Collections & Archives at the time the letters were donated, remarked that the white cadet's interactions with Carver "shows foresight in a time when segregation was the norm."[20] Reel, who was the university historian at the time, added, "Clemson felt perfectly comfortable to bring a distinguished African-American scientist to campus during a time when that was neither acceptable nor socially proper in South Carolina. . . . This was a very clear moment of progress."[21]

The interaction between Carver and the cadet should not be surprising, however, and Clemson's "very clear moment of progress" was miniscule at best. Carver's letters to the Clemson cadet reveal he was mentoring white students at other universities as well, including several from Yale and another who lived in New York.[22] We would also do well to remember that South Carolina Low Country planters entrusted their rice fields to the enslaved Africans they purchased from the rice-growing regions of West Africa—including "the 'Rice Coast,' the 'Windward Coast,' the 'Gambia,' and 'Sierra-Leon'"—who were skilled in producing the cash crop.[23] Additionally, Blacks who were deemed to be outwardly accommodating toward whites, notably Booker T. Washington, were afforded opportunities to engage with white audiences and some white prominent politicians. After Washington delivered a speech at the Cotton States and International Exposition in Atlanta in 1895, he dined with President Theodore Roosevelt and his family in the White House in 1901. This event led Clemson trustee and US Senator Tillman to assert that "we shall have to kill a thousand niggers to get them back to their places."[24] If indeed Carver's speeches at Clemson could be characterized as "a very clear moment of progress," why didn't Clemson invite other notable Black agricultural scientists to speak to its students? Instead, administrators relegated Black wage workers to "Negro houses" that lacked indoor plumbing well into the 1930s;[25] minimized the contributions of talented agricultural agents who labored in the segregated extension service program run by the US Department of Agriculture; hired prominent but "respectable" Black musicians beginning in 1920 to perform at student-organized segregated social events; and resisted desegregation until 1963 when Gantt won a class-action lawsuit to gain admission to Clemson. To further complicate matters, local oral history suggests that Clemson invited Carver to speak only after the Seneca Institute, a school for African Americans in the nearby town of Seneca, had brought the acclaimed scientist to the Upstate for a lecture.

Clemson Colleagues Collaborate on Call My Name: Success and Failure

While pursuing initiatives with community members and organizations and with consulting firms, I returned to explorations of collaborations with Clemson colleagues. David White, director of Environmental Informatics, Cyberinfrastructure Technology Integration, had invited me to join the Geographic Information System panel at Clemson's Cyberinfrastructure Expo 2014 to talk about my interest in creating story maps for the Clemson campus and community. That invitation led to a collaboration for *Mapping the Clemson Story: Reconnecting Time and Place through Historical Narrative,* a project funded by a grant from Clemson's Humanities Advancement Board. We intended to create a layered map that revealed changes on the land where Clemson University was built over time, beginning in the Cherokee era. We gained access to digitized historic maps from Clemson's Special Collections & Archives and hired a graduate student with expertise in GIS to create the maps, but we were unable to fully realize our goal. The limitations of technology and primary documents and lack of time prevented us from sustaining momentum. However, the project led to the creation of a map that depicts the Fort Hill Plantation fields superimposed over the current Clemson campus.

A more fruitful collaboration occurred from an unlikely pairing when Bostic connected me with the Clemson Athletics' Creative Solutions team,

Jonathan Gantt, Nik Conklin, and Jeff Kallin, to investigate social media options for raising the profile of my project. After learning about Call My Name, they scheduled a meeting with me to further discuss my project, which resulted in their creating a list of options for me to explore. Adobe Spark offered a user-friendly platform that enables users to create media—websites, social media posts, flyers, posters, and such—that look professionally designed. With a bit of trial and error and practical tips from my research assistants, I developed a launch site to introduce and provide updates about the project (www.callmyname.org). As visitors scroll through the site, the story of African Americans slowly unfolds from free Africans and enslaved people of African descent who labored on the Calhouns' Fort Hill to the exhibition that will present the interwoven history of Black people at Clemson University and in nearby communities as an African diasporic narrative. We also created a Facebook page that functions as a digital archive. Each day, Sundays through Fridays, research assistants publish a post that provides information about one of the six generations, including a primary source. The number of people who have liked the page has increased from under one hundred to more than one thousand two hundred since the page was created in 2016.[26]

I had initially imagined creating a website to showcase my project, but the process to create one proved too onerous. I contacted Clemson Computing and Information Technology (CCIT) about the feasibility of having space on the university's server. They sent me a long form with many technical questions that I could not answer. Also, CCIT staff informed me that space on the server would be provided but no assistance with the website upkeep. I decided to move forward and hire an administrator to maintain the site. Call My Name project manager Marjorie Campbell initiated the process by contacting professors associated with Clemson's new Center of Excellence, informing them that I was leading a project regarding the role and importance of African Americans in Clemson's history. She emphasized the backing of the president's office, the provost, the Clemson Foundation, and alumni donors for my research and accompanying projects. Campbell initially requested an informational type of site under the umbrella of Clemson University. Planners of the new Center of Excellence for Digital Media and Learning were still waiting to officially open, but they assured us they had discussed my project as one of the first they would support.[27] As plans for the new Center lagged, however, we reached out to Clemson's Creative Services for assistance. Instead of creating a website, they suggested that I develop a blog that would be hosted on the Clemson University website.[28] But an intern from the Pearce Center for Professional Communication had already created an aesthetically appealing blog for my research, which my projects had outgrown. Creative Services staff convinced me to migrate my blog to their site, which meant it needed to be branded as Clemson media, conforming to a particular style and colors. My blog lost its unique flavor and my interest. If I did not want to post or read about my own work, who else would be interested in reading it?

Next, Campbell and I considered setting up a website on my college's faculty research page. The web developers were using a platform called Cascade that was fairly user-friendly, with the capacity of creating simple but elegant sites. But we did not know who should request, create, and maintain the site, and my college's webmaster did not have time to assist me.[29] I then attempted to hire a private contractor, but the web designer abruptly stopped communicating with me after showing initial interest in the project. Our final option was to meet with Clemson's Procurement Services staff to investigate the possibility of an outside developer. Two companies presented bids worth hundreds of thousands of dollars just to create the sites, options that were not financially feasible for a humanities project.

By this time, Clemson Athletics' Creative Solutions team informed me that the staff at Adobe headquarters liked my project's Spark page and had included it in a feature story for their electronic newsletter. They also invited me to attend the EDUMAX 2016 conference in San Diego, California, and talk about my use of Spark products for my research. As I traced my journey to Adobe Spark at the conference through the fits and starts of seeking technological assistance from Clemson, I did not realize CCIT staff were watching the session live back at Clemson. I soon received an email asking me to detail my experience.[30] The new staff were surprised by the insurmountable hurdles that had been placed before me and promised to assist me moving forward. By this time, however, I preferred working with the Clemson Athletics Creative Solutions team. They were enthusiastic about and interested in my project and offered specific cost-effective tools my research assistants and I could utilize for my work, mostly without technical assistance. Somehow word spread about our collaboration, and I soon began receiving requests from other Clemson media specialists for the list of tech tools my consultants had provided for research in the humanities.

Based on the success of the Spark page, I considered developing an app, circling back to the technology I had initially considered when launching the project. I would begin with a simple African American heritage walking tour of campus but would eventually develop an app that would include archival material, oral histories, photographs, and videos. The director of the Mobile Innovation team indicated the cost of apps ranged from five thousand to two hundred thousand dollars, an estimate range that did not give me the confidence I needed to move forward with development.[31] I also tried working with a Clemson professor who taught an app development class, but we could not create a design that reflected the complexities of the project. Eventually, I created a Call My Name tour using Knight Lab's StoryMap online platform.[32]

However, I did contribute to the development of a new Clemson app in 2015: CU on Foot. Content developer Data Tolentino-Canlas, then a graduate student in the RCID program, invited me and several other Clemson professors, including Andrea Feeser and Chenjerai Kumanyika, to create new narratives for several historic sites alongside a few that had been recorded by Reel. I was assigned the Fort Hill Plantation, Gantt Circle, and the Carillon Gardens. Our goal was simple: share an introduction to the university's complex history within the constraints of a brief narrative available on a mobile app. The nearly three-minute narrative I recorded for Fort Hill traces the historical arch of the land from the colonial period through the founding of the university, identifying multiple white owners as well as the variety of enslaved persons who lived and labored on the land. We also noted the absences of markers at significant historical sites associated with African American history on campus, which included the locale of the slave quarters for field hands at that time. An assortment of photographs of Fort Hill accompanied the narrative, ranging from Thomas Green Clemson sitting in a rocking chair on the porch of the house to the SLBI, which used the house as the backdrop for their *Taps* yearbook photograph in 1975 as many white student organizations had done before and after desegregation. My third narrative for the app, which provided a brief overview of the origin and purpose of the Carillon Gardens, was fairly straightforward Clemson history regarding a site established to honor students and faculty who have made significant contributions to the university. Including it was a deliberate choice on my part to show that my interest in Clemson history is focused on but not limited to the African American experience.

The narrative for Gantt Circle runs nearly one and one-half minutes longer than the others; I successfully lobbied for extra time to provide a more complete introduction to one of the most significant and complex events in Clemson history—which the institution characterizes simply as "Integration with Dignity." Pulling visitors into the site by emphasizing the irony of how Gantt entered a building named after Tillman, a white supremacist who advocated the lynching of African Americans, which is located just behind a statue of university founder Thomas Green Clemson, a Confederate veteran who fought to preserve a slaveholding society, we situated Gantt's courageous act within its wider historical context. We reintroduced the desegregation of Clemson as part of efforts by civil rights activists to press South Carolina to move with all deliberate speed, nearly a decade after the 1954 *Brown v. Board of Education* US Supreme Court decision. Listeners learned of Gantt's participation in a sit-in while he was in high school and his nearly three-year quest to enroll in Clemson. Collaboration fostered the development of an insightful, inclusive, honest narrative that powerfully exemplified the need for Clemson to commit to sharing its complete and complex story.

Clemson Student Researchers Contribute to Call My Name

As Call My Name further coalesced into a project, I sought more opportunities to involve students in my research initiatives. As a faculty-in-residence in the spring of 2015, I hosted a dinner for students in my apartment, during which I expressed a need for research assistants. Edith Dunlap, an English major who had taken a few of my literature courses, immediately expressed an interest in joining my team. Soon she was assisting with writing posts for Generation 4—Wage Workers; Generation 5—Musicians; and Generation 6—Integration, categories for the Call My Name Facebook digital archive. During the 2015–16 academic year, Edith worked alongside eleven other undergraduates and a graduate assistant, Emily Boyter, on my Creative Inquiry (CI) team that explored various aspects of Clemson University history. We met in the reading room of Clemson University Libraries' Special Collections & Archives twice weekly. Rather than restrict my undergraduate researchers to African American history at Clemson, I encouraged them to explore topics of interest to them. Dunlap challenged herself to examine the complexities of Tillman's character through an examination of his relationship with his wife, Sallie Starke Tillman, as evidenced through his personal correspondence. She found him to be a loving and affectionate husband, who struggled with everyday challenges, such as dealing with an alcoholic son, while devoted to a political career that kept him frequently away from home.

Most of my CI team members focused on Clemson's African American history, however, which gave them a sense of the expansiveness of African Americans' contributions to the university's development and led to some unexpected discoveries. One student critiqued Clemson's "Integration with Dignity" mantra, which characterizes Gantt's desegregation of the University as a simple, peaceful transition: through the creation of a StoryMap, the student traced Gantt's transformation from a young socially conscious man growing up in segregated Charleston into a determined and persistent college student, who utilized the legal system to gain entry into a higher education institution that had rebuffed his efforts to earn an architecture degree in his home state. Another student shifted the focus of the integration of Clemson athletics from sports frequently associated with Black athletes, such as football, basketball, and track and field, to the documentation of the first Black student-athletes in soccer, tennis, diving, wrestling, and volleyball within the first ten to twenty years of desegregation.

Some of the more surprising discoveries students made concerned white students' efforts to bring Black musicians to campus to perform for social events and their racist representations of Black people in student-sponsored activities prior to and immediately after integration. CI team member Samuel Wilkes, whom I eventually hired as a research assistant, focused his research on the Clemson student-run Central Dance Association's (CDA) efforts to hire prominent Black performers for annual dances and concerts. By combing through the organization's papers and accounts of the events in the digitized student newspaper the *Tiger* and the student yearbook *Taps,* Wilkes discovered that student organizers worked for more than ten years before they were able to successfully negotiate an agreement to bring Duke Ellington to campus in March 1955. Yet when Allen and Bray referred to the event in *Clemson: There's Something in These Hills,* they included only a picture of Ellington and no reference to its source. The letters Wilkes examined also yielded evidence of the challenges the CDA faced in selecting Black musicians who would be acceptable performers on a campus located in the most conservative part of a state in the Jim Crow South. As he turned his attention to the yearbooks, Wilkes also found photographs of individuals wearing Ku Klux Klan hoods and blackface, incidents that had never been acknowledged in Clemson's official histories.[33]

Another CI Team member, who focused on African Americans' participation in Clemson's Cooperative Extension Service, found evidence of their extensive contributions to the program, which had not been appropriately recognized in the university's official histories. The extension program is associated with the development of land-grant institutions in the late 1800s to share research-based data regarding agricultural practices and technological innovations with the public. Clemson University lifetime trustee and South Carolina representative Frank Lever cosponsored legislation in 1914, the Smith-Lever Act, to create the Cooperative Extension Service to ensure that federal, state, and local governments worked collaboratively to facilitate the sharing of agricultural and homemaking research and resources throughout the state. Clemson was designated as the headquarters for this work in South Carolina. Because it was a segregated higher education institution at that time, however, the extension service office for African Americans was established at the Colored Normal Industrial Agricultural and Mechanical College of South Carolina (now South Carolina State University), a land-grant, historically Black higher education institution in Orangeburg. In keeping with the requirements of the second Morrill Act in 1890, which stipulated that, for former Confederate states, either race not be used as criteria for college admission or that separate but equal institutions be established for Black and white students, the institution was founded shortly after Clemson. The earlier Morrill Act of 1862 had allocated land in each state to establish an educational institution for training residents in agriculture, home economics, mechanics, and other practical professions. As the undergraduate researcher began looking for documents about the persons who worked in the program, she wondered how she would determine their races. "Dr. Thomas," she soon called out, "they are separated by race." When the lists were initially created for annual program reports, African American extension employees were identified separately in groups such as "Negro Agricultural Agents," "Negro Home Demonstration Agents," or "Negro Stenographers." The archivists who created the cataloging system for the papers preserved the segregated system. As we further examined the reports the "Negro" extension employees created, we discovered disparities in resources as well as compensation. More often than not, when Clemson University historians and the Clemson Extension staff who have shared the history of the Cooperative Extension Service, however, they have seldom acknowledged the impact of the institution's segregated and unequal practices prior to the Civil Rights Act of 1964 or the loss of employment opportunities African Americans experienced when operations were consolidated at Clemson University. Clemson alumnae Carmen V. Harris wrote extensively about the state's cooperative extension program in her 2002 doctoral dissertation "A Ray of Hope: Blacks in the South Carolina Extension Service, 1915–1970" and later publications.[34] More recently, historian William C. Hine included detailed accounts about Black extension employees' work in *South Carolina State University: A Black Land-Grant College in Jim Crow America*.[35] After integration, the offices for the segregated extension program for Black agents was closed and all operations consolidated at Clemson although many of the agents could not move to the Upstate where the new offices were located.

Occasionally, my team's findings were emotionally overwhelming. We were sitting around the conference room table in Special Collections & Archives discussing our discoveries after class when a CI team member drew our attention to the stereotypical depiction of a young African American boy in a *Taps* yearbook. I suddenly realized another one of my student researchers was crying.

"Why?" she asked aloud. "Why would they do that to him?"

I dismissed my other undergraduates and lingered with my student, sharing her pain and anger at the misrepresentation of a Black boy deliberately inserted on a page in a yearbook by white students who would never see him as an equal. How do I explain the time when racist images like these were normal? They appeared on food packaging, like Uncle Ben's rice and Aunt Jemima's pancake mix, as well as on laundry detergent boxes and wrappings for bars of soap. Yet these images still appear on university and college campuses, online, and in American communities. They reappear quickly when Clemson's Black football players perform poorly during a game or when an ivy league–educated couple become America's first Black president and first lady. They reappear when students dress in blackface or when respected members of the Black community are depicted as apes. I assert that Ameri-

Clemson College extension agent (left) making a site visit with a South Carolina dairy farmer, 1950. Courtesy of Clemson University Libraries' Special Collections & Archives.

cans cannot understand and challenge how Black people are still dehumanized unless we examine the historical trajectory that stretches back to the shores of Africa and the inauguration of the transatlantic slave trade.

This encounter with history reminds me of the challenges of engaging students with Clemson history. I have attended meetings where mentioning the Confederates as anything but heroic provokes resistance from some white participants. Some Clemson staff members have told me that they have heard from Clemson students who believed my work in recovering the history of African Americans at the university was tarnishing the institution's brand as a progressive, twenty-first century higher education institution. Some students have asked me why I teach at a predominately white university if the environment is so challenging for a Black faculty member to navigate. Nevertheless, I have persisted in devising ways to reach Clemson students because I am beginning to see the positive effects of my research. And I'm a sixth-generation South Carolinian with personal and professional commitments to this work.

Other Clemson students have shown an interest in and willingness to support the Call My Name project. Pearce Center for Professional Communication interns have assisted with creating digital media, designing a publication, planning public events, and managing advertising campaigns.

In the fall of 2017, the Undergraduate Student Senate invited me to give a presentation, which ended up being a week after they held a marathon impeachment hearing to determine if they would unseat their African American vice president. He retained his office, but I wasn't sure the timing was right to give a talk. After receiving assurances that the senators still wanted me to speak, I engaged with Clemson's student leaders about Call My Name, framing the discussion through the lens of Black children and youth. The students learned about enslaved persons like less-than-a-year-old Caty, whom the Calhouns had owned on the Fort Hill Plantation; the sixteen children described as "half-hands" who had worked alongside freed men and women, former slaves, as sharecroppers for Thomas Green Clemson during Reconstruction; thirteen-year-old boys like Wade Foster, who had been assigned to the Clemson convict workforce; teenaged girls like Jane Edna Harris, who had babysat the children of Clemson professors; young musicians like twenty-two-year-old Maurice Williams and his backup singers, the Zodiacs, who had performed at Clemson; and twenty-year-old Harvey Gantt, who resorted to filing a class-action lawsuit so that he and other African American students could complete degrees at a public higher education institution in their home state. I ended my presentation with a challenge for the students to find ways to engage with the University's complete and complex history. I would not dictate how that engagement should be enacted, but as young leaders, I encouraged them to think about and devise ways they could ensure student involvement in documenting and presenting Clemson history.

But just before I issued my challenge, I shared one of the surprising outcomes of my research into Clemson history—the discovery that my family has a connection to the university. Students who had been attentive leaned forward as I related details of the possible familial relationship between John Edward Wannamaker, one of Clemson's first lifetime trustees, and Lucretia Wannamaker Earle, my paternal great-great-grandmother, both from the Orangeburg, South Carolina, District. I tell them DNA testing points to a genetic link between me and John Wannamaker's parents. I inform them I have hired a team of genealogists to help determine my great-great-grandmother's status: my daddy described her as white, but one of my cousins insists she was enslaved. The genealogists believe the evidence thus far points to enslavement for my white-skinned great-great-grandmother.

Indeed, the history of South Carolina is written on my skin—the history of slavery and its legacies in my family.

Section Four

God showed Noah the rainbow sign
It won't be water but fire next time.
CHARLES JOHNSON, "IT'S GONNA RAIN"

Fire!

Two extant inventories of enslaved persons who labored on the Fort Hill Plantation include Sawney and his family. His is the first name inscribed on each, followed by the names of his family members, beginning with Tilla. In the first inventory, created for the deed for the sale of the Fort Hill Plantation from Floride Calhoun and Cornelia to Andrew Pickens Calhoun, fifty-nine-year-old Sawney, and fifty-year-old Tilla have six children: Ned, 25; Nicholas, 18; Jonas, 16; Jim, 12; Matilda, 10; and Chapman, 8. In the 1865 inventory created after Andrew Calhoun's death at the end of the Civil War, only seventy-one-year-old Sawney and sixty-two-year-old Tilla are listed together.[8]

The "dangerous old Negro" and his wife survived slavery and enjoyed freedom from the Calhouns.

But what became of their children, Issey and Sawney Jr. along with their siblings? Some appear to be listed separate from their parents on the 1865 inventory.

Fire!

In the fall of 2017, Clemson University installed three new South Carolina historical markers on campus as evidence of the intentions of Clemson trustees' Task Force on the History of Clemson to create a complete public narrative. Although one of the signs acknowledges the origins of the land as the site of the Cherokee town of Isunigu, only the name of Sawney, Calhoun's favorite slave, appears on the markers.

The gristmill branch of Mill Creek had been named Sawney's Branch in his honor but was later renamed Hunnicutt Creek. Nobody seems to know why the creek was renamed. The waterway begins near Highway 76, the road that connects the cities of Clemson and Anderson, South Carolina, and flows into branches that intersect with two-thirds of campus. One branch cuts through the Seneca River Basin, the last remaining parcel of the former Fort Hill Plantation fields, where Sawney and some members of his family once toiled. Men and boys who labored on the predominately African American convict crew used clay from the creek to mold bricks for the university's earliest build-

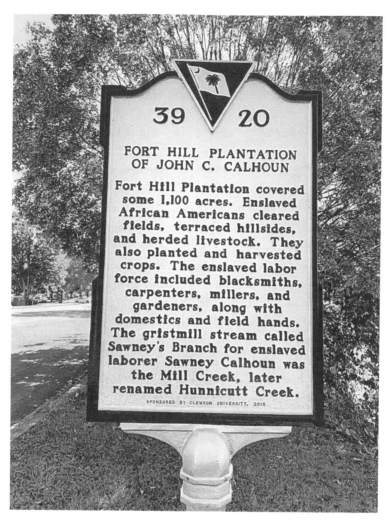

The recently installed South Carolina historical marker for the Fort Hill Plantation on the site of the former plantation fields in the Seneca River Basin on the Clemson University campus, 2016. Photo by the author.

ings between 1890 and 1915.[9] In the 1940s, some of Clemson's African American wage workers lived in houses raised on stilts in the area.[10]

Clemson's College of Agriculture, Forestry, and Life Sciences (CAFLS) has received a one hundred thousand dollar grant for the restoration of Hunnicutt Creek. They have also been awarded a one million dollar grant to expand the organic farm in the Seneca River Basin that was established in 2001. The press release about the latter grant noted that the Bottoms "lies between Hartwell Lake and Perimeter Road on the Clemson University campus and is the location of Clemson's Student Organic Farm and Community Supported Agriculture Program (CSA). It is also land that was first farmed by Cherokee Indians, then by John C. Calhoun and Thomas Green Clemson."[11] The communications director for CAFLS says he didn't know the history of the basin but was simply basing his description of the land's history on information that was given to him by others. After I discussed the omission with CAFLS faculty and staff, I accepted their invitation to be a consultant on their project to tell the full history of the Seneca River Basin.

The managers of Clemson's organic farm have obtained approval from Clemson's board of trustees to rename the land "Calhoun Fields" in honor of John C. Calhoun. But Calhoun didn't legally own the land until his mother-in-law Floride Colhoun died in 1836 and left the property to his wife, who transferred the title of the property to him. Which means he only owned the land for about fourteen years, as he died in 1850.

Sawney tilled that soil from about 1825 to 1865, around forty years.

Two of his children attempted to purify the land of enslavers with fire.

Yet the Clemson campus marker identifies the land as "Calhoun Fields," current site of the Student Organic Farm, agronomic crop and water quality research, and environment engineering.

But neither sign says anything about Sawney's wife or children. Their whereabouts after they gained freedom at the end of the Civil War are currently unknown. We will continue searching until we find them. And we will continue sharing stories about Sawney Jr.'s and Issey's resistance to slavery.

Fire!

Response: The Fire This Time

EMILY BOYTER AND EDITH DUNLAP

The stories of Old Sawney and his children, Issey and Sawney Jr., can evoke a variety of reactions depending on the perspective from which they are viewed. Most people are aware of many of the obvious atrocities associated with slavery, looking for the familiar markers of families separated, human beings commodified, bodies beaten and killed. They can be less aware of the subtler patterns, however: the way white people's voices are centered at the expense of the voices of people of color. This phenomenon often leads to the misrepresentation of Black families and communities, especially during the time period of chattel slavery in the United States, since most Black people in America were illiterate due to the laws prohibiting their education at the time. The experiences of Old Sawney and his family ask us to read against the grain, to find the empty spaces in the story by quieting the white voices that are so intent on telling these stories in self-serving ways. Many aspects of the story have been ignored or hidden for years, with *The African-American Experience at Fort Hill* brochure suggesting that the fire Issey set was accidental, despite clear confirmation in the Calhoun family's private correspondence that the fire was set intentionally. Although we do not know why Sawney Jr. set fire to the overseer's tent, it is likely that he did this intentionally as well.

Fire!

It's a cry with the potential to cause chaos beyond the physical destruction it accompanied. The white Calhouns who told these stories made sure to keep them as close to home as possible for fear of inciting riots on other plantations. By keeping other Blacks, both enslaved and free, ignorant of the resistance that was happening on Fort Hill, white plantation owners were able to "protect" their (human) investments and their farms. Even in the twenty-first century, we see the effort being made to cover up acts of arson. In 2016, when the Clemson University board of trustees reviewed recommended text for new historical markers to be placed around campus, they approved signage that mentions only the fact that there was once a stream named Sawney's Branch, after Old Sawney. No mention is included of his wife and children or of his children's acts of resistance.

Fire!

Old Sawney himself has been portrayed in a certain way in narratives written by white people: as a contented servant favored by his benevolent master. A 1950 biography of John C. Calhoun written by Margaret L. Coit paints an idyllic picture of Calhoun's childhood: "A solitary walk through the woods in the fall, carrying a rifle; a hot afternoon at the side of the creek, his long hands tensed on the rod, and the Negro, Sawney, asleep at his side."[1] Coit goes on to claim that "[y]ears later, John's playmate, Sawney, basking in reflected glory, would gleefully recall: 'We worked in the field, and many's the time in the brilin' sun me and Marse John has plowed together.'"[2] Coit borrowed this quote from Colonel William Pinckney Starke's "Account of Calhoun's Early Life," published in 1899. Starke gives no indication whether he recorded this recollection from personal experience or from some other source. In Coit's narrative, Old Sawney's words are framed twice, first by Starke and next by Coit. Old Sawney's actual words, never mind his thoughts and feelings, are not the point of Coit's narrative; he is merely a character—a prop, even—in her story about John C. Calhoun. Coit demonstrates her bias by referring to Old Sawney as "John's playmate," by talking about how he basked in Calhoun's "reflected glory," and by describing his tone as "gleeful." If not for his seemingly fond remembrances, Old Sawney would likely have not even been included in Coit's narrative at all. However, her characterization of him makes him a safe, pleasant, unchallenging presence—a portrayal belied by the disruption caused by Old Sawney and his children.

Fire!

Reading about Old Sawney and the fires that were undoubtedly and intentionally set by two of his children reminds us that some of those who were enslaved did not stand idly by as their freedoms, their dignities, and their physical bodies were grossly violated and exploited. Rather, they fought by any means necessary to have their voices—which were mostly silenced—heard. Issey's "privilege" as an enslaved house servant allowed her access to the most intimate parts of the Fort Hill Plantation, giving her an especially personal knowledge of the day-to-day operations inside her owners' home. Similarly, Sawney Jr. knew that to see the doctor regularly was an advantage not afforded to most enslaved persons, so he made sure to use the opportunity wisely, attempting, on one occasion, to burn down the overseer's tent. The deflection of Issey's arson attempt was never meant to protect her, no matter how Floride Calhoun characterized her actions. Instead, the Calhouns intentionally spread falsehoods in order to keep the white public's fear of slave revolts at bay. For John C. Calhoun, maintaining this façade would have been extremely important because of his major political roles and proslavery stance. His son Patrick Calhoun's failure to obey his mother's instructions to burn the letter outlining the facts of Issey's attempted arson is the only reason we know the truth. If not for Patrick's negligence, the fire would have continued being misrepresented as a mere accident and would not have given Issey the voice for which she so bravely risked her life.

Issey and Sawney Jr. could both have been hanged for attempted arson.[3] She and her brother knew the consequences of their actions, but they decided to openly resist anyway. Perhaps John C. Calhoun was embarrassed by their actions, which called into question his effectiveness as a "good master." Because of their actions, we believe both of Old Sawney's children are heroes. Despite the burdens of slavery being ever-present around them, their spirits did not waiver. Instead, their acts of resistance have been solidified in history and have lent voices to the enslaved African Americans at Fort Hill.

Sawney Sr.'s, Issey's, and Sawney Jr.'s narratives remind us that white masters (and others who profited from the bondage of other human beings) often told narratives about loyal enslaved persons to fool themselves more than anyone else. Old Sawney's children's actions beautifully disrupt that narrative by shifting to the forefront the deliberate actions of two members of an enslaved family who were discontented with their lot as laborers on a plantation where they would never reap any substantial benefits.

Honestly, who can blame them?

Fire! Fire! Fire!

CHAPTER 4

The Impact

Clemson History as Public History

～～～

We find the song "Dixie" to be insulting
and very embarrassing when used at rallies, games, etc.
How can we "legally" do away with it?
CLEMSON STUDENT LEAGUE FOR BLACK IDENTITY

We are a product of our history—even the history we don't like
to think about.
JAMES W. LOEWEN

"RHON, YOU NEED to look at this," my friend Cheryl Bowie-Thomas directed my attention to the television.

"Not at Mother Emanuel," I cried.

I was vacationing with friends in Orlando, Florida, on June 18, 2015, when we awakened to the news of a shooting in Charleston at the Emanuel African Methodist Episcopal (AME) Church during a prayer service the previous evening. A self-avowed white supremacist had issued a call for a race war by murdering nine African Americans: Cynthia Hurd, the Reverend Sharonda Coleman-Singleton, Susie Jackson, Ethel Lance, the Reverend Clementa Pinckney, Tywanza Sanders, the Reverend Daniel Simmons, and Myra Thompson. He spared three persons in the room, Felicia Sanders and her eleven-year-old granddaughter and Polly Shepherd. Pinckney's wife Jennifer and their six-year-old daughter Malana escaped death by hiding under a desk in a room adjacent to her husband's office at the church.

The murders happened in Charleston, one of the most historically significant locations in the nation, known for the self-determination and spiritual nourishment of Black people, as well as for the rebellious intentions of American citizens. Here in 1816, Morris Brown founded the Emanuel AME

against closing the doors that Pinckney had opened through his work as a pastor and politician. His sacrifice must lead to reconciliation, ministers on the stage admonished as the choir sang:

No weapon formed against me shall prosper, it won't work
No weapon formed against me shall prosper, it won't work
Say No weapon formed against me shall prosper, it won't work
Say No weapon formed against me shall prosper, it won't work
God will do what He said He would do
He will stand by His word
And He will come through
God will do what He said He would do

As the choir kept singing hymns and gospel songs, such as "I Cannot Tell It All," and politicians and clergy were taking extra time to reminisce about the man who walked the talk, we learned from a *Wall Street Journal* reporter sitting behind us that the program was delayed due to President Barack Obama's decision to stay in Washington until the Supreme Court ruling on same-sex marriage had been announced. When he arrived, we felt his presence before we saw him enter: excitement rippled through the crowd when the Secret Service agents wearing dark suits and large earplugs swarmed through the arena. And when Obama leaned forward unexpectedly and sang a verse of "Amazing Grace" at the end of the eulogy, he pulled us all into a world of possibilities where grace could heal wounds, dry tears, and transform our broken nation.

Black Lives Matter at Clemson University, Too: Student Activists Renew Demands for Clemson to Change Its Public History

Indeed, new wounds, fresh tears, and excruciating pain had surged through America, particularly within Black communities, during the summer of 2013, when a spike in the number of deaths of unarmed Black men and women at the hands of police officers galvanized the #BlackLivesMatter movement. The term first appeared on Facebook in a post after the acquittal of George Zimmerman for the murder of Trayvon Martin. That year, Patrisse Khan-Cullors, Alicia Garza, and Opal Tometi cofounded the Black Lives Matter Foundation, Inc., which has become a "Global Network . . . a chapter-based, member-led organization whose mission is to build local power and to intervene in violence inflicted on Black communities by the state and vigilantes."[2] The hashtag gained traction on Twitter after a white police officer fatally shot Michael Brown in the summer of 2014.[3] How would the nation and Clemson University respond?

Carson's previously mentioned "See The Stripes" spoken word poem, published online in August of 2014, had reflected Clemson students' increased engagement with #BlackLivesMatter as they and their allies began protesting in solidarity with movement organizers. One of the first indicators of the impact of Carson's work was a revamping of the Fort Hill plantation house tour. That fall, Clemson's Historic Properties Department introduced an updated tour that provides a more holistic perspective of the Fort Hill Plantation, including insights into the lives of the enslaved and enslavers, overseers and visitors.

Clemson students persisted in demanding changes in how the university shared its history. On January 29, 2015, the Graduate Student Senate passed a resolution penned by Ryan Gagnon, a doctoral student in Parks, Recreation, and Tourism Management, seeking a name change for Tillman Hall. He characterized Tillman as "an evil man and an avowed racist. What's ironic to me is that Tillman's name is here when he was broadly opposed to any type of minority education." The proposal was forwarded to Clemson's Office of Student Affairs, which is tasked with presenting student concerns to the board of trustees.[4] That same day, Clemson University Libraries' Special Collections & Archives posted "Naming Tillman: Consulting Primary Sources," an online exhibit that traced the history of the naming of Tillman Hall. Clemson trustees approved the name in 1946 when Tillman's son, Benjamin R. Tillman, believed his father's legacy was being forgotten and the Dixiecrat Party, which advocated states' rights and segregation, was— through the efforts of Clemson alumnus Strom Thurmond—on the rise across the nation.

While some students demanded a change in building names, others like those affiliated with Clemson's Coalition of Concerned Students were still waiting for the board of trustees' response to their demands, which the vice president for student affairs had promised during their demonstration on the steps of Sikes Hall about a month earlier. The matter may have been discussed at the February 6, 2015, board meeting, but student concerns were not referenced in the minutes, and no response was provided after the meeting.[5]

Within a week of the board meeting, Clemson's Faculty Senate supported the graduate student initiative by passing a resolution requesting that Clemson trustees change the name of Tillman Hall. Faculty senators justified their resolve to have Tillman's name removed from the building by characterizing him as an "avowed racist," and stating that "this is at odds with the university's mission and values, and reflects poorly upon it."[6] Rather than respond to the Faculty Senate, Graduate Student Senate, or student activists directly, however, then Clemson board of trustees chair David Wilkins provided a statement to *The Greenville News*: "While we respect the many differing opinions of our graduates, our students, our faculty and staff regarding this matter, the Clemson University Board does not intend to change the names of buildings on campus, including Tillman Hall."[7] The board further claimed that South Carolina's Heritage Act prevented them from seriously considering changing the name of one of the oldest buildings on campus.[8] What Wilkins failed to explain was that in 2000, as Speaker of the House of Representatives in the South Carolina General Assembly, he had brokered this compromise bill to remove the Confederate flag from atop the state house dome and install it near the front of the building. Legislators agreed that a two-thirds vote of both the house and senate was needed to make changes to certain monuments and memorials associated with wars, African American heritage, and historical figures throughout the state.[9] Historian James W. Loewen asserts, "We are a product of our history—even the history we don't like to think about."[10] The history of slavery and its legacies still impacts South Carolina, influencing how we share and preserve—as well as avoid—painful aspects of the past we'd rather forget.

Undaunted, the Clemson Undergraduate Student Government's Council on Diversity Affairs and the *Greenville News* sponsored a debate March 10, 2015, to examine whether or not the name of Tillman Hall should be changed. Invitations were extended to Clemson president Jim Clements, university administrators, the trustees, and state legislators, but none accepted the opportunity to join about four hundred community and campus members who turned out for the event. Some invitees said they had previous commitments; others indicated they were out of town.[11]

For some members of the Clemson community, the trustees' continued evocation of the Heritage Act to prevent them from attempting to change the name of Tillman Hall was simply an excuse not to engage in the difficult work of reconceptualizing public memorials on campus. In July 2015, nine past Faculty Senate presidents penned an opinion piece, "We Have the Appetite to Rename Tillman. Do You?" for the senate's online "Open Forum":

> While renaming Tillman Hall will, in isolation, fail to secure a sustainable and more inclusive future for the University, it is far more than symbolic. It is an affirmation that honoring those whose station and legacy were achieved in significant measure via the vilest actions of intolerance has no place at Clemson University now or in the future— even as the history, university-related role, and scholarly study of those same individuals must have an indelible role in our educational mission. It is an affirmation that community matters; that ignorance can be replaced with enlightenment; that the administration and our Board have a special responsibility as stewards of our institutional culture; and that we can hold, recognize, adapt to, and share changing values.[12]

Despite faculty and student support for the name change, Clemson trustees would not consider the issue.

While debates about campus memorials and renaming Tillman Hall widened and strengthened, a group of faculty, staff, and alumni were developing an application for the three aforementioned new South Carolina historical markers on campus. The group that spearheaded this drive included James Bostic Jr. (Clemson alumnus and former trustee), William Hiott (historic properties director), Barry Anderson (campus planner), Jeremy King and Denise Anderson (presidential fellows), and me. Our discussions focused on how to use state historical markers to better commemorate Native American and African American history at Clemson. We believed the university needed to adopt a means to acknowledge this history not simply for the campus community but also for the residents of and visitors to South Carolina. The group initially considered one marker for both the site of the Fort Hill Plantation quarters for the enslaved and the nearby stockade for incarcerated laborers but eventually recommended three. The first would stand close to the spot where the stockade had been located near the Strom Thurmond Institute; the flip side of the marker would note the space where the quarters for the enslaved persons had been located near the current Lee Hall complex, which houses the School of Architecture and Department of Art. The second historical marker (mentioned in chapter 3) was slated for installation in the Seneca River Basin area (also called Calhoun Fields and Calhoun Bottoms) near the Athletic Complex and Lake Hartwell, where the Cherokee settlement of Isunigu once thrived and where enslaved persons and sharecroppers labored in the Fort Hill Plantation fields. The final marker would commemorate the burial ground for Black laborers, enslaved persons from Fort Hill, and Black convicts who helped build Clemson. These markers signaled our desire for an earlier starting point for Clemson's historical timeline, moving it from Thomas Green Clemson's birthday on July 1, 1807, to the era of the Eastern Band of the Cherokees, who lost their lives and their land after siding with the British during the American Revolution. The markers also signaled a significant shift to a public acknowledgment of the university's indebtedness to Black laborers for its existence.

The spring 2015 semester ended with no support from the administration for changing the name of Tillman Hall and no response for the demands from the Coalition of Concerned Students. These demands had included changing the names of "offensively named buildings" such as Tillman Hall and adding a diversity/university history component to CU 1000, an introductory course that new students must complete during their first semester at Clemson.[13]

Although Clemson's trustees had steadily resisted requests for open forums with the campus community and calls for change in the name of Tillman Hall, suggesting that there were other, more meaningful initiatives the University could implement, the murders at Mother Emanuel proved to be the catalyst for major changes in South Carolina and Clemson University's public history initiatives. On July 8, 2015, at 2:15 A.M., the South Carolina House approved a Senate bill to remove the Confederate flag from its prominent position adjacent to a statue of Benjamin Tillman on the SC state house grounds. That evening on the Clemson campus, someone removed the American flag and replaced it with a Confederate battle flag on the pole situated behind the Thomas Green Clemson statue near the entrance to Tillman Hall. Two days later during a family trip to San Antonio, Texas, as I watched the live televised broadcast of the ceremony, which involved an elaborate lowering and folding of the flag by SC state patrol officers, I wondered how others who revered or abhorred the Confederate flag would respond.

Charleston Murders Compel Clemson Trustees
to Initiate Campus History Project

Clemson's trustees had unanimously approved the resolution for the removal of the Confederate battle flag and soon thereafter issued a statement regarding their intentions to reconsider the institution's public history in a resolution titled "Sense of the Board Regarding Accurately Portraying Clemson University's History." After commending the General Assembly for the removal of the Confederate flag, the trustees declared in part,

> The sense of the Board of Trustees is that such actions and views of Benjamin Tillman are repugnant to our values and our fundamental purpose of being a high seminary of education;
>
> The Board of Trustees reaffirms that Clemson University should be known as a Top 20 Public University and for its outstanding students, faculty, and staff not by the racist actions a century ago; and
>
> There is a need for a task force of members of the Board to work closely with the President and administration on how to best preserve and tell the complete history of Clemson University. This task force is charged with the engagement of stakeholders to include students, faculty, administration and alumni to receive their input. The task force is charged with creating a comprehensive plan to include, but not limited to, any recommendations regarding curating our historic buildings and memorials, developing better ways to acknowledge and teach the history of Clemson University, and exploring appropriate recognition of historical figures. This task force will serve for a period of six months at which time it shall expire unless extended by the Chairman of the Board of Trustees and will report its progress and any recommendations to the Board at its quarterly meetings.[14]

Members of the trustee task force included David Wilkins, chair; David Dukes; Louis Lynn; Bob Peeler; Kim Wilkerson; board chair Smyth McKissick, ex officio; and Allen Wood, ex officio, along with Maxwell Allen, Clemson University president's chief of staff.

It had taken the murders of nine African American parishioners by a self-avowed Confederate battle flag–admiring white supremacist to convince

as a weave house, meal house, blacksmith shop, and slave quarters. Lee had also identified the footprints of the Fort Hill Plantation slave quarters and the building that had served as the overseer's kitchen. He recommended acquiring farm machinery, tools, and other artifacts, some of which were in the college museum, to enhance the "Little Williamsburg" experience. The grounds would be landscaped with period shrubbery and trees, streets would be lighted with oil lamps, and the site enclosed with a rail fence. Architecture students would be required to engage with the site as part of their studies. Lee summed up his rationale for the restoration as follows:

1. Museum preserving the early farm life of South Carolina
2. Laboratory for students of the Department of Agriculture
3. Preservation of John C. Calhoun buildings
4. Center of social activities
5. Headquarters for prominent visitors
6. Cultural inspiration for entire community
7. Attraction of tourists from distant points with resulting publicity
8. Relatively low cost of construction[17]

His recommendations for a colonial village were not implemented for reasons that are unknown. The log cabins were likely destroyed as new campus buildings were erected. The Altamont Plantation was razed in the 1940s; its ruins are in the 17,500-acre Clemson Experimental Forest. The Hanover House, now managed by Clemson's Department of Historic Properties, is located in the South Carolina Botanical Garden situated adjacent to Clemson's main campus. The Woodburn Plantation still sits on Clemson land several miles from campus but is managed by the Pendleton Historic Foundation, which rents the grounds for weddings and private events from April through October, fulfilling one of Lee's original goals for this structure in his proposed historic village.

Clemson trustees adopted a radically different approach than Lee's for their history project, which included updating the founders' biographies on the university website and installing new historical markers on campus. They authorized revisions of "the biographies of Clemson's founders, including but not limited to Thomas Green Clemson, Anna Maria Calhoun Clemson, Benjamin Tillman, John C. Calhoun and Floride C. Calhoun. Additional historical figures, who will also require updated biographies, should

Harvey B. Gantt surrounded by reporters on the day he registered for classes and desegregated Clemson, 1963. Photo courtesy of Cecil Williams.

be considered."[18] Although the list of founders, key historical figures, and notable people include Floride Bonneau Colhoun Calhoun and Anna Maria Calhoun Clemson, the biographies still focus mostly on white male founders. Additionally, trustees maintained control of the content by authorizing themselves to give final approval of the text. In *Invisible Founders: How Two Centuries of African American Families Transformed a Plantation into a College*, anthropologist Lynn Rainville insists that we acknowledge Black people as founders of universities like Sweet Briar College—and Clemson— which were built on plantations and where descendants of enslaved persons still labor for higher education institutions like these.[19] Yet the stories of Clemson's Black founders—enslaved persons, sharecroppers, incarcerated laborers, wage workers, and musicians—are still omitted from the university's list of founders and key historical figures. Only one person of color, African

American Harvey Gantt, who desegregated Clemson in 1963, is identified as one of the institution's "Notable People."[20] Nevertheless, some progress was made in embracing Clemson's full history. The implementation team created a website to keep the public updated as we fulfilled the history task-force's recommendations.[21]

For the built landscape, the trustee task force recommended the installation of markers that identified historical buildings on campus, the oldest of which were constructed by convict laborers. They requested "more prominent signage of each historical building" and "better, more prominent signage for Gantt Circle that provides historical context about Harvey Gantt and why the circle bears his name."[22] Eleven nine-foot, brown signs were installed for each of the buildings listed in the National Register of Historic Places, as well as new granite signage for Gantt Circle. Each inscription provides the building's name, a brief history of the structure, and its role in Clemson's growth and development. Although the names of several significant people associated with Clemson history appear on the new campus markers, including its founder Thomas Green Clemson and its first Chemistry professor Mark Hardin, all references to African Americans, except Harvey Gantt, are classifications—slaves, domestics, sharecroppers, and convicts—although many of these laborers can be identified by name. However, the board approved language for a new granite marker about Gantt's desegregation of Clemson that recognizes its own role in officially naming the horseshoe-shaped road that loops around the statue of Thomas Green Clemson in front of Tillman Hall Gantt Circle. Nevertheless, Clemson has joined the Universities Studying Slavery consortium, signaling a willingness to continue seeking ways to research, document, and incorporate the story and legacy of slavery at the higher education institution into its public history.[23]

In the mid-1990s, after Lee's vision for a "Little Williamsburg" had faded and decades before the trustees' plans to acknowledge complete Clemson history was formulated, an African American anthropologist initiated archeological fieldwork at historic sites on campus; and a group of African American faculty and staff attempted to create the Clemson University Black History Project to fill in this gap in University history. In 1992, anthropologist Carrel Cowan-Ricks completed an excavation of the Fort Hill cemetery during the South Carolina First Annual Archeology Week. She held public meetings to share her findings, including one where she gave a talk titled "Calhoun's Pre-Emancipation African Americans."[24] Clemson Black faculty and staff had more expansive project goals in seeking "to develop a system for interpreting the rich and diverse history of African Americans and their contributions to Clemson University and South Carolina. The ultimate goal of the project is to identify and honor Black Clemson University pioneers—students, athletes, staff, and faculty."[25] The project was funded by a grant from Clemson's Office of the Vice Provost and supported by the President's Commission on the Status of Black Faculty and Staff. The project team sought to archive historical material about African American faculty, staff, and students at Clemson; document the historical development of cultural and educational programs for African American constituents; and create media and print materials to preserve the history of African Americans at Clemson. Its advisory committee included a director, faculty from the School of Architecture and the Department of History, a production-research assistant, athletic staff, the director of the Charles H. Houston Center for the Study of the Black Experience in Education, the president of the Black Faculty and Staff Association, the director of multicultural affairs, the research and planning administrator for access and equity, an administrative assistant from the Strom Thurmond Institute, the director of marketing and education for the Brooks Center for the Performing Arts, the dean of student life, and the records manager. The group considered a collaboration with the Clemson University Black Legends & Legacies program to examine the theme of "Clemson University Blacks—Diversity, Dignity & Desegregation: Factors Influencing the Presence of African Americans at Clemson University, 1954–1981." Legacies were defined as "CU programs targeted to black student staff [sic]."[26] Despite adequate project team members and funding, the CU Black History initiative did not meet its goals and objectives. As with Lee's proposal, no one is sure why their plans for preserving campus history associated with Black people were not realized.

Brown University's Impact on Slavery and the University Projects

Nearly thirty years later, I developed the Call My Name project just as higher education institutions in America were beginning to closely reexamine their ties to slavery and its legacies, prompted in large part by the work of Brown University's Steering Committee on Slavery and Justice. In 2003, then BU President Ruth Simmons appointed a group of students, faculty, and administrators to a steering committee to not only research the institution's connections to slavery and slave trading but to recommend how the university could engage with the public in considering how the legacies of slavery are impacting American life. Their work culminated in the issuance of a report that includes an overview of the history of Brown's relationship to slavery, a discussion of international engagement with retrospective justice, and a synopsis of the current slavery reparations debate in the United States. The committee intended their report to be utilized as the basis for continuing the dialogue at Brown and across the nation about the history and legacies of slavery in America. Despite Brown's groundbreaking work, other universities and colleges, including Clemson, were initially reluctant to commit major institutional resources for similar initiatives. In the decade that followed, however, public and private higher education institutions, including Harvard University, the University of Virginia, Davidson College, the University of Glasgow, and the University of Mississippi, have launched their own initiatives.

BU has continued and expanded its work, including establishing the Center for the Study of Slavery and Justice, hosting an annual conference, and bringing an array of scholars to campus to discuss topics connected to its work. In the spring of 2018, I accepted an invitation to make a presentation about Call My Name at the center's *Race, Memory and Memorialization* Conference. The aim of the conference was "to examine the activism behind the Southern Freedom Movement and critically question the ways in which slavery and the Civil Rights Movement have been represented through memorials and exhibitions."[27] As I stopped by the memorial to enslaved persons, stepped onto the green named in honor of Simmons, and visited the historic house where the scholarly research center operates, I better understood the importance of marking the built landscape with Black history and finding an appropriate means to institutionalize the long-term work of campus history projects.

Clemson University's Uneasy Relationship with Its Complete History

During much of the time prior to Clemson trustees' engagement with campus history, instead of reexamining its complex complete story, the administration had focused on publishing new official public narratives. The first text, a biography titled *Thomas Green Clemson*, edited by Clemson professor of humanities and English Alma Bennett, was released in 2007 in celebration of the bicentennial of Thomas Clemson's birth. The book is comprised of essays about the university's founder written by fifteen contributors, mostly Clemson faculty, staff, and administrators. It features one chapter, "Race, Reconstruction, and Post-Bellum Education in Thomas Green Clemson's Life and World" by Clemson historian Abel Bartley, which includes some information about the institution founder's life as a slaveholder and Confederate Army officer. The chapter, however, offers few new details about the enslaved people who labored on the Fort Hill Plantation that Thomas Clemson managed or those whom he purchased for his own Cane Brake Plantation in Saluda, South Carolina.[28] The second publication was Reel's two-volume set, *The High Seminary*. In extolling the merits of volume 1, former Clemson president James Barker asserts, "[Reel's] book is destined to become the standard reference for understanding Clemson's founding and early years up to July 1, 1964."[29] Barker offers a similarly enthusiastic endorsement of the second volume: "Once again, Dr. Reel has documented the facts and shared the fascinating, personal stories that make history come alive during the decades of Clemson's climb into the top ranks of American public universities."[30] The *South Carolina Historical Magazine* published an equally positive review of volume 2 of Reel's history, written by educator and historian and Clemson alumnae Leslie Wallace Skinner of the South Carolina Department of Education: "As I read the second volume of *The High Seminary* on the thirtieth anniversary of my undergraduate graduation from Clemson, I found myself filled with renewed admiration for the author and his work. . . . At times the topics are intricate, but the writing is informative and entertaining, with Reel retaining his sense of humor throughout the book. Twice, I laughed out loud" (74–75).[31] Although all three books are good sources of general information about the university and its founder, none have attracted critical review.

Ironically, the trustees' interest in Clemson history after the murders of parishioners at Mother Emanuel emerged just as the group I was working with was seeking approval for three new SC historical markers, a process that can take more than a year. Hiott had broached the idea for the markers with the SC Department of Archives and History, learned they were supportive of the project, and began drafting the text for the signs. They provided preliminary approval of the text prior to our presentation to the president's executive leadership team. We then were advised to submit the proposal to the University Advisory Committee on Naming of Land and Facilities. We secured their approval, which included recommended tweaks for the text to be inscribed on the markers. When the proposal was forwarded to the trustees, they requested Clemson history professors' engagement in fact checking and further copy editing. As the markers entered the final approval stage, Bostic and I requested that the ages of the convict laborers, thirteen to sixty-seven (at the time, I had not verified twelve-year-old Simon Davis's court and prison records), be included. Some of the trustees resisted, however, due to their discomfort in publicly displaying the age range of incarcerated boys who had helped build Clemson. I even prepared a one-page, single-spaced overview of the history of convict labor at Clemson, in consultation with Clemson historians, for their review, which only seemed to strengthen the trustees' resolve to exclude the age range from the markers. The trustees eventually approved the markers but insisted that the incarcerated men and boys, whom their predecessors had leased, be described simply as a "predominately African American state convict crew."

Some Clemson trustees' discomfort with historical facts led to the obfuscation of the reality that most of the convicts who helped build the university were young men, forced to create a higher education institution they could never attend and to live under oppressive conditions brought about in large part by Clemson trustee Tillman. When I make presentations about the founding of Clemson and ask audience members to describe who comes to mind when they hear the word "convict," the consistent response is "murderers," "rapists," and "hardened criminals." Audience members are always surprised when I inform them that Clemson's convict workforce was comprised primarily of Black young men and boys as young as thirteen who had frequently been convicted of some form of felonious theft and sentenced from a few months to a life of hard labor in the state penitentiary. Never-

CLEMSON UNIVERSITY

HARDIN HALL

*The oldest remaining academic building on campus,
Hardin Hall was completed in 1891 to serve as the
Chemistry Building. It is named for Mark B. Hardin, the
first chemistry department chairman who served terms as
acting president in 1897, 1899 and 1902. As one of the
original campus facilities, Hardin Hall was constructed
by a predominantly African-American state convict labor
crew using local materials, including bricks they made
from nearby clay soil and granite foundations reclaimed
from the demolition of the slave quarters used on the Fort
Hill plantation prior to the Civil War. It was added to
the National Register of Historic Buildings in 1990.*

ESTABLISHED

1891

Listed on the National Register of Historic Places

The recently installed Clemson University historical marker for Hardin Hall, the institution's first academic building constructed between 1890 and 1891 by a predominately African American convict crew, 2018. Photo by the author.

theless, the historical markers provided the start of a deeper engagement with Clemson history. But the university would need more effective learning devices to share its complete history with the public.

Descendants Participate in New Clemson University History Initiatives

When Clemson broke ground for the historical markers in April of 2016, Eva Hester Martin and her daughter Valerie Martin-Lee, descendants of Sharper and Caroline and their daughter Matilda, who were enslaved on the Fort Hill Plantation, were our special guests. As I stood in the oversized white tent watching people trickle in around me, someone slipped up behind me and grabbed my hand. I turned to see former Clemson president Barker, who had resisted my initial request for the university to reexamine its history shortly after I arrived at Clemson about eight years earlier. We shook hands and exchanged smiles. No words were necessary. We both knew this event could have been part of his legacy. I immediately turned my attention back to Eva Martin, ensuring that she and her family were comfortably seated.

The day was marked by celebratory public events and quiet reflective moments. After Bostic and I unveiled full-size reproductions of the markers, we joined trustees, Clemson administrators, and the Martins in turning over reddish dirt, using shovels with orange handles and gold blades. During his remarks, Clemson president Clements declared, "The story of Clemson University's founding is one of great vision, commitment, and perseverance. However, it is also a story with some uncomfortable history. And, although we cannot change our history, we can acknowledge it and learn from it, and that is what great universities do."[32] At the end of the ceremony, Eva Martin, who was celebrating her ninetieth birthday, remarked to a local television reporter that she was glad she had lived long enough to see Clemson's recognition of her family's contributions to its history. When she later walked into my classroom to share her story with students enrolled in my African American literature course, history came to life. Clemson students conversed with a woman whose grandmother had been enslaved by the Calhoun family. They encountered living, breathing history. They were confronted with concrete, indisputable evidence that enslaved persons once labored on the land where their beloved Clemson was built.

The Martins' visit to campus unexpectedly enabled me to connect with another descendant family. When I returned to my office after the groundbreaking ceremony, I found a message from Patricia Fruster, requesting that I call her. Fruster had seen a photograph of her ancestors, Frances and Thomas Fruster, standing in front of the Fort Hill plantation house, featured in a televised news story about Eva Martin's participation in the groundbreaking ceremony for the historical markers.

"Is she part of my family?" Patricia Fruster asked.

My only explanation was that the local television station had inserted a picture of former enslaved persons without requesting information about their identity.

Connecting with Patricia Fruster enabled me to invite her and her family to participate in a series of Call My Name project events and Clemson history program. When I recommended that she record an interview for the StoryCorps initiative sponsored by Call My Name, she chose her cousin Eric Young, a Clemson alumnus. A few months after the interview, Eric and his wife and parents accepted my invitation to travel to Clemson to participate in Call My Name's Contemplative African American Heritage tour of the campus, providing insights about how their family's stories as descendants and alumni are tied to Clemson history. The tour was developed with a grant from Clemson's Office of Inclusion and Equity. Then the Frusters agreed to take part in the university's first "History in Plain Sight Day" in the spring of 2017, a partial fulfillment of the trustees' recommendation for an annual Clemson History Week. The Frusters interspersed gospel songs with family stories at the event held on Bowman Field in front of Tillman Hall. Audience members also heard Clemson students read letters written by Thomas and Anna Clemson and by Clemson alumni who fought on the front lines of World War II.

Some Student Concerns about Clemson History Addressed, Others Persist

Other initiatives have drawn Clemson closer to addressing student concerns and fulfilling the trustees' goal of sharing the university's complete history. In April of 2016, African American students found hanging bananas on an "African Americans at Fort Hill" banner near the center of campus; they had been placed there to link Black people to monkeys. Clemson president Clements sent an email describing the incident as "hurtful, disrespectful, unacceptable" and distributed a report regarding diversity and inclusion initiatives.[33] But after waiting more than a year for answers from the administration to their demands after the #StudentBlackOut march, student activists and their allies staged a sit-in inside Sikes Hall. Protesters were allowed to stay overnight in the building, but Clemson administrators ordered them to leave Sikes by 5:30 P.M. on the second day of the demonstration. When five refused—D. J. Smith, Khayla Williams, Ian Anderson, A.D. Carson, and Rae-Nessha White—they were arrested for trespassing but released the same evening. The protestors moved the sit-in outside to the front steps, keeping a twenty-four-hour vigil that included sleeping on the steps and in tents until they suspended the protest on day nine. During that time, the more than one hundred student protestors received support from faculty, staff, and their peers. Campus Recreation, Clemson football players, and Greek organizations were among those who offered encouragement or assistance. The student activists also were taunted and harassed by members of the campus and local communities. For example, white Clemson student Jamie Moore, who issued an anonymous death threat against the protesters on Yik Yak, was arrested and subsequently suspended, though he was allowed to take his exams and complete the semester.[34] On the final day of the sit-in, President Clements distributed an email response to their demands that included timelines and point persons.[35] Carson would later create a timeline that placed the Sikes sit-in within a global context of events that impacted Black lives.[36]

In the fall of 2016, in response to students' demands and President Clements's desire for better space for the multicultural center, the Harvey and Lucinda Gantt Multicultural Center was relocated from cramped quarters in the Edgar Brown University Union building to refurbished, spacious

While a Clemson University police officer tasked with maintaining order looked on, more than one hundred student sit-in protesters waited outside Sikes Hall for the release of fellow protesters A.D. Carson, Khayla William, Ian Anderson, Rae-Nessha White, and Darien Smith, who were arrested after refusing to leave the building, 2016. Photo courtesy of Edith M. Dunlap.

offices on the second floor of Brackett Hall. But the students had requested a building for the center. Two years later, David Markus, an archeologist and visiting lecturer in the department of sociology, anthropology, and criminal justice, provided his students with training for a six-week archeological field school, the first Clemson has offered. In the summer of 2018, the team conducted a dig in the area between the rebuilt Fort Hill kitchen and the Shoeboxes residential hall, where plantation outbuildings are believed to have been situated; they located footprints of a building and several artifacts dating back to the antebellum period.[37] The field school was held again for Markus's students in the summer of 2019, leading to the discovery of a larger building footprint and more artifacts. The Department of Historic Properties had worked with the South Carolina state archeologist for an excavation of the same site a few years earlier.

Clemson is further sustaining engagement with its history by considering a recommendation from the History Implementation Team to renovate the Trustee House, one of the buildings in the historic district built by incarcerated laborers, for use as a history center. Historic Properties staff have long desired more space for offices, visitors, and exhibits. The house is ideally located between the Fort Hill plantation house and Hardin Hall, the oldest academic building on campus. Campus planning staff have developed architectural drawings for the renovation project that include a new addition to the back of the structure that would provide classroom, exhibit, and reception space. Glass panels would enable guests to see the history of the university on the landscape, from the soil upon which the Eastern Band of the Cherokees walked, to the two-story white plantation house enlarged by enslaved carpenters during the antebellum era, to the red brick buildings built mostly by incarcerated laborers. The provost has also created the Seneca River Basin Sustainability Initiative to develop a preservation plan for the last piece of historic land on campus where academic buildings have not been erected and parking lots have not been installed. Clemson would honor many different peoples who have lived on and cultivated the land, while utilizing the space as a learning lab where the organic farm will provide research opportunities for students and faculty and sustenance for the campus and local communities.

New student initiatives will likewise ensure that Clemson continues to refine its approach to documenting and sharing its history. During the spring of 2017, several honors students began a conversation they characterized as "Considering Calhoun: An Open Discussion about the Namesake of the Honors College" to gather students' opinions about the name of the college and to gauge student interest in changing the name of the program to the Clemson Honors College. About two years later, students and faculty circulated petitions inviting members of the campus community to support the name change. The more than two hundred students and alumni who signed the petition argued that "[r]emoving 'Calhoun' so that the name is 'Clemson Honors College' would not remove his legacy from the campus.

. . . Calhoun is and will remain a prominent figure at Clemson and in its history, notably in that his plantation home still sits in the middle of our campus."[38] At the beginning of the fall 2019 semester, petitioners were still waiting for the provost to announce the administration's decision regarding their request. Additionally, the undergraduate student government had recently created an inclusion and equity committee. One of the committee's first actions was to pass a nonbinding resolution in August 2018 against the display of the Confederate battle flag on and around campus, after the SC Secessionist Party held a flagging on a pedestrian bridge and along US Route 123, Calhoun Memorial Highway, a few miles from campus. Up until January 2019 when the organization disbanded, the Secessionists staged flag-waving events throughout the state to protest the legislature's failure to keep its promise to secure a new place for the display of the Confederate battle flag following its removal from the state house grounds. In endorsing the resolution, the Undergraduate Student Government declared, "We stand against the adverse notions the Confederate flag brings to a campus pushing for inclusivity, and . . . we . . . do stand against the display of the Confederate flag and believe this sentiment should be expressed to our students, faculty, administration, and surrounding Clemson community."[39] Secessionist organization members and their supporters invited Clemson student leaders to discuss South Carolina history and threatened to stage a major flagging on campus during the academic year.[40] The students declined; the major flagging event never materialized.

Engaging the Local Community:
Let's Talk Race in the City of Clemson

Not only have several students and faculty become more engaged in Clemson history initiatives, community members have become increasingly interested in learning more about the local and university history and in cosponsoring events that give them opportunities to engage with researchers. Courtney Green, whom I met through her husband Jerad Green, associate director for multicultural programs in Clemson's Harvey and Lucinda Gantt Center, had asked me to lead several African American heritage tours of campus for community groups. Then in the fall of 2018, she invited me to facilitate a community dialogue, "Let's Talk Race," the kind of conversation I had in mind when I informed Lester Holt that I believed the country needed to engage in a national discussion about the topic. She had brought a steady stream of local residents, including young couples and stay-at-home moms with small children, for the campus tours, which stopped only because I went on research leave. For the community discussion held at the CAAAM, we agreed to list the Call My Name project and my affiliation with Clemson as part of the publicity materials. The museum would be open for visitors to view exhibits for about an hour before the program began. I would speak for thirty minutes, followed by a question and answer period and small group discussions. Courtney Green asked me to focus on important history of the area and the campus as it relates to race. The planning team's goal was to encourage attendees to make connections between the history and legacies of race manifested in the city of Clemson, as well as to consider how to achieve equity and justice in their communities.

I decided to frame my comments around my *Black Clemson* exhibition project, which links stories about Blacks in Clemson University history with narratives of those who lived in nearby communities. In the spring of 2018, the Whiting Foundation awarded me a Public Engagement Fellowship to create an exhibition about the Black experience at Clemson University and in local communities in order to create a space in which attendees can participate in conversations about this slice of American history and devise ways to move toward solutions for the continued challenges of race relations in America. Since we didn't have an exhibit or enough suitable artifacts to jumpstart those discussions, I decided to utilize storytelling to engage our audience, a practice Black feminist Jewel Amoah argues is "a tradition based on the continuity of wisdom . . . [that] functions to assert the voice of the oppressed . . . not merely a means of entertainment."[41] This type of storytelling is revolutionary. Indeed, "Narrative is radical, creating us at the very moment it is being created," according to Toni Morrison.[42]

As people began to arrive for the program around 5:30 P.M., I wondered how the radical narratives I would share about Black people in Clemson history would create us, the 150 local residents who had filled every seat and were standing around the back walls of the auditorium. Talking for twenty-five minutes without a PowerPoint had seemed daunting when I began. However, as I worked my way through the presentation, weaving the stories of Black Clemson with the challenges of fostering better race relations in the divisive age of US president Donald Trump and with my experiences as a sixth-generation South Carolinian and a descendant of slaveholders and enslaved persons, we nearly ran out of time for small-group discussions. The narrative that seemed to resonate most with the audience was my experience in purchasing a house when my husband and I moved to South Carolina in 2007. We decided to conduct all our business online and through telephone conversations as research has shown that African Americans customers do not always receive fair treatment in the real estate business. When we received the paperwork, we discovered our broker had checked the box by "white" for our race and noted that he had made the determination via telephone. But he had not asked us our race. Perhaps he assumed we were white based on our incomes, jobs, and new neighborhood, as well as our voice inflections. Being accused of "sounding" or "acting" white was not new to me: some of my Black classmates in high school who did not know me very well believed my bookworm, congenial persona was evidence of my aspiring to be like the smart white students at our predominantly white boarding academy. After consulting with my brother Carlton, a real estate attorney, who was handling the closing, my husband and I decided not to correct the broker's errors. We simply signed the papers and tucked the photocopies of our drivers' licenses he had requested at the bottom of the stack.

When the Let's Talk Race audience began asking "What's next?" questions, I offered practical advice: to become more involved in their local communities, to seek out opportunities to engage with people of diverse backgrounds, and to be more accepting of racial differences. Several members of the audience also encouraged participants to vote, to elect officials and support legislation that help create and sustain a diverse and inclusive community. After the program, Elizabeth Maxon, a CAAAM volunteer, posted a snippet of the program she had videotaped on Instagram with this caption:

I love Clemson. I know it's not perfect, but I love it. And on a night like tonight I am so encouraged that the people in my community have a desire to face the issue of race with interest and compassion. Dr. Rhondda Thomas was a wise and kind guide as we explored where we have come from and how that impacts where we are going. Yes, it's true. We can all do this simple thing—talk about it (and do plenty of listening too).

Clemson Seeks New University Historian: Should I Apply?

As I expanded my outreach to local communities, I wondered if I should seek a larger platform for my work at Clemson. I had been thinking about applying for the university historian position. Then an email arrived in my electronic inbox on March 27, 2019:

> The Office of the Provost is now accepting applications and nominations for the position of University Historian. This appointment, reporting directly to the Executive Vice President and Provost, will serve as a key authority on issues relating to historic interpretation, representation and commemoration for the Clemson community and will be responsible for compiling and disseminating new scholarship relating to Clemson's past.

Should I apply? I contacted one of the three faculty members on the search committee, seeking clarification about the nature of the appointment. Would it be a joint appointment or full-time? Temporary—maybe a three-year, renewable appointment—or permanent? We both hoped it would be a temporary, renewable appointment to attract a wider variety of candidates. I had to make a decision quickly as applications were due in ten days.

About an hour after the announcement was distributed, a colleague in the English department emailed me: "Are you applying for this? If you are not, I might." When we talked later, we decided both of us would apply.

Within thirty minutes of receiving my first colleague's email, another colleague, my former department chair, sent me a message: "For what it's worth, Rhondda, I think you would be a very strong candidate for this position, particularly as it's described (and seems to me re-described) here. Happy to confer." We began to confer in an email exchange. In previous conversations, I had always insisted that preserving my ability be an early African Americanist scholar—who included Black history and culture at Clemson as part of her research agenda—would be the basis for my work-related decisions. My colleague assured me that I had successfully figured out how to balance my local, national, and international interests. "Being an English professor can be enough," my colleague assured me. Would successfully applying for the university historian position permanently disrupt that balance I had worked for nearly twelve years to achieve? The job would require me to devote nearly all of my time to researching and documenting Clemson history. What would happen to the Call My Name project?

As I carefully reread the announcement attached to the Provost's email, I noticed it described the position as a "joint appointment." Perhaps I could continue teaching and researching early African American literature after all.

I decided to apply. I was beginning to think I should be engaged in the process, even if I were not selected.

One week after I received the email announcement about the university historian position, I attended a Council on Diversity and Inclusion meeting, where the provost talked briefly about the search. He emphasized the administration's desire for candidates who could devote all their time to the position. After following up with my colleague who had encouraged me to apply, I asked the provost for clarification about the joint appointment nature of the position. The university historian would retain faculty status but would be expected to focus on the administrative and service responsibilities of university historian, with very few teaching or research responsibilities.

A series of events the following day clarified my thinking regarding the viability of my seeking the university historian appointment. The day began with my facilitating a thesis defense for an English honors student, Brendan McNeely, who is also a Call My Name research assistant. In addition to his first reader and me, Brendan had invited three of the most intellectually gifted faculty members in our department to engage in a discussion about his work. Before the defense began, as my colleagues and I conversed about memorialization and campus history, I realized how much I had missed engaging with them while I had been on sabbatical and research leave for nearly two years. After Brendan brilliantly defended his thesis, I rushed to the Hendrix Center to serve with Clemson's president as cohost for the annual spring forum sponsored by the Commission on the Status of Black Faculty and Staff. As I facilitated the reports from the Commission and our constituents' Q&A with the president and members of his executive leadership team, I realized how much I was looking forward to the organization's expanded role. We had decided to restructure the organization as the Commission on the Black Experience in the fall of 2019, adding students, alumni, and the local community to its constituency. Immediately after the forum,

I gave Monica Williams-Hudgens, the mixed-race granddaughter of Strom Thurmond, and her husband, Gerald, an abbreviated African American heritage walking tour of campus, which began at the Fort Hill plantation house and ended at the Strom Thurmond Institute. I then rushed to the Memorial football stadium, West End Zone, to assist my Pearce Center intern team with completing the setup for the Call My Name *Book of Names Launch*. The event would showcase—to stakeholders, supporters, Black alumni and retirees, and descendants—the research my student assistants and I had been conducting for the project during the past twelve years. Attendees viewed primary documents, including records of convict labor on loan from the SC Department of Archives and History, at stations representing the six generations of African Americans in Clemson history. The site overlooked the football field, which had been meticulously prepared for the annual spring game. It is situated adjacent to a grassy hill (no longer present) where African Americans were forced to sit during games, a place known as "nigger hill" during the Jim Crow era. From our vantage point, we could also see the hill on the opposite end of the stadium where the mostly Black football team and their coaches now run down to the field on game days. Guests also examined the *Book of Names*, which identifies hundreds of people of African descent, enslaved and free, who have labored on Clemson land, as well as the students, faculty, and staff who came to the university after desegregation. The printed book will be distributed throughout the state and around the world in an electronic version, to facilitate the crowdsourcing phase of the Call My Name initiative. We hope people will see familiar names and help us fill out more stories of African Americans in Clemson history.

By the end of the day, it was clear to me that being an early African Americanist who includes a Black Clemson history project as half her research agenda is who I need to be. *Call My Name* called my name.

Reframing Call My Name through the Lens of the African Diaspora

But the exhibition preview also convinced me that my goals for *Black Clemson* were still mediated through the experiences of African Americans connected with the history of the University at the expense of the community. I hoped my fourth visit to the National Museum of African American History and Culture in the spring of 2019 would help me to reenvision my project. As I headed to Heritage Hall on the lower level of the museum, I felt as if I were entering the bowels of a slave ship. I needed to think through my assertion that Black Clemson history is Black American history and American history. I hoped the exhibits would help me understand how these stories are all bound up together. As I moved through the oversized glass doors that led to the exhibit area, I thought about the Door of No Return at Cape Coast Castle, which now functions as the Door of Return for Black people from the African Diaspora. Maybe *Black Clemson* could function as a door of return to the history that many would rather forget or gloss over. As I entered the lobby, the first photograph I saw was of Thurgood Marshall, who argued the *Briggs v. Elliott* case for Clarendon County public schools in South Carolina, which became part of the landmark *Brown v. Board of Education* decision. Marshall seemed to be smiling at me from the photo collage, beckoning me to explore American history in South Carolina through a Black filter. Near him was a photograph of educator and activist Mary McLeod Bethune, a South Carolinian, and an image of the familiar painting of Olaudah Equiano, likely Carolina-born, but dressed as an Englishman. The South Carolina story is foundational for this national Smithsonian museum, for American history.

As I entered the elevator and watched the years imprinted on the walls roll back to the 1400s as we descended to the lowest level, I realized immediately that *Black Clemson* history does not begin in 1825 on Calhoun's Fort Hill Plantation. It starts with freedom in Africa, with Polydore and Mennemin, "the Africans," and the ancestors of other enslaved Black people who worked alongside them. They helped create the African Diaspora and were part of the largest forced migration in human history. Instead of designing the exhibition around the experiences of African Americans at the university from slavery through desegregation, *Black Clemson* will follow a historical arch, telling stories about the experiences of Black people in the Greater Clemson, South Carolina, area in freedom, enslavement, emancipation, segregation, and desegregation.

Call My Name is the product of this history, particularly Black local history that has been ignored or omitted. But telling these stories requires financial resources. The grant and gift I received from the provost and the Bostics enabled me to transform an idea into a research project. Two NEH grants had given me opportunities to strengthen partnerships with Clemson's Humanities Hub and local community organizations through the creation of the Call My Name Coalition. SC Humanities and Whiting Foundation grants provided a means for me to consult with historians Cecelia Moore and Megan Taylor-Shockley and StudioDisplays to create the concept for a traveling exhibition. But I had applied and failed to receive a major NEH Public Humanities grant to fund the completion of the project in 2017. I then missed the opportunity to reapply in January of 2019 due to miscommunication regarding deadlines during the government shutdown. In the months that followed, I checked the NEH website periodically to see if new applications were being accepted. The grant was especially attractive because awardees could receive up to $400,000 for the implementation phase of an exhibition project. On July 5, 2019, I discovered NEH was accepting new applications for the grant. When I asked Lee Morrissey, my principal coinvestigator for Call My Name's two other successful NEH grant applications, if he had time to assist in preparing the proposal, he replied, "Yes. Let's." Our exhibition team includes scholars from five universities, the Call My Name Coalition, and the Upcountry History Museum in Greenville, South Carolina. We submitted our application on August 14, 2019. On Tuesday, April 7, 2020, we learned NEH awarded Call My Name a $400,000 exhibition public humanities implementation grant. The exhibition is slated to open at Clemson University in January of 2022.

Together—my research team, Clemson University, and local communities—we will call names, we will share stories, and we will create a complex and inclusive community history.

Section Five

Let your motto be resistance! resistance! RESISTANCE! No oppressed
people have ever secured their liberty without resistance. What kind of
resistance you had better make, you must decide by the circumstances
that surround you, and according to the suggestion of expediency.
HENRY HIGHLAND GARNET

Call: Post-desegregation Clemson

RHONDDA ROBINSON THOMAS

Resistance.

Nearly seven years after Gantt came, almost every Black student left campus in protest.

In October of 1969, sixty of the nearly sixty-five African American students then enrolled at Clemson left campus in "fear and complete panic," according to newspaper accounts published throughout the nation.[1] Clemson's student newspaper the *Tiger* reported, "Black students vacate campus for protection . . . to remove the threat of physical violence."[2] A year earlier, Black students had returned to campus in the fall, just four months after the assassination of Martin Luther King Jr., determined to transform Clemson into a more welcoming and inclusive place.

Clemson University's public commemoration of integration frequently begins and ends with Harvey Gantt's enrollment as the first African American student on January 28, 1963. On the anniversary of integration in 2019, Clemson president Clements tweeted, "Today marks the 56th anniversary of Harvey Gantt enrolling at Clemson. Thank you, Mr. Gantt, for changing Clemson for the better."[3] A South Carolina historical marker on campus installed near Tillman Hall, the building where Gantt registered for classes, describes the historical event as "Integration with Dignity." Many Clemson supporters laud then president Robert C. Edwards for orchestrating Clemson's peaceful transition from a segregated college for white, mostly male students to a desegregated institution with one Black male student. Few acknowledge that South Carolina was the last state to integrate its higher education institutions nearly a decade after *Brown v. Board of Education*, the US Supreme court case that outlawed segregation in public schools. The university rarely discusses the fact that Gantt's admission resulted from a class-action lawsuit that the institution fought all the way to the US Supreme Court. Moreover, most people know very little about the first decade of integration at Clemson as the university's African American student population slowly grew from one student to almost one hundred. Most were Black males. Clemson had become coeducational in 1955 to avoid closure as white male interest in attending a military college waned after the brutalities of World War II. When Gantt desegregated Clemson, he enrolled in a higher education institution that was not only all white but pervasively white male—administrators, faculty, staff, and students, many of whom had grown up in the Jim Crow era of white male supremacy in South Carolina. Two of the first three Black female alumnae, Dorothy Ashford and Delores K. Barton, who completed four-year degrees at Clemson, report that they experienced some challenges, but they believe their male counterparts bore the brunt of racism during the early years of desegregation.

A year before their protest in 1969, Black students had organized Clemson's first Black student organization, the SLBI, to "promote courses in Black History, the study of Black culture and art, and the study of the Black man in today's society" and invited any student who supported the organization's purpose to join.[4] Meetings were initially held off campus at the Newman Center, the gathering place for Clemson's Catholic Student Organization.

By this time, the campus climate was increasingly hostile for Black students. In the dining hall, for example, white students were pelting Black male students with food during their meals. The first time African American alumnus James Bostic Jr. recounted the story, he characterized the perpetrators as "the people."

"Were they students, Dr. Bostic?" I asked gently.

"The people would throw food at us," he insisted.

The next time Bostic shared the experience about three years later, he identified the perpetrators as white male students but added that they threw food at Black male students every day for three months. Initially, Bostic and his friends sat at their table, heads down, daring not look a white male adversary in the eye.

The *Taps* yearbook photograph of the Student League for Black Identity, Clemson University's first African American student organization, 1975. Courtesy of Clemson University Libraries' Special Collections & Archives.

Resistance. *Fight back, against the odds.*

African American alumnus Titus Duren, who enrolled during Bostic's senior year, recalls that he and a few of their Black male classmates considered retaliation against their antagonists but immediately backed down, realizing they were outnumbered. Having come of age in Jim Crow South Carolina during the 1950s and early 1960s, they also feared lynching for Black young men who might harm a white male. President Edwards intervened only after the students followed his instructions to identify the culprit. One day, one of the Black male students dared to look up when the pelting began and identified their white male adversary, who was expelled from the college within twenty-four hours. The food throwing stopped permanently, according to Bostic.

But Black students were still forced to hear the Tiger band play "Dixie," which they characterized as "insulting and very embarrassing," and to see white students proudly display a large Confederate battle flag at official University events.[5] Additionally, at athletic games, white students hurled racial epithets at Black players on opposing teams. During a basketball game against Florida State in February 1969, "white students jeered pickaninny, nigger, jungle bunny, boy, Willy, Leroy, and coon at players of Florida State team at b-ball game," according to Evron Laitala, a white Clemson student, who wrote a letter to the editor that was published in the *Tiger*. Charles A. Williams, a Black Clemson student, also wrote a letter that appeared in the same issue of the *Tiger*, defending his decision not to stand for or sing the national anthem at games where he heard Blacks called "LEROY." He declared, "Until I can be unchained and given my freedom, America does not mean —— to me."[6] Furthermore, campus police officers placed Black male students under surveillance, monitoring their movements in public space. In the classroom, Black students sat in the front row to shield themselves from harassment from white students who sat behind them. When they considered which classes to enroll in during registration, they consulted with each other, avoiding professors deemed to be racist. One student recalls being given an F in a course during his senior year that prevented him from graduating. When he confronted the professor about his grade, the faculty member responded, "Some people are superior, and others are inferior," and slammed the door in his face. The student believed he had no recourse but to retake the class and graduate a semester late.

But the SLBI fought back. Within a year of its establishment in 1968, its members initiated a meeting with Clemson administrators, presenting discussion questions to President Edwards regarding the status of Black life and learning at Clemson, the recruitment of Black students and athletes, the introduction of more classes that examined Black life, history, and culture, the opportunity to invite Black speakers, "radical and non-radical," the hiring of more Black faculty, and the inclusion of more Black literature in the library.[7] They also sought to end the display of the Confederate battle flag and the playing of "Dixie" at official university events and expressed concerns about a skit that included stereotypical depictions of African Americans. Clemson's *Taps* yearbook featured pictures of white students still performing at university-sponsored events in blackface during the decade following integration.[8]

The administration placated Black students by giving them their own building on campus, which students dubbed the "Black House," for social events; providing them with a car to drive to Seneca to participate in social events held in a room on the second floor of a drugstore owned by Harold E. Hill, an African American pharmacist; and adding a Black History course taught by William F. Steirer Jr., a white historian in Clemson's Department of History. Administrators encouraged Black students to utilize the "Black House" especially after sporting events to avoid contact with racist drunk white students and community members. But when the SLBI demanded that the Clemson traditions associated with the Confederacy be discontinued, 3,300 Clemson students signed a petition to keep them, and President Edwards publicly supported the continued use of these relics of the Lost Cause. In a letter to the editor of the *Tiger* directed at the SLBI, white Clemson students John Richards and Sandy Edge insisted, "Yet please note that these things are Clemson traditions and you are not. They have been here for many more years than you and will remain long after you are gone if the majority of the students have their say about the matter."[9]

Resistance. *Take your stand.*

The SLBI refused to back down. While they fought for the removal of these Confederate symbols, they organized talk-ins, open forums to discuss topics of interest and benefit to the campus community. In 1969, they hosted a talk-in that examined "The White Problem in America." "The only way we can do this," explained Raymond Huff, chair of the project committee, "is to have the whites on campus participating with real [truthfulness]. SLBI is trying desperately to be recognized as a vehicle for advancement toward racial [equality] and moral justice."[10] They organized all-Black intramural sports teams, determined to dominate on the field and the court as well as to excel in their classes. On Friday evenings, Black male students would gather in a friend's room in Johnstone Hall, drink wine, and decompress after surviving another week at Clemson. But come Sunday night, they were devoting their time to studying.

In the fall of 1969, the SLBI scored a major victory when the white student–run Spirit Committee agreed to discontinue the playing of "Dixie" and displaying of the Confederate battle flag during official University events beginning in 1972. Many white students had insisted they preferred to honor these symbols of the Confederacy at Clemson rather than the presence of Black students. Shortly thereafter, Clemson also stopped using the Country Gentleman mascot, a white male student dressed up like a southern planter, preferring the Tiger.

The SLBI continued their work of transforming Clemson into an integrated place until it was reorganized as a cultural group called *Pamoja*, a Swahili word meaning "togetherness," in 1980. By this time Black fraternities and sororities had been established on campus.

Clemson would not have another campus-wide Black student organization until 2010 when the Black Student Union was established "to PROMOTE, CELEBRATE, and EMBRACE Black Culture on Clemson University's campus while instilling a sense of pride in the community."[11] Many Black students recall coming to Clemson primarily to earn their degrees without engaging in activism to improve the campus climate. Without a support system of Black and white faculty, staff, and administrative allies, students focused on completing their education. By the early twenty-first century, however, the percentage of African American students at Clemson had increased from merely 1 percent, or sixty students, to about 6.5 percent, about twelve hundred students. Clemson learning spaces like the Gantt Multicultural Center provided programming, events, and activities that included celebrations of Black history and culture. Black students still wanted more than an education. They increasingly demanded equal access to all opportunities that can enrich their Clemson experience.

In the fall of 2019, a small group of Black Clemson students staged a protest near Sikes Hall demanding "Black Space." Some are still waiting for and expecting to have their twenty-first-century version of a Black House.

Resistance. *Speak up.*

Response: A Tale of Parallels

SHAQUILLE FONTENOT

Though forced to inhale the thick air of racism that swirled in and out of every body, every building, and every thought, James Bostic Jr., became an alumnus of Clemson University.

My chest tightened as I read about the behavior of the white male students, their own insecurities the root of their deep hatred. Did the chests of Bostic and his friends tighten, too, as chunks of food bounced off their backs? Were they tight with anger, or stricken with fear, as racial epithets slung across slick tongues toward them? Would their resistance taper off? Would they fight back? Could they breathe?

Resistance. *The will to stay.*

Given the setting and social climate of the time, it is refreshing to know that Black Clemson students were still able to implement an amazing amount of change as a result of their frequent and direct resistance. Establishing a unified Black voice during the late 1960s required extreme organization, enormous resilience, and effective positioning against the dominant white Clemson voice. The sea of whiteness that connected the staff and student body at the time, also made it abundantly clear that Clemson's Black students had few, if any, allies. This meant the odds were against Black students not only in the classroom but at all times, sometimes even in their own minds.

Resistance. *The will to survive.*

Despite this, Black students established the SLBI and demanded a space for Black identity and existence at Clemson. The SLBI worked to shift Clemson's social climate through strategic action directed at both the administrative and student body levels. I am grateful for their unrelenting work, which laid the foundation for my own Clemson experience.

Resistance. *The will to fight.*

It has become evident, particularly at good ol' boy institutions and organizations, whose histories are marred by bigotry and hatred, that blemishes of the past can and will be buried under new, fabricated narratives. This includes categorizing statues in memory of racists and bigots "tradition," regardless of how these present-day reminders make student, staff, and faculty feel.

When I was at Clemson, the feelings of otherness weren't as prominent during my first two years as they were during my last two years on campus. As a freshman, I joined many organizations and saw enough sprinkles of Black and brown students to feel as if I were protected and in a safe place. Although I was the only Black student in many of my classes, there were enough shiny objects, classes, and activities to keep me on a certain track. I realized later that this track was established the way it was for a reason. This was a track that supported the comfort of ignorance.

Resistance. *Just do your work.*

When on-boarded as a student, I was never exposed to Clemson's real history. The diversity course I completed during my freshman year consisted of making a PowerPoint presentation with an "ethnic" friend and taking a few pictures. I never thought about how Clemson's past would impact my studies or my everyday experience as a student. My blackness just got me the occasional drunken comment from a white frat boy about how I was "pretty for a Black girl." Later, it got my life threatened.

A year later, I came face to face with the "otherness" I had managed to ignore. While I was visiting a friend who was a student resident assistant, someone dropped a whole, raw chicken in front of her doorstep. Later that night, she saw a comment on the anonymous messaging platform, Yik Yak, that read "hope you enjoyed the chicken, nigger."

Resistance. *You're not welcome here.*

This is when I knew: we were dealing with a much bigger beast than I thought. It was right around this time that I began to explore Clemson's history for myself. I remembered thinking that there was no part of Clemson's founding story that asked me to be there, and since I was there anyway, I was going to make sure everyone knew I deserved to be.

Resistance. *Here to stay.*

I was very blessed to be positioned at Clemson when I was. During the height of the Black Lives Matter protests, I was taking an African American literature course with Rhondda Thomas. She taught me how to properly research, examine historical documents, and look at new ways to connect the Black experiences of the past with those of today. I became one of many student-activists and organizers who demanded visibility for the Black student body and urged the administration to take a serious look at how we could change Clemson University for the better.

Resistance. *Armed with history.*

I don't remember getting a lot of sleep during that time. We met late at night in undisclosed locations to discuss the campus climate. We wrote to media outlets about racist campus parties, incidents of blackface, harassment toward Black students, and unwelcoming spaces. We protested and stood in solidarity with student organizations across the United States. We leveraged social media to organize events and meetings with university staff and to facilitate dialogue between students and faculty.

Resistance. *We built this.*

We had the advantages of digital media and overall societal shifts as well. What did the Black Clemson students of the late 1960s have besides each other?

Fighting a fight you didn't ask to fight is something that is often required for progress. And so they decided to progress. It's funny how a system not built for us reacts when we realize it. We simply wanted Clemson to make a clear and direct statement that hatred, harassment, and racism would not be tolerated on our campus and would not be upheld by any Clemson University policy, system, monument, or action.

I realized that the "allowances" that pacified Black students in the past were the same ones used to pacify us while we were on campus. For us, publicity luncheons and meet ups sponsored by the administration that included free sandwiches made the message very clear, very quickly: let them create organizations and let them speak up, but don't let them rock the boat.

Resistance. *Rocking the boat anyway.*

Clemson's leadership told us that although students could express their views and opinions, they must not "cross the line and become harassment or intimidation, just as rallies and protest marches must not cross the line to lawlessness."[1] This language suggested our protests were a "lawless" act. Administrators even positioned Black alumni to reassure us that "it's not that bad" and that we were making it more difficult for other Black students to be accepted into Clemson if we spoke up.

Resistance. *Taking the risk.*

The pacifist language came after very public protests highlighted the harsh racial climate on Clemson's campus and our university's reluctance to shut it down. Much as the students in the late 1960s were driven to change as a result of the assassination of Dr. King, who was called a Communist, inciter of violence, and threat to national security, so the Black student body of the 2010s was moved by the deaths of young Black men like Trayvon Martin, Mike Brown, and Eric Garner, who were called thugs, nobodies, and deemed disposable by society.

Resistance. *Honoring the slain.*

The feelings of otherness surged to new levels when we got looks from once friendly classmates, who were not so friendly after our protests, and after public threats on digital messaging and communication apps like Yik Yak and Twitter stacked up in our inboxes and littered our timelines.

During the 1960s, in the Clemson student publication, the *Tiger*, racist white students blatantly told members of the SLBI that they were not in alignment with Clemson tradition. Half a century later, when we protested against the university's response to the threats we received, members of the student body asked us, "If you don't like it, why don't you just leave?"

Resistance. *This is our place, too.*

Prior to this period in my life, I had no idea how many lies were presented in the public-facing version of Clemson's history. I learned that financially and socially, rich families flourished as result of their ability to control the Black body. Denying Black people agency was, and still is, a profit center in America.

Resistance. *We are not merchandise.*

Dr. Thomas's courses made it clear to me that the techniques and tactics used to oppress and pacify Black people in the past are still in use today.

From an activism standpoint, the parallels in our approach to action shows me that at a core level, the Black students of Clemson's past endured similar experiences to the ones we did. During both periods, we advocated for more diverse staff, we asked for racist monuments and nomenclature to be removed, we requested a willingness to address our basic needs as a community. To me, it seems we were all just asking for the freedom to simply exist, in all our blackness, without threat, without abuse, and with the support of our institution.

Resistance. *Living freely.*

I remember as we drafted our grievances to the university before a protest, we used language like "woefully inadequate and insecure" to describe the lackluster response from university staff and personnel, who feebly attempted to address our concerns. I wish more students would realize the power they have at their respective institutions to shift the status quo. You are paying to be at your school. You have to demand action to shift policies. Publicity luncheons, Black Houses, or polite emails cannot silence you.

Resistance. *To free sandwiches that ain't free.*

At Clemson, I recognized that the otherness I felt each day was not a feeling unique to me. I had the luxury of support from other students and close faculty and staff members who also supported our desire for change. My experiences at Clemson shifted the way I think about time and make me more mindful of the language I use when navigating through dominant white male spaces.

Today, I proudly wear my Clemson ring to remind myself of everything I went through to get where I am today. It is also a reminder of everything the Black students before me went through to call Clemson University their alma mater. As a result of my time at Clemson, I am much more aware and sensitive to the strategic and calculated ways my agency is stripped away each day as a Black woman. The SLBI has shown me that we are still connected, and no matter what I have to endure, I can maintain my agency and incite change with faith and collective power. So can you.

Resistance. *We will not be silenced.*

Coda

The Power of Calling a Name

◇◇◇

> For my people standing staring trying to fashion a better way
>   from confusion, from hypocrisy and misunderstanding,
>   trying to fashion a world that will hold all the people,
> all the faces, all the adams and eves and their countless generations
> MARGARET WALKER, "FOR MY PEOPLE"

> History is not everything, but it is a starting point. History is a clock that
> people use to tell their political and cultural time of day. It is a compass
> they use to find themselves on the map of human geography. It tells them
> where they are but, more importantly, what they must be.
> JOHN HENRIK CLARKE

> We shall not, we shall not be moved.
> We shall not, we shall not be moved.
> Just like a tree that's standing by the waters
> We shall not be moved.
> NEGRO SPIRITUAL, "WE SHALL NOT BE MOVED"

"Hush, hush, somebody's calling my name." I was surprised to hear the first line of "Hush" playing over the speakers as I walked from the wings of the Greenville One Center toward the red circle in the center of the stage. The music had not been included in rehearsal the previous afternoon. But hearing a snippet from the Call My Name project's theme song energized me. I'd been given twelve minutes to distill twelve years of research into my TEDx talk, "The Power of Calling a Name." As I turned toward the audience, I saw my friend Gail Wilson and her boyfriend, Victor, smiling back at me. Then as I scanned the audience, I noticed some people staring at the screen where the Fort Hill Plantation fields SC historical marker had been prematurely projected. I'd just have to pretend this was planned.

"Good morning," I began. I felt my body relax as the sound of my voice reverberated through the room. "American historian John Henrik Clarke once made a profound statement about stories. Here's what he said." The quote encapsulated the belief that undergirds my work: members of the Clemson community must use our complex history to better understand our past, present, and future. Just before I walked out on stage, however, the speaker before me talked about the power of storytelling, a talk that resonated with me as I situate myself as a storyteller rather than a historian. That belief slipped into my Ted Talk as I immediately realized I had substituted "stories" for "history" in my opening line. But I kept talking.

A few years earlier, Gail had insisted that I give a TED talk: "You're the one that should be doing this, Rhondda." We were standing in the lobby of the Dale F. Halton Theater in Charlotte, where she had just completed her talk, "The Tao of Reduce, Reuse, Recycle," for TEDx 2017. Gail is a gifted public speaker, who had been involved in theater productions during our high school years. I was usually more comfortable reading a book or writing an essay than giving speeches. Indeed, my early attempts at public speaking frequently proved disastrous. Either I couldn't stop giggling, like the time I gave an impromptu speech in high school about the first time I wore pantyhose, or my mind went blank, like the time I couldn't remember the opening lines of the poem "It Couldn't Be Done" by Edgar A. Guest for a recitation during a youth program at my church. My greatest successes with public speaking had been when I was the only student in my eighth-grade class to memorize and recite Max Ehrmann's poem titled "Desiderata" and when I flawlessly delivered my eighth-grade graduation speech with coaching from Mrs. Doris Gully, the resident elocution expert at Berean Junior Academy. After I started wearing prescription glasses in high school, my classmates nicknamed me "professor." When I fulfilled my childhood dream of becoming an English professor, I learned to be at ease in facilitating discussions about literature in seminar rooms or lecture halls. But give a twelve-minute talk in front of a room full of strangers while cameras rolled and a live feed beamed my words around the world? I could not imagine myself standing in the bright red circle on a TEDx stage sharing a compelling idea.

But here I was at TEDx Greenville 2019, continuing with my talk: "I believe that only by calling the names and sharing the stories of those whose lives and labors were essential for our existence can we create a complete and complex community history."

By this time, Call My Name had become an "idea worth spreading," not only at Clemson and in South Carolina but around the world. I had decided to take Gail's advice and rework my idea into a TED talk. I soon learned there was a TEDx group near me in Greenville, South Carolina. I missed the deadline for the 2018 program but submitted a proposal for the TEDx 2019 that would explore the theme of "Unknxwn." I believed Call My Name could help ensure that the names of African Americans in Clemson history were never unknown.

I submitted my application online. And then I waited.

Within a few days, I received an email welcoming me to the first round of the speaker selection process. In one hundred words or less, I would need to convince the event organizers that my idea could "change a mind, a community, the world, . . . a life" and that I was qualified to share it. I sent them this pitch:

> In this compelling talk, Rhondda Thomas calls the names of marginalized individuals whose labor was essential for the founding of Clemson University, a respected and beloved Upstate education institution. These stories—including those of Susan, who was enslaved on the Fort Hill Plantation; Pinckney, a sharecropper who worked on Fort Hill during Reconstruction; and Sam, a 13-year-old from Greenville County who was among nearly 700 convicts assigned to build Clemson—enables us to see them as humans, not categorize them as laborers. Only by calling their names and sharing their stories can we create a complete and complex community history.

I was confident in my ability to give the talk, having been a professor for twenty-seven years, one whose research and teaching focused on early African American literature and culture. By this time, I had also given forty-two presentations about Call My Name in a variety of venues and had been awarded prestigious grants to support my research. I also believed my personal connection to the Upstate as a Spartanburg, South Carolina, native and sixth-generation South Carolinian positioned me as a credible and compelling speaker.

TEDx Greenville organizers responded positively to my idea.

And then I waited.

About two months later, I was informed I had advanced to the final round.

I was asked to make a three-minute video of my "idea worth spreading." My Clemson colleague Wanda Johnson filmed the segment on the front porch of the Fort Hill plantation house. As I talked about the practice of slavery and its legacies on Clemson land and the necessity of calling the names of Black people whose labor was essential for the University's existence, I stood facing Calhoun's plantation office where he penned proslavery and states' rights speeches. When Johnson later inserted a picture of Clemson trustee John Wannamaker next to my great-great-grandmother Lucretia Wannamaker Earle, I realized their body types were strikingly similar: oval faces, long limbs. Just like mine.

Within two weeks, I received the news: "CONGRATULATIONS, Out of more than three hundred nominees, your project has been selected to be presented at TEDx Greenville 2019: Unknxwn. We couldn't be more excited to share your talent with our community!! . . . Again, CONGRATS!! I look forward to working with you as the weeks progress. Brace yourself for some fun!"[1] I must admit, at this point, "fun" was not a word that came to mind when I thought of prepping for the TEDx stage. When I talked with one of the event organizers, I confessed to being quite nervous, which he assured me was normal. The antidote for fear—memorize my talk; practice it daily. I devised a plan to commit my talk to memory in chunks under many different conditions, including while walking on the treadmill as others lifted weights and talked loudly nearby; while staying in an Airbnb in Washington, DC, which was located near a hospital where sirens interrupted my rehearsals; and while completing aquatic exercises at 5:30 A.M. in the YMCA Anderson, South Carolina, pool.

My intense practicing paid off. As I delivered my talk, I noticed audience members leaning forward, as if they were anticipating every word.

As I neared the end, I reemphasized my compelling idea: "Believe in the power of calling a name." The audience applauded enthusiastically as I exited the stage.

About six weeks after TEDx Greenville, videos of the talks began appearing online. After waiting a week for mine to appear, I searched for and found it on YouTube—under the name "Rhondda Robinson-Thompson." As the video began, a caption popped up that read "Rhondda Robinson" just as I began my talk. On the back of the stage behind me, my name was projected as "Rhondda Robinson Thomas." How could I talk convincingly about the power of calling a name when TEDx gave me three different identities?

Rhondda R. Thomas giving her talk titled "The Power of Calling a Name" at TEDx Greenville UNKNXWN, 2019. Photo by the author.

By the time I discovered the video, more than sixty people had found and watched it, despite the fact that the recording cut off abruptly about one and one-half minutes before the end of my talk. I soon learned there had been an issue with the live feed, which the technicians were attempting to resolve.

This experience seemed like a metaphor for some of the research challenges associated with the Call My Name project. People of African descent have suffered the indignities of having names imposed on them in slavery and freedom, from the names of significant rulers like Caesar to reinforce their subordinate state in society to the moniker "Mammy" for women who could only be viewed in the role of a loyal servant-mother figure. Others changed their name, like Sharper, who replaced his surname, Calhoun, with Brown after leaving the Fort Hill Plantation at the end of the Civil War.

Still others chose new names for themselves; but racial classifications, like "African American," and characterizations, like "Black Southern woman," imposed on them by society obfuscate their identities.

The TEDx Greenville team eventually recovered and published the correct and complete version of my talk. Family, friends, and strangers have sent me messages expressing their appreciation of my idea worth spreading: call the names of African Americans in Clemson University history, as well as the people who laid the foundation for your own communities.

When I arrived at Clemson in 2007, the University was not a place where I could thrive. After I learned that the institution was built on Calhoun's former Fort Hill Plantation; that it was founded by a diplomat and scientist who had also been an enslaver and Confederate officer; and that it was established by influential white businessmen selected as trustees, who were Confederate veterans or had close ties to the Confederacy and embraced and enforced white supremacist ideologies, I was faced with the choice of leaving or staying and being the change I wanted to see.

I stayed.

I have kept the promise I made when I first saw the inventory of enslaved persons who were sold with the Fort Hill Plantation in 1854: to share their names and stories with the Clemson community and the world. In the poem "For My People," Margaret Walker writes, "For my people standing staring trying to fashion a better way / from confusion, from hypocrisy and misunderstanding, / trying to fashion a world that will hold all the people, / all the faces, all the adams and eves and their countless generations."[2] When I began the Call My Name project, I simply desired to know the names of enslaved persons who had lived and labored on the Calhouns' Fort Hill Plantation. As I learned more about the history of African Americans at Clemson and in local communities, I began to see their story as part of an African Diasporic narrative. Walker's poem beckons us to place this story within an even wider context, with roots that stretch back to creation and extend into eternity through generations of African peoples who have contributed and will continue to contribute to Clemson history.

Every time I call the name of an African American in Clemson history, I reaffirm my belief in the power of calling a name.

Postlude

Call: Reconciling My Lineage to Strom Thurmond

MONICA WILLIAMS-HUDGENS

After accepting an invitation to talk publicly about my family's lineage and legacy at Clemson University on February 4, 2015, I should have felt great relief in sharing a sixty-year-old family secret. This event in the *Race and the University* series sponsored by the College of Architecture, Arts, and Humanities was to be a triumphant moment that would surely lead to my being completely free. My talk title was straightforward: "Reckoning the Strom Thurmond Lineage with my Family's Legacy." My dad and siblings had privately discussed the topic for over six decades, but my mother, Essie Mae Washington-Williams, had not allowed us to converse publicly about our connection to her father, South Carolina senator Strom Thurmond. Up until that point, my life experiences demanded that I should carry on as if nothing devastating had been stirred up in my heart. *Piece of cake*, I thought. I really believed I would nail my presentation with my well-prepared speech and PowerPoint notes.

A few hours before I was to speak in Clemson's Tillman Hall auditorium, however, I was offered the opportunity to take a campus tour. During that two-hour tour, I learned about Benjamin Tillman, John C. Calhoun, Strom Thurmond, enslaved persons, convict laborers, and Clemson's Confederate connections. Thus, when the time for my talk rolled around, I was somewhat mentally and emotionally paralyzed by the truths I'd just heard about who, what, and how South Carolina and Clemson were built and maintained. Amazingly, I had taken Black history classes in junior and senior high school and during my first year of college in Los Angeles. However, the Black history I learned during the campus tour enabled me to walk in Black people's shoes through a close and personal account of what and how they endured the atrocities of slavery and Jim Crow laws. I was shocked and angry, and I knew that my transformative moment of "Reckoning the Strom Thurmond Lineage with my Family's Legacy" was not going to happen that evening.

As I was called to the podium to speak, I gazed at the attendees gathered to hear me share my story. The sheer number of people who had purchased my mother's book and who showed up for this speaking event made me realize how the past and present issues of racism and separatism are still having their impact on the South. At that moment I could not help but feel embarrassment and a little shame as the biracial granddaughter of James Strom Thurmond. These feelings had not occurred to me since I was a child and first learned that my grandfather was a white southerner. Taking charge of my feelings, I decided to focus on the positive attributes of my immediate family and not dwell on the negative characteristics of my grandfather.

My talk actually ended up being more of a history lesson about how well my family had done in spite of the fact that Strom Thurmond had fathered my mother outside of wedlock and despite his absolute lack of respect for my Black grandmother, Carrie Butler. He jeopardized both of their lives at many different levels in a very violent, racist, and separatist America. My talking points at Clemson turned totally in the direction of what my mother had given to her children: Essie Mae Washington-Williams's "legacy of discovery of who and what we are, continuing the journey of life, love, family building, enduring hardships, and positively embracing the future." And above all she admonished, "Judge not the ethnicity of the person, but scrutinize the character."

I knew that when my talk was over, the Q&A would begin. My mind wandered during my presentation, speculating on what questions members of the audience would ask. Fortunately, the first few questions were tame, but someone finally asked, "Did Strom Thurmond rape your grandmother?" Knowing I had asked the same question of my mother when I was fourteen, I expected it to come up. I offered the pat answer my mother always used: "I was told that my grandmother never portrayed herself as a victim when she was in the presence of Strom Thurmond or in her conversations about him." But in my thinking and learning as a woman's advocate, I knew that the relationship was inappropriate, even if not rape. As the Q&A ended, I breathed deeply and relaxed.

Before retiring for the evening, I decided to catch up on my emails. At midnight, I received an email from a woman who had attended my speaking event. She introduced herself as a great-granddaughter of Benjamin Ryan Tillman, South Carolina's rebel white supremacist politician, who helped to usher in the age of Jim Crow. She explained how horrified she was to even think about publicly acknowledging her kinship to Tillman and asked me not to share her identity. She wanted to know how I could publicly speak about my lineage and relationship to Strom Thurmond. I then realized I had not reconciled or come to true terms with my family's connection to the *real* Strom Thurmond and his racist southern roots. But I didn't have time to resolve the matter before a speaking engagement at another South Carolina higher education institution.

The next day I traveled to Rock Hill, South Carolina, where I spoke at Winthrop University and took in even more South Carolina history. I used the same PowerPoint and prepared speech that I shared at Clemson. However, I was much more relaxed during my talk at Winthrop than at Clemson. I thought my relaxed posture could be due to the fact that I was speaking to an audience that included a larger number of students and a good mix of staff and community members, as well as my having the opportunity to correct mistakes I had made at Clemson during my presentation.

The Q&A went well, or so I thought until a student asked the question, "Should the name of the Strom Thurmond Building be changed?" I quickly provided the same answer I gave to the same question posed at Clemson, "We could change it to the Essie Mae Washington-Williams Building." I was joking, and the student realized I was being insincere. Later I learned that she wrote for the campus newspaper. I wish I had answered her question sincerely. I soon learned I would be sharing lunch with her, Black honor students, and members of the Black Student Union.

Lunch with the students gave me a flashback of my tour of Clemson.

Members of the Black Student Union shared their racist experiences at Winthrop. They included stories of blackface parties hosted by white students, who could not understand why their Black peers were upset, and dangerous hazing of Black students during inductions into sororities, which ended badly for some pledges.

After nearly four days in South Carolina, I eagerly returned to my home in Kitsap County, Washington. I was fortunate to have invited two of my daughters on this trip, not knowing that they would be my only true comfort during the flight home. I found myself more unsettled about my lineage than ever before. From February 2015 until June 2015, I could not discuss my visit to South Carolina with coworkers, friends, or family. During those months, I became somewhat isolated from what I loved so much about Kitsap County: scenic views of blooming flowers, evergreen trees, lovely waterways, beautiful mountain ranges—and a superficial type of peace regarding race relations. Despite this superficiality, inclusion and reconciliation were goals for the common good of western Washingtonians.

As I reflected on my experiences at Clemson and Winthrop, my mind turned to my mother, who had transitioned from her earthly life on February 3, 2013. Ironically, I had sought to make peace with my past by speaking publicly about my family history for the first time on the second anniversary of her death. Many times before my mother passed, she had strongly suggested that I move to South Carolina to continue my work in social justice and education. I had been graced with the privilege of working with and advocating for women and children who were survivors of domestic violence. Additionally, I had been a teacher for many Head Start programs throughout my life. Advocating for these causes meant lobbying at the state capital and in family court for survivors' rights, including victim compensation and Temporary Assistance for Needy Families for those who were escaping violence. My mother felt that after I had advocated for human rights so adamantly in Los Angeles and the Great Northwest, the time had come for me to share my views in her home state. She was passing the baton of education and reconciliation to her children.

While experiencing this emotional turmoil and unrest about my family history and the next phase of my advocacy work, I made a spontaneous decision: by May 31, 2015, I moved all my belongings to Columbia, South Carolina. I believed relocating to my mother's home state would be the step that was essential for my vindication as a descendant of sons and daughters of the Confederacy and as the granddaughter of James Strom Thurmond.

Settling into my new life in Columbia actually went well—until June 17, 2015. On my thirty-seventh wedding anniversary, the mass shooting at Mother Emanuel AME Church occurred. Strom Thurmond's legacy of racism, separatism, and segregation was still alive in South Carolina. Although he had insisted to my mother repeatedly that he was not a racist, that day I knew for sure he was. He may very well have changed his views over the years due to the fact that he had a Black daughter and Black grandchildren, who had to deal with racism and Jim Crow that extended beyond southern borders; but his public espousal of racist ideologies took root in South Carolina and the nation.

More than four years after my visit to and speaking engagement at Clemson University, I still found myself deeply reflecting on the public image and personal persona of my maternal grandfather, James Strom Thurmond. At times I am weary and confounded as I wonder if I have experienced any real or meaningful reconciliation about my family's connection to him. While I have had many personal transformative moments over the past few years, I cannot help feeling as if my life has become even more complicated since my grandfather's death in 2003. I have great difficulty finding ways to reconcile the devastating legacy of inequity, division, and political ramifications he left behind for South Carolinians, as well as leaving his sons, daughters, and grandchildren to contemplate and hopefully come to terms with their Thurmond lineage.

I have recently sought to find reconciliation by working with United Way of the Midlands and the AmeriCorps Economic Mobility VISTA (Volunteers in Service to America). AmeriCorps VISTA members "bring passion and perseverance where the need is greatest: to organizations that help eradicate poverty. [They] serve as a catalyst for change, living and working alongside community members to meet our nation's most pressing challenges and advance local solutions."[1] The goal and objective of the project are to empower individuals and families living in poverty to obtain employment and improve their financial education and management skills. By building the capacity of the United Way and community partners to engage volunteers who will support and enhance its programs, the project provides job training and placement. It also offers other skill development services, financial education and coaching, tax preparation programs, and increased access to financial services.

In addition to helping South Carolinians achieve economic mobility, I have been seeking ways to improve race relations in my mother's home state. I recently accepted an invitation to join the University of South Carolina's Collaborative for Race and Reconciliation and its premier program, The Welcome Table SC. The Collaborative's bold mission is "to foster racial reconciliation and civic renewal through on-going dialogues in classrooms, boardrooms, and community rooms. The Collaborative's work focuses on inclusiveness and the participation of individuals who are committed to exchanges of personal reflections about their lives and the desire to build bridges among participants and, in turn, to bring about real and lasting change."[2]

I believe The Welcome Table SC and AmeriCorps VISTA are my opportunities for transformation and reckoning. I am reconciling my lineage to Strom Thurmond by participating in organizations that advocate and facilitate real change in South Carolina. I can now say my work of reconciliation has begun. Indeed, I am fulfilling my mother's legacy and creating my own.

Response: Where There's a Will . . .

RHONDDA ROBINSON THOMAS

It's the last day of the fall 2019 semester. I am walking hurriedly down the staircase located on the back of Tillman Hall—or Old Main as I prefer to call the building—having sought a quick exit from the space I least like on the Clemson University campus. My dislike stems primarily from the building's namesake: self-avowed white supremacist and influential South Carolina politician "Pitchfork Ben" Tillman, one of the institution's first lifetime trustees. A politician whose racist policies had an enormous negative impact on Black South Carolinians, including my family. As I descend from the fourth floor to the ground level, I suddenly realize I am enclosed by red bricks that were handmade and fired by African American men and boys: those whom Clemson trustees leased from the South Carolina state penitentiary to help build this structure in 1893 and then rebuild in 1894 after a fire. I carefully begin scanning the bricks, searching for fingerprints or initials as I go down each flight of stairs. I am hoping to find some legible mark that will connect the unknown brickmakers to the nearly seven hundred men and boys whose names are inscribed in the registers of convicts the state penitentiary assigned to the Clemson College work detail. The bricks memorialize their lives and work, beckon us to honor their contribution to Clemson history. By the time I reach the first floor, however, it feels as if the brick-lined stairwell is functioning like a conduit. It's directing my attention to the day Clemson opened in 1893 when 446 white male cadets began classes with their white male professors after registering in this beautiful red brick building erected by Black men and boys. Those Black laborers would be locked up in a stockade on campus after completing their labors and eventually sent back to the penitentiary in Columbia, South Carolina, or released. Those Black men and boys would never learn in the classrooms, eat in the mess hall, recover in the infirmary, live in the houses, or worship in the chapel they helped build.

As I round the corner and head for the building's front exit, the four-paneled exhibit in the lobby that explores the history of Old Main pulls me momentarily back into the present. I am looking at the fourth "Modern Era" panel that focuses on the building's induction into the National Register of Historic Places and the series of organizations and academic units that have been housed therein, currently the Eugene Moore School of Education and ROTC. As I continue walking toward the door, I realize I am viewing the exhibition in reverse order. The panel "Clemson Desegregates" featuring Harvey Gantt comes into view, which traces Gantt's successful journey from the US Supreme Court, where he won his battle for admission to the university, and then to the city of Charlotte, where he served as mayor, established an influential, multicultural architecture firm, and created an arts center. As I reach the mid-point of the lobby, I catch a glimpse of the next panel, "Old Main Renamed," which provides an overview of the events leading up to the trustees' naming of the building for Tillman in 1946. It also highlights the more recently appointed trustees' characterization of Tillman's racist, violent views as "repugnant to our values" in a 2015 resolution they issued after the murders of nine parishioners at Mother Emanuel. Finally, as I reach the door and see the first panel, "Early History of Old Main," I'm reminded that Tillman gave the keynote when the building was dedicated in 1893, that it housed the administration offices, and that it was built by a predominately African American state convict crew. As I move outside Old Main, I step on the spot where, after registering for classes on January 28, 1963, Gantt stood looking into a sea of reporters, who filled in the space; and where five hundred white cadets had gathered in 1904 to raise the Confederate flag and hear the college band play "Dixie"; and just behind the space where a statue of Thomas Green Clemson would be installed in 1941.[1] It's the kind of experience Monica Williams-Hudgens suggests leaves you "mentally and emotionally" paralyzed by the "truths" you learn "about who, what, and how South Carolina and Clemson were built and maintained." When I lead Call My Name campus tours, I describe this space as the most contested place on campus. A place where you must crane your neck to see the "Tillman Hall" metal nameplate attached near the highest point of the building just under the clock tower, as if someone wished to force generations to continuously look up to Tillman. A place where many current Clemson students refuse to read the inscription on the founder's statue out of the superstitious belief that they won't graduate if they do. A place where the truth must set us free to courageously look directly at Thomas Green Clemson and critically examine Clemson's complex history in order to become the diverse vibrant community we aspire to be.

When I first arrived at the university in 2007, I frequently heard admirers of the university's founder marvel that Thomas Green Clemson included no stipulations regarding the race or gender of students who could attend his college in his will. Indeed, he wrote,

> My purpose is to establish an agricultural college which will afford useful information to the farmers and mechanics, therefore it should afford thorough instruction in agriculture and the natural sciences connected therewith—it should combine, if practicable, physical and intellectual education, and should be a high seminary of learning in which the graduate of the common schools can commence, pursue and finish the course of studies terminating in thorough theoretic and practical instruction in those sciences and arts which bear directly upon agriculture.[2]

Thus, some came to believe the agricultural scientist, former US diplomat, and Confederate veteran was a visionary who intentionally created a legal loophole that would eventually allow women, African Americans, and members of other marginalized groups to earn degrees at Clemson. In the late nineteenth century, however, few African American South Carolinians were graduating from segregated, underfunded common schools. The prevailing sentiment among white leaders was "[t]o educate a Negro is to spoil a laborer and to train up a candidate for the Penitentiary."[3] However, if Clemson had intended to include a provision for African American students to enroll in his college, why didn't administrators admit African American brothers Spencer Bracey and Edward Bracey when they applied to Clemson in

1948, fifteen years before Harvey Gantt initiated his successful quest to gain admission?[4]

Until recently, the primary source of Thomas Green Clemson's ideas about how race might impact his college is his October 29, 1878, letter to William Wilson Corcoran, which he wrote just after white Democrats regained control of the statehouse. Clemson expressed his concerns about the possibility of African American representatives becoming the majority in the SC state legislature again, at a time when Blacks outnumbered white South Carolinians, which would enable them to determine who could enroll in the public higher education institution he had founded.[5] In effect, those Black legislators could decide to integrate Clemson.[6]

A more recently recovered source that provides insights regarding his views about race— written nearly five years earlier than his letter to Corcoran—appears in his correspondence with Mary Amarinthia Snowden. On November 23, 1873, in a letter written at Fort Hill in Pendleton, South Carolina, Clemson clearly articulated his ideas about race relations to Snowden, founder and treasurer of the Ladies Calhoun Monument Association (LCMA). The LCMA was established shortly after John C. Calhoun's death in 1850 and, by the time the Civil War began, had raised seventy-five thousand dollars to erect a memorial in Charleston near the Citadel for the South's most ardent proslavery advocate. They installed their first monument in Calhoun's honor in Marion Square in 1877. The group also organized an annual Great Bazaar in Columbia, South Carolina, to raise funds for the Confederacy.[7] In his letter to Snowden, Clemson asserted,

> Ever since my residence in the South, now about forty years I have seen and felt, that our people peculiarly required this [education], in order to hold, or retain their proud position, in the rank of nations. Since the war our dreadful condition has made it more than imperative, if we would not lapse into barbarism, and be entirely overwhelmed by the foreign race, which now governs us, for we must not make a mistake, the negro is not "a black white man," but a race entirely distinct from ours, in all physical and mental attributes—in my opinion not capable of reaching a high degree of civilization, and certainly never the same as that

of the white man. Our only hope to make a stand against the degrading torrent, that is fast overwhelming us, is by cultivating to its utmost our superior intellectual faculties, yet at this very moment, we are, and have been neglecting the ordinary culture of civilized nations, and unless we act speedily, the men of the rising generation, will come on the stage even less armed than ourselves to compete in the deadly struggle before them.[8]

Clemson believed Blacks and whites were so dissimilar that they were of different races both physically and intellectually, ideas in line with those espoused by Josiah Clark Nott, advocate of polygenism and scientific racism in his 1854 *Types of Mankind: or, Ethnological Researches Based upon the Ancient Monuments, Paintings, Sculptures, and Crania of Races, and upon Their Natural, Geographical, Philological, and Biblical history.* His only hope was "our superior intellectual facilities": the embrace and teaching of white supremacist ideology.

Thus, Clemson designed a "high seminary" that would provide the education he believed white men needed to become men like Calhoun, who would maintain their superior status over African Americans, whom he believed were incapable of being civilized. The proslavery statesman would serve as the model man for this "regeneration."[9] His ideals seem closely aligned with his father-in-law's characterization of slavery as a positive good and with the Confederacy's motivation to perpetuate a society in which enslaved African Americans were the primary unpaid workforce. In employing the language of war for this "regeneration," Clemson intimates that the primary weapon for this new battle for civilization is superior, segregated education for white males at educational institutions like his "high seminary," though he also expressed support for the development of a separate "female branch" for the education of white women.[10] Indeed, it appears that Thomas Green Clemson never intended for African Americans to attend the agricultural college he and his wife Anna wished to be established on the Fort Hill Plantation. Sentiments expressed in this letter further suggest that Clemson would likely have been very supportive of the decision of the college's trustees—mostly government officials and professionals who were also Confederate veterans, whom he had selected and identified by name in his will—to lease a predominately African American convict crew from the state to build the higher education institution. The Black convicts' rightful place was creating the infrastructure for the advancement of white men's civilization, just as their enslaved forefathers had done from the inception of slavery in the Americas to its reestablishment as convict leasing, which was slavery by another name.[11]

From 1890 to 1963, Clemson trustees and administrators followed the higher education founder's blueprint with few exceptions, permitting African Americans to work on the labor force that supported their educational system but refusing to provide a seat in the classroom until forced to do so. Gantt's enrollment in Clemson led not only to the admission of other African American students but to the hiring of faculty, staff, and administrators as well. In 1969, Regina Thompson in the Department of Nursing became the first tenure-track African American faculty member hired at Clemson. Thirty-eight years later, I followed in Thompson's footsteps, teaching at a historically white university that was never designed with either of us in mind.

For the fall 2019 issue of *Clemson World*, Karen Land wrote an article about my work, titled "The Power of Calling a Name," that epitomizes just how far the university has moved from its founder's intentions. The publication shares stories about the higher education institution with alumni and friends three times each year, conveying "the determined spirit of Clemson's alumni, faculty, staff and students" and offering "a glimpse into the personality of the institution through the stories and images of her people."[12] Land traced the trajectory of my journey from curious postdoc to the founding director of Call My Name. Members of the editorial staff and I were pleasantly surprised when the article was featured as the lead story on my college's home webpage for about three weeks. Shortly thereafter, as I was searching for some information on the home page of Clemson University's website, I realized the article was the banner story. One reader described the story and my research as "remarkable." Another stated, "Thank You for your COURAGE to Speak 'TRUTH'!!!" Still another, one of my former students, wrote, "Dr. Thomas inspired me in my own work as a teacher." Another reader remarked, "Thank you, Dr. Thomas, for shedding light on a subject that a lot of people just want to keep buried."[13] As I reflected on this notable turn of events, I could not help but remember that when I arrived at Clemson in 2007, I could not easily find links to the university's history through its website.

In February 2020, my community partners, Shelby Henderson and Nick McKinney, assisted with efforts to shed more light on this narrative by creating an exhibition preview, *Call My Name: The Making of the Black Clemson Community*, based on the research my team has been conducting. The exhibition featured two sets of interrelated stories. The first examined the predominately African American convict workforce, whom Clemson trustees leased to help build a college for white cadets. It included information about George Shaw, a convicted laborer who settled in the Clemson area after he was released from the state penitentiary. The second shared the stories of African American musicians who performed at Clemson prior to and during the decade after desegregation and of African American entrepreneurs Horace and Gertrude Littlejohn, whose Littlejohn's Grill in the city of Clemson was where African American musicians performed on the Chitlin' Circuit and African American travelers could find safe overnight accommodations during the Jim Crow era. Students enrolled in my African American literature and American literature courses, as well as those who are taking the first-year composition course, also conducted research for Call My Name, completing projects for their classes and creating content for the project's social media pages and the project website. A postdoctoral fellow, La'Neice Littleton, will join the project team in the fall of 2020 for a two-year stint.

Clemson's campus history project is moving into its next phase with the appointment of a new university historian, Paul Anderson, and the presentation of the Clemson History Implementation Team's final report to the trustees. Anderson, who previously taught in Clemson's Department of History, was appointed in May 2019 and is developing multiple means for members of the Clemson University and local communities to be engaged with the institution's history project. One of the first initiatives was assisting William T. Billbrough, undergraduate student senator, in gaining approval for a new Clemson history course. Anderson, Bostic, and William Hiott, historic properties director, are working with me in assisting a group of Clemson students, led by Sarah Adams and Morgan Molosso, to create a proposal for the installation of a memorial for the enslaved and convict laborer cemetery. Anderson was present when Cathy Sams, chair of the Clemson History Implementation Team, made the final report at the trustees' October 2019 meeting. The report indicates that the following principles guided the Implementation Team's work:

» Support the institutional priorities of Clemson University and the goals of the ClemsonForward strategic plan.
» Adhere to the guiding principles established by the Board of Trustees Task Force on the History of Clemson.
» Tell the Clemson story as completely, accurately, and honestly as possible and practical.
» Continue to keep constituents engaged and informed as the plan is developed and implemented.
» Be a national model in researching, teaching, recognizing and celebrating all aspects of university history.[14]

The report includes recommendations for the creation of a sustainability plan to ensure that the work of documenting and sharing Clemson's complete history continues through the offices of the university historian, historic properties, and university planning and design with the assistance of student interns, promotions, and a proposed new history center. While the Implementation Team completed the trustees' checklist of history projects, we also developed a long-term interpretative plan that received a Historic Preservation Award in 2018, given by Preservation South Carolina and the South Carolina Department of Archives and History.[15]

Changes are currently being implemented to chart a new course for Clemson University that our founder Thomas Green Clemson could not have imagined when he envisioned the creation of a "high seminary of learning" for white males in South Carolina in 1889.[16] He could not have foreseen the day when an African American female professor would be teaching early African American literature at an integrated Clemson. He could not have imagined a determined African American professor like me spearheading a research initiative to document the stories of the African American people he enslaved and employed. He could not have envisioned the struggle at Clemson to create a campus climate in which everyone feels welcome, always.

Item 4 of Thomas Green Clemson's will states his "desire that the dwelling house on Fort Hill shall never be torn down or altered, but shall be kept in repair, with all the articles of furniture and vesture that I hereinafter give for that purpose, and shall *always* be open for the inspection of visitors" (emphasis mine).[17] For more than a century, Clemson honored its founder's wish, creating a tour that emphasized architecture, artwork, and antiques. Unlike their predecessors—Clemson cadets who considered a tour of Fort Hill to be an essential component of their education—many current Clemson students believe a visit to the house brings on a curse that will prevent them from graduating.

In February 2020, Giovanni Gibbs, an intern with Clemson's Department of Historic Properties and undergraduate Pan African Studies major, created an African American Heritage tour of Fort Hill that may finally break the "curse" students associate with visiting the house. The Call My Name team and Historic Properties staff collaborated with her on the project. During the tour, Gibbs called the names and told the stories of persons whose forced labor was essential for the development of Fort Hill and Clemson University—including Issey, who started a fire in a Fort Hill bedroom, and Susan, who slept with a string Anna Calhoun Clemson tied around her wrist each night. In so doing, she created another way for visitors to inspect the house and learn from the stories of slavery and its legacies at a land-grant higher education institution in Upstate South Carolina. During the tour, I learned that Historic Properties staff are creating new and more inclusive interpretative signage for the house. Call My Name will work to ensure the tour Gibbs created is always available for visitors who come to Fort Hill.

A few weeks later, during Women's History Month, Call My Name hosted a program featuring two of the first three Black women who earned four-year degrees from Clemson in 1969: Dorothy Ashford and Delores K. Barton. (The third woman, Laverne Williams-White, is deceased.) Attendees for the event, "To Be Young, Gifted, Black and Female at Clemson University," packed the Academic Success Center, filling every seat, sitting on the steps, standing along the walls. Ashford and Barton recalled being selected by their high school guidance counselors to attend Clemson. They described the challenges of being double minorities—both Black and female, when the university had been coeducational for only a decade at the time they enrolled. They laughed when sharing the excitement of panty raids in the dorms and smiled when explaining how they made friends with white female students by finding commonalities, such as liking the same shoe style. They provided highlights of their distinguished careers at IBM. When we came to the end of the hour-long program, Ashford asked to have the last word. She began by reading a quote from *Time* magazine's special issue, "100 Women of the Year, A Century Redefined 1920–2019":

> Each generation inherits a history, focused through the lens of those who came before it. . . . In the words of Edith P. Mayo, a curator emeritus at the Smithsonian National Museum of American History, "When you're invisible, people assume that you've done nothing."[18]

And then she turned toward me and added, "Thank you for calling our names . . . and making us visible."

Call their names, Clemson, *always*.

Contributors

EMILY BOYTER is the administrative coordinator for Clemson University's Department of English. She earned her MA in English from Clemson in 2016. After finishing her degree, she worked as a community college teacher, a health coach, and a researcher for the Call My Name project.

EDITH MARIA DUNLAP graduated from Clemson University in 2016 with a BA in English writing and publication studies and a minor in Pan African studies. She was Call My Name's first research assistant. Dunlap has a passion for multiple photographic genres and is currently pursuing a career in creative media.

SHAQUILLE FONTENOT graduated from Clemson University with a BA in English in 2014. She has since worked as a marketing consultant and as a Teach for America instructor. Fontenot is currently employed at Cedar Wolf Media in Charleston, SC, a data-based brand and strategy company of which she is a founding partner.

THOMAS MARSHALL earned a BA in English from Clemson University in 2020. He devoted his collegiate career to ensuring college access, specifically for students of color. His long-range plans include returning to work on Capitol Hill, where he spent the summer of 2019 as a Congressional Black Caucus Foundation intern.

BRENDAN MCNEELY earned a BA in English from Clemson University in 2019. He is currently transforming his senior thesis, which examined the memorialization of riots and revolts in the years immediately following World War I, into a book project. McNeely has worked with the Call My Name project since 2017.

MICHAEL LEMAHIEU is an associate professor of English at Clemson University. He is the author of *Fictions of Fact and Value: The Erasure of Logical Positivism in American Literature, 1945–1975*. LeMahieu's current project on Civil War memory in literature from the civil rights movement to the contemporary moment has been supported by fellowships from the American Council of Learned Societies and the National Endowment for the Humanities.

MONICA WILLIAMS-HUDGENS is a social justice advocate, activist, writer, educator, and community organizer in the domestic violence field. She earned a BS in human services and MS in organizational management and leadership from Springfield College. Her work as a social change agent reflects the rich family legacies her parents, Julius Thomas Williams and Essie Mae Washington-Williams, left for their children. Williams-Hudgens is also the granddaughter of the late Senator Strom Thurmond, the second-longest serving member of the US Senate.

ERIC D. YOUNG graduated from Clemson University in 1995 with a BS in Financial Management–Real Estate and earned a Project Manager Professional (PMP) certification in 2016. He is a direct descendant of Thomas and Frances Fruster, who were enslaved on the Fort Hill Plantation on which Clemson University was built. Young currently is employed by Wells Fargo as an investor reporting analytics consultant within the Commercial Mortgage Servicing Group. He is also a member of the award-winning gospel choir Donald Lawrence & the Tri-City Singers.

Acknowledgments

It takes a village to support the Call My Name project. Special thanks to the following folks and organizations in my village that have provided a steady source of support for me, my team, and this enormous undertaking.

Research assistants, supporters, consultants, donors, family, and friends: Maxwell Allen, Paul Anderson, Susanna Ashton, James E. Bostic Jr., Edith H. Bostic, Cheryl Bowie-Thomas, Joy Bivins, Emily Boyter, Vernon Burton, Brenda Burk, James Burns, A.D. Carson, Joshua Catalano, Marjorie Smith Campbell, Susan Chastain, Jim Clements, Joann Clark-Brown, Kim Cliett-Long, Ebony Coletu, Nik Conklin, Camille Cooper, Will Cunningham, Allison Daniel, Marissa Davis, Edith Dunlap, Katherine Eaves, Andrea Feeser, Jonathan B. Field, Ashley Cowden Fisk, Shaquille Fontenot, Jonathan Gantt, Rick Goodstein, Lee Gill, Marion Gill, Marlyn Grant, Jonathan Green, Terence Hassan, Dan Harding, Shelby Henderson, William Hiott, Susan Hiott, Wanda Johnson, Bob Jones, Karen Land, Katy Koon, Michael LeMahieu, Kyra Lobbins, Jeff Kallin, Bessie Kemp, Robert Kemp, Cheryl Kinsuzu, Barbara McCaskill, Nick McKinney, Brendan McNeely, Ty Miller, Cecelia Moore, Lee Morrissey, Linda Norman, James Orlick, Carla Peterson, Barbara Ramirez, Carl Redd, Altheia Richardson, Nathan Riggs, Gail Slocumb-Brittan, Dana Thorpe, Brenda Tindal, David White, Samuel Wilkes, Kesha Williams, Gail Wilson.

The Pearce Center for Professional Communication, intern team, Department of English, Clemson University: Lauren Andrews, Caroline Cavendish, Allison Daniel, Tayler Green, Carlyle Griffin, Raven Guerra, Nygaele McGeathey, Sallie McLeod, Hannah Rohaley, Melissa Rau, Nicolaus Sherrill, Saavon Smalls, Carter Smith, Brianne Stanback.

Community and organization partners: Bertha Lee Strickland Cultural Museum, Seneca, South Carolina; Clemson Area African American Museum, Clemson, South Carolina; Lunney Museum, Seneca, South Carolina; National Humanities Alliance, Washington, DC; Pendleton Foundation for Black History and Culture, Pendleton, South Carolina; Upstate History Museum, Greenville, South Carolina.

Archives: Clemson University Libraries' Special Collections & Archives; Clerk of the Court, Abbeville County South Carolina; Department of Historic Properties, Clemson University; Library of Congress; National Museum of African American History and Culture; Lake Hartwell Country (formerly Pendleton District Commission), Pendleton, South Carolina; Recorder of Deeds, Anderson County, South Carolina, and Pickens County, South Carolina; South Carolina Department of Archives and History, Columbia, South Carolina.

Creative media partners: Clemson University Athletics Creative Solutions Team; Next Elevation Company, Columbia, South Carolina; Shaquille Fontenot; Pearce Center for Professional Communications, Clemson University; StudioDisplays, Pineville, North Carolina; SmithWorks, Charleston, South Carolina.

Funding resources and grant agencies: African American History, Culture, and Digital Humanities, University of Maryland; Dr. James and Edith Bostic; Clemson Commission on the Black Experience; Clemson University Foundation; College of Agriculture, Arts, and Humanities, Clemson University; National Endowment for the Humanities; Office of Inclusion and Equity, Clemson University; Office of the Provost, Clemson University; South Carolina Humanities; Whiting Foundation.

Clemson University collaborators and supporters: Clemson Department of Historic Properties; College of Architecture, Arts, and Humanities; Clemson University Libraries; Clemson University Libraries' Special Collections & Archives; Department of English; Department of History; ENGL 4820/6820; African American Literature to 1,920 students, Fall 2019; Harvey and Lucinda Gantt Multicultural Center; The Humanities Hub.

My publisher: Special thanks to Teresa Magnum, Meredith Stabel, Annie Valk, and other staff of the Humanities and Public Life Book Series at the University of Iowa Press for the support and enthusiasm they provided for this project.

My family: I am most grateful for my husband William L. Thomas Jr., who encourages and supports me in living my God-sized dreams. I am also grateful to my siblings and their families—Monika Robinson and Sam Wade and Elijah and Malik; Carlton and Ingrid Robinson and Micah and Leah; and Donald and Sherlene Robinson and Justin and Tara—whose belief in me reflects the strong and loving belief of our parents, Earle B. and Naomi W. Robinson, in us.

Notes

FOREWORD

1. James Daley, ed., *Great Speeches by Frederick Douglass* (Mineola, NY: Dover, 2013), 34.

PREFACE

1. John F. Callahan, *In the African-American Grain: Call-and-Response in Twentieth-Century Black Fiction* (Urbana: University of Illinois Press, 2001), 19.

2. Toni Morrison, Nobel Lecture, December 7, 1993, The Nobel Prize in Literature 1993, accessed January 15, 2020, https://www.nobelprize.org/prizes/literature/1993/morrison/lecture/.

CALL: THE BLACK FRUSTER FAMILY'S CLEMSON CONNECTION

1. Lucile Williams and Leah Grier Interview, No. 108. W. J. Megginson, *Black Heritage in the Upper Piedmont of South Carolina Project*, MSS 282, Clemson University Libraries' Special Collections & Archives, Clemson, SC, accessed November 16, 2019, http://media.clemson.edu/library/special_collections/findingaids/manuscripts/Mss282BlackHeritage.pdf.

2. Inventory and Valuation of the Estate of Colonel A. P. Calhoun, Thomas Green Clemson Papers, Box 5, Folder 2, Clemson University Libraries' Special Collections & Archives.

3. "Thos Fruistu," 1880 United States Federal Census, https://search.ancestry.com/cgi-bin/sse.dll?dbid=6742&h=42516630&indiv=try&o_vc=Record:OtherRecord&rhSource=7602; and "Thomas Frooster," 1900 United States Federal Census, https://search.ancestry.com/cgi-bin/sse.dll?dbid=7602&h=59303381&indiv=try&o_vc=Record:OtherRecord&rhSource=60525.

4. G. Anne Sheriff, Robert Dodson, and W. J. Megginson, *African American Cemeteries of Pickens County, SC* (privately published, 2007), 51, 69, http://www.oldpendleton.scgen.org/Surnames/PDF%20Survey%20Scans/Book-7%20Blacks/Blk_Cemeteries.pdf. The inscription for Frances Fruster gives her name as Annie.

5. Maya Angelou, "Still I Rise," in *And Still I Rise: A Book of Poems* (New York: Random House, 1978), *The Poetry Foundation*, accessed January 15, 2020, https://www.poetryfoundation.org/poems/46446/still-i-rise.

6. W. J. Megginson, *African American Life in South Carolina's Upper Piedmont 1780–1900* (Columbia: University of South Carolina Press, 2006), 243.

7. Interview, Juanita Webb, August 26, 2019; Lucile Williams and Leah Grier Interview, *Black Heritage in the Upper Piedmont*, MSS 282, Cassette 2, Clemson University Libraries' Special Collections & Archives.

RESPONSE: HUSH, OH, HUSH, SOMEBODY'S CALLING MY NAME

1. "Confederate Flag Pole," *Blakely-Early County, Chamber of Commerce*, accessed December 18, 2019, https://www.blakelyearlycountychamber.org/tourism/step-in-to-the-past/.

2. Confederate Soldier's Memorial, Blakely, GA, waymarking.com, accessed December 3, 2017, http://www.waymarking.com/waymarks/WMNRY_Confederate_Soldiers_Memorial_Blakely_GA; and *Vanishing Georgia*, accessed December 18, 2019, https://dlg.galileo.usg.edu/cgi-bin/vanga.cgi?query=id%3Aear034-82&_cc=1&Welcome.

3. Luther Lyle, email to Andrea Feeser, April 17, 2020.

4. Jerome Reel, *The High Seminary: A History of the Clemson Agricultural College of South Carolina, 1889–1964*, vol. 1 (Clemson, SC: Clemson University Press, 2009), 5.

5. Megginson, *African American Life*, 56.

6. Reel, 1:15.

7. *The African American Experience at Fort Hill*, Department of Historic Properties, Clemson University, Clemson, SC, accessed November 16, 2019, https://www.clemson.edu/about/history/properties/documents/Race%20Exhibit.pdf.

8. Ernest Ingersoll, "The Calhoun Summer Home," *Century Magazine* (April 1881): 892, accessed December 3, 2017, http://www.unz.org/Pub/Century-1881apr-00892?View=PDF& apages=0084.

9. "Fort Hill," Clemson University, Clemson, SC, accessed December 19, 2017, https://web.archive.org/web/20070203064550/http://www.clemson.edu:80/wel-come/history/forthill/index.htm.

10. Ken Scar, "Clemson to Celebrate Legacy Month with Special Events in November," *Newsstand*, Clemson University, Clemson, SC, November 2, 2015, accessed December 19, 2017, http://newsstand.clemson.edu/mediarelations/clem-son-to-celebrate-legacy-month-with-special-events-in-november/.

11. Harriet Hefner Cook, *Fort Hill: John C. Calhoun Shrine* (Clemson, SC: John C. Calhoun Chapter, United Daughters of the Confederacy, 1970).

12. *History of African Americans at Fort Hill: 1825–1888*, Department of Historic Properties, Clemson University, Clemson, SC, accessed December 19, 2017, https://web.archive.org/web/20070313175753/http://www.clemson.edu:80/welcome/history/forthill/africans.htm.

13. John Ernest, "Life beyond Biography: Black Lives and Biographical Research," *Commonplace* 17, no. 1 (Fall 2016), accessed November 22, 2017, http://commonplace.online/article/life-beyond-biography/.

14. Ernest.

15. "The Clemson Story: History," Clemson University, Clemson, SC, 2014, accessed December 19, 2017, https://web.archive.org/web/20140704153539/http://www.clemson.edu/about/history/index.html.

16. "Notable People," Clemson University, Clemson, SC, 2014, accessed December 19, 2017, https://web.archive.org/web/20140710093203/http://www.clemson.edu/about/history/notable-people.html.

17. Deed to Real & Personal Estate, Thomas Green Clemson Papers, Clemson University Libraries' Special Collections & Archives.

18. Inventory and Valuation of the Estate of the late Col. A. P. Calhoun, Thomas Green Clemson Papers, Box 5, Folder 2, Clemson University Libraries' Special Collections & Archives; Jerome Reel, *The High Seminary: A History of Clemson Agricultural College of South Carolina, 1889–1964*, vol. 1 (Clemson, SC: Clemson University Press), 25–26; and *The African-American Experience at Fort Hill* presentation, Department of Historic Properties, Clemson University, Clemson, SC, accessed April 21, 2020, https://www.clemson.edu/about/history/properties/documents/Race%20Exhibit.pdf.

19. "John C. Calhoun's Home Life," *Anderson Daily Mail* (Anderson County, SC), October 23, 1926; reprinted from a Baltimore newspaper article of August 1849.

20. Mary Prince, *The History of Mary Prince, a West Indian Slave. Related by Herself. With a Supplement by the Editor. To Which Is Added, the Narrative of Asa-Asa, a Captured African* (London: F. Westley and A. H. Davis, 1831), 38.

CALL: OF STRING AND MAMMY

1. "Thomas Green Clemson," Department of Historic Properties, Clemson University, Clemson, SC, accessed December 13, 2017, https://www.clemson.edu/about/history/bios/thomas-g-clemson.html.

2. Myrtle Herlong, "Aunt Susan Richardson," May 24, 1958, Department of Historic Properties, Clemson University, Clemson, SC.

3. Zora Neale Hurston, *Their Eyes Were Watching God* (New York: Harper & Row, 1990), 14.

4. Herlong, "Aunt Susan Richardson."

5. Herlong.

6. Herlong.

7. Robert Jefferson Norrell, *Up from History: The Life of Booker T. Washington* (Cambridge, MA: Harvard University Press, 2009), 66.

8. Micki McElya, *Clinging to Mammy: The Faithful Slave in Twentieth-Century America* (Cambridge, MA: Harvard University Press, 2009), 3.

9. Herlong, "Aunt Susan Richardson."

10. Herlong.

RESPONSE: BLACK LIVES HAVE ALWAYS MATTERED

1. Elizabeth Belser Fuller, *Anderson County Sketches* (Anderson, SC: Anderson County Tricentennial Committee, 1969).

2. Saidiya Hartman, *Lose Your Mother: A Journey along the Atlantic Slave Route* (New York: Farrar, Straus and Giroux, 2007), 16.

3. Natasha Trethewey, "Elegy for the Native Guards," in *Native Guard* (Boston: Houghton Mifflin, 2006), 44.

4. Fuller.

5. Fuller.

6. 56 Cong. Rec. S3218 (March 23, 1900).

7. Abram J. Ryan, *Poems: Patriotic, Religious, Miscellaneous* (New York: P. J. Kenedy & Sons, 1896), 125.

8. State Song of Maryland, *Maryland*, accessed November 7, 2019, https://sos.maryland.gov/mdkids/Pages/StateSong.aspx.

9. *Maryland*.

10. Henry Kirke Brown to Mrs. H. K. Brown, January 12, 1862, Henry Kirke Brown Papers, Library of Congress, Washington, DC, 1412.

11. John C. Calhoun, "Document: Slavery a Positive Good, February 6, 1837," Teaching American History, accessed September 24, 2019, teachingamericanhistory.org/library/document/slavery-a-positive-good/.

12. Brown to Brown, Henry Kirke Brown Papers, 1412–13.

13. John C. Calhoun, "Speech on Reception of Abolition Petitions," February 6, 1837, 418, *The Constitution Reader*, accessed April 21, 2020, http://www.constitution-reader.com/reader.engz?doc=constitution&chapter=OEBPS/Text/ch75.xhtml.

14. Hartman, 6.

CHAPTER 1

1. In 1989, when Lucille Clifton visited the Walnut Grove Plantation in Spartanburg, South Carolina, located about an hour north of Clemson University, she was the only person of color on the tour, and the guide didn't mention slavery. When she asked the guide to check the plantation's inventory, he discovered ten enslaved men but speculated that there may have been more since enslaved women and children weren't acknowledged in the document. Clifton wrote "At the cemetery, walnut grove plantation, south carolina, 1989" to commemorate her expe-

rience. Lucille Clifton, *Quilting: Poems, 1987–1990* (Brockport, NY: BOA Editions, 1991), 11–12; Bill Moyers, "Lucille Clifton," in *The Language of Life: A Festival of Poets*, ed. James Haba (New York: Doubleday, 1995), 81–83.

2. Jane Edna Hunter, *A Nickel and a Prayer*, ed. Rhondda Robinson Thomas (Morgantown: West Virginia University Press, 2011), 41, 43, and 45.

3. The Creative Inquiry program at Clemson University provides opportunities for undergraduate students to conduct team-oriented research with a professor or advanced graduate student, who serves as their mentor. More than 33,400 students have participated in more than one thousand projects since the inception of the program in 2005. See the Creative Inquiry website for more information about the program. Creative Inquiry, accessed November 7, 2019, https://www.clemson.edu/centers-institutes/watt/ creative-inquiry/about/.

4. Maggie Wilkins, "Architecture Project to Revitalize African-American Landmark," *Tiger*, March 7, 2003, 3.

5. Bertha Lee Strickland Cultural Museum, accessed November 7, 2019, https://www.blscm.org.

6. Susanna Ashton, "Texts of Our Institutional Lives: Don't You Mean 'Slaves,' Not 'Servants'?: Literary and Institutional Texts for an Interdisciplinary Classroom," *College English* 69, no. 2 (November 2006): 157.

7. Clifton, 11–12.

8. Ashton, 169.

9. Ashton, 169–71.

10. Quotation is found in the legend below the picture in the lower right corner. "Fort Hill: The Beginning of a Legacy," Department of Historic Properties, Clemson University, accessed November 7, 2019, https://www.clemson.edu/about/history/properties/documents/1.pdf. The description of Fort Hill does not include references to the enslaved persons who labored and lived on the property for seventy-five years. "Fort Hill: The Beginning of a Legacy," *The Historical Marker Database*, HMdb.org, accessed November 7, 2019, https://www.hmdb.org/marker.asp?marker=51284. Additionally, the Fort Hill Plantation is not currently listed on the Pickens County page of the South Carolina National Heritage Corridor website. "Pickens County," South Carolina National Heritage Corridor, accessed April 21, 2020, https://www.revealsc.com/pickens-county-sites. See also Fort Hill Marker.

11. See Thomas Green Clemson Papers, Box 5, folders 5 and 7, Clemson University Libraries' Special Collections & Archives.

12. Orville Vernon Burton, "African American Status and Identity in a Postbellum Community: An Analysis of the Manuscript Census Returns," *Agricultural History* 72, no. 2 (Spring 1998): 216.

13. Burton, 216–17.

14. See Thomas Green Clemson Papers, Box 5, folders 5 and 7.

15. Clemson Papers.

16. The 13th Amendment states, "Neither slavery nor involuntary servitude,

except as a punishment for crime whereof the party shall have been duly convicted, shall exist within the United States, or any place subject to their jurisdiction."

17. Reel, "Building the School," in *The High Seminary*, 1:69–98.

18. Marion Chandler, email to Rhondda R. Thomas, October 9, 2013.

19. The 13th Amendment.

20. Lyn Riddle, "Research Honors the Lives of Convicts Who Built Clemson," *Greenville News*, April 17, 2014, accessed November 7, 2019, accessed November 17, 2019, http://www.greenvilleonline.com/story/news/local/2014/04/17/research-honors-lives-convicts-built-clemson/7855017/. The headline for the story has since been changed to "Clemson's Convict Laborers Studied."

21. Leon Wiles, email to author, April 18, 2014.

22. Author, email to Leon Wiles, April 18, 2014.

23. James Barker, "The Sacred Soil of Bowman Field," in *Clemson: There's Something in These Hills*, eds. Trent Allen and Kevin Bray (Clemson, SC: Fort Hill Press, 2006), 182–83.

24. Barker.

25. "Treaty of Hopewell, 1785," *Cherokee Nation*, accessed November 7, 2019, http:// www.cherokee.org/About-The-Nation/History/Facts/Treaty-of-Hopewell-1785.

26. "Black Heritage in the Upper Piedmont of South Carolina Project Collection: A Register—1982, 1989–1990," Clemson University Libraries' Special Collections & Archives, accessed November 7, 2019, http://media.clemson.edu/library/special_collections/findingaids/manuscripts/Mss282BlackHeritage.pdf.

27. "Documenting the African American Experience at Clemson," Clemson University Libraries, Clemson, SC, accessed November 7, 2019, https://digitalcollections.clemson.edu/explore/ collections/dcaae/.

28. Ebony Coletu, "Biographic Mediation," *Auto/Biography Studies* 32, no. 2 (2017): 384–85, accessed November 7, 2019, http://dx.doi.org/10.1080/08989575.2017.1289018.

29. Lynn Haessly and Harvey Gantt, "Oral History Interview with Harvey B. Gantt, January 6, 1986," Southern Oral History Program Collection (#4007), Documenting the American South, University of North Carolina, Chapel Hill, NC, accessed November 7, 2019, http://docsouth.unc.edu/sohp/C-0008/menu.html.

30. Kali Kupp, "The African American Experience at Clemson," accessed November 7, 2019, https://sites.google.com/site/hon221finalproject/home.

31. Kupp.

32. Thomas Green Clemson to William Wilson (W. W.) Corcoran, October 29, 1878, Thomas Green Clemson Papers, Box 5, folder 14.

33. Clemson to Corcoran.

34. Henry H. Lesesne, "University of South Carolina," *South Carolina Encyclopedia*, University of South Carolina, Institute for Southern Studies, last modified April 24, 2019, http://www.scencyclopedia.org/sce/entries/university-of-south-carolina/.

35. David J. Watson to R. F. Poole, "Bldgs and Grounds Committee and Sub-Committee on Names, May 14–15, 1946," Holmes Collection, Mss 1, Box 1, Folder 7 and President Robert F. Pool Committee Files, Series 7, Folder 6, Clemson University Libraries' Special Collections & Archives.

36. Nathaniel Cary, "Clemson Won't Rename Tillman Hall, Board Chair says," *Greenville News*, February 12, 2015, accessed November 7, 2019, https://amp.greenvilleonline.com/story/news/education/2015/02/11/clemson-rename-tillman-hall-board-chair-says/23238993.

37. Cary.

CALL: LOVE, DUKE ELLINGTON

1. George Bennett, personal interview, December 23, 2019.

2. Norman E. Campbell to Tom E. Stanley, November 30, 1938, Central Dance Association Papers, Clemson University Libraries' Special Collections & Archives.

3. Bob Bundy to the Chairman, September 27, 1929, Central Dance Association Papers.

4. Bob Bundy to Tom Stanley, December 5, 1938, Central Dance Association Papers.

5. In 1955, *The Negro Travelers' Green Book*, a directory of businesses in the United States, Bermuda, Canada, the Caribbean, and Mexico that welcomed African American business and vacation travelers during the Jim Crow era, listed two tourist homes in Greenville, SC: Dr. Gibbs Tourist Home, 914 Anderson Road, and Miss M. J. Grimes Tourist Home, 210 Mean [sic] Street. Victor H. Green, ed., *The Negro Travelers' Green Book: The Guide to Travel and Vacations* (New York: Victor H. Green, 1955), 61, accessed December 24, 2019, https://digitalcollections.nypl.org/items/2a146d30-9381-0132-f916-58d385a7b928. Many Black musicians, including Duke Ellington, who performed for Black and mixed audiences at Textile Hall in Greenville, would also stay at the Mrs. W. H. Smith Tourist Home in the Southernside neighborhood. Ramon M. Jackson, personal interview, January 9, 2020, and Green, ed., *The Negro Travelers' Green Book: The Guide to Travel and Vacations* (New York: Victor H. Green, 1954), 61, accessed January 9, 2020, https://digitalcollections.nypl.org/items/3c85ba30-9374-0132-9292-58d385a7b928.

6. Tom E. Stanley to Harold F. Oxley, February 27, 1939, Central Dance Association Papers.

7. For more details about Littlejohn's Grill, see Vince Jackson, *The Littlejohn's Grill Story: Blues, Jazz and Rock 'n' Roll in Clemson, SC* (Clemson, SC: SugarCane, 2008).

8. Board of Trustees, Minutes of the Meeting of the Board of Trustees of the Clemson Agricultural College held in the President's Office, Clemson, S.C., June 18, 1948, 754–56. *TigerPrints*, accessed December 24, 2019, https://tigerprints.clemson.edu/cgi/viewcontent.cgi?article=1431&context=trustees_minutes. Special thanks to Cathy Keaton, an undergraduate researcher, who discovered the information

about the Bracey brothers' attempt to enroll in Clemson while she completed a Call My Name biography project in my early African American Literature course during the fall 2019 semester.

9. Personal interview, Harry Bolick, December 12, 2019.

10. Harvey G. Cohen, *Duke Ellington's America* (Chicago: University of Chicago Press, 2010), 311.

11. "Duke Ellington to Play for the Military Ball," *Tiger*, February 24, 1955, 1; and "Military Ball Begins Friday Night at Nine O'Clock," *Tiger*, March 24, 1955, 1.

12. "Military Ball."

13. George Bennett, personal interview.

14. Bennett interview.

15. Hans Engelmann wrote the music for "Melody of Love" in 1903, and Tom Glazer added lyrics in 1954. The recording of the song by the Four Aces appeared on the Billboard Chart in January of 1955, where it stayed for seventeen weeks, peaking at number eleven. "Melody of Love," *Songs with Earlier Histories than the Hit Version*, accessed October 2, 2019, http://www.songswithearlierhistories.com/melody-of-love/.

16. Bennett interview.

17. "Financial Statement Central Dance Association Military Dance Series March 26 and 27, 1955, Receipts," *Tiger*, April 21, 1955, 1.

18. Central Dance Association Papers, Clemson University Libraries' Special Collections & Archives.

19. "Wynton's Interview on EBONY—Entertainment and Culture," Wynton, Wynton Marsalis Enterprises, accessed January 15, 2020, https://wyntonmarsalis.org/news/entry/wyntons-interview-on-ebony-entertainment-and-culture.

RESPONSE: "WORLD-FAMOUS" DUKE ELLINGTON, THE CENTRAL DANCE ASSOCIATION, AND THE *TIGER*

1. "Roving Reporter: Dance Weekends Draw Opinions," *Tiger*, February 15, 1963, 1.

2. "Brook Benton Brings Ballroom Blues Beat," *Tiger*, February 15, 1963.

3. *Tiger*, December 19, 1960, 5–6.

4. "Committee Votes to End Use of Confederate Flag," *Tiger*, October 24, 1969, 1.

5. *Oxford English Dictionary*, s.vv. "jazz, n." and "jazz, adj." 2.b.

6. "Roving Reporter," *Tiger*, February 15, 1963, 1.

7. Tom E. Stanley to N. E. Campbell, November 28, 1938, Central Dance Association Papers, Clemson University Libraries' Special Collections & Archives.

8. Stanley to Campbell.

9. "Integration with Dignity" is a widely marketed phrase on Clemson's campus, adorning the SC historical marker that commemorates Gantt's admission to the college in addition to being inserted in many of the publications about this event. See Skip Eisiminger, ed., *Integration with Dignity: A Celebration of Harvey Gantt's*

Admission to Clemson (Clemson, SC: Clemson University Press, 2003), as well as Reel, *The High Seminary*.

10. The *Tiger*, September 1, 1978, 12; and the *Tiger*, September 8, 1978, 11.

11. James Weldon Johnson, ed., *The Book of American Negro Poetry* (New York: Harcourt, Brace, 1922), x.

CHAPTER 2

1. *George Washington's Mount Vernon*, Mount Vernon's Ladies' Association, 2019, accessed October 7, 2019, https://www.mountvernon.org.

2. Craig Wilder, email to Lolita Buckner Inniss, November 8, 2013.

3. According to the "Clemson Tigers" website, "[l]aunched in 1999 as a marketing campaign by the university to assist in promoting Clemson throughout the entire state of South Carolina, 'Solid Orange' created new symbolism to represent and reinvigorate the sense of pride and family unity that are cornerstones of Clemson's philosophy. The motto for the campaign became *Solid Orange: It's about Pride*, and the central theme was honorable conduct, symbolized by the wearing of orange at athletic events and on Fridays," https://clemsontigers.com/clemson-officials-remind-fans-to-be-solid-orange/. See also "Solid Orange," accessed October 8, 2019, http://www.clemson.edu/solid-orange/.

4. A.D. Carson, "Project Overview," *See The Stripes* [Clemson], accessed November 10, 2019, https://aydeethegreat.com/see-the-stripes/.

5. Carson, https://www.dailykos.com/stories/2014/8/20/1322622/-Clemson-Student-Exposes-Historic-Racism-At-University-With-Provocative-Video.

6. See Steve Siebold, "NCAA's Football Slavery Scheme," *HuffPost*, January 5, 2018, accessed October 14, 2019, https://www.huffpost.com/entry/ncaas-football-slavery-scheme_b_5a4fec40e4b0f9b24bf31727; Billy Hawkins, *The New Plantation: Black Athletes, College Sports, and Predominantly White NCAA Institutions* (New York: Palgrave Macmillan, 2010); William C. Rhoden, *Forty Million Dollar Slaves: The Rise, Fall, and Redemption of the Black Athlete* (New York: Crown, 2006).

7. "Wesley Bolling," Gov. Benjamin R. Tillman's Papers, Petitions for Pardon, Florence-Horry Counties, Folder 14, South Carolina Department of Archives and History.

8. A.D. Carson, "Clemson Student Exposes Historic Racism at University with Provocative Video," *Daily Kos*, August 20, 2014, accessed November 10, 2019, https://www.dailykos.com/stories/2014/8/20/1322622/-Clemson-Student-Exposes-Historic-Racism-At-University-With-Provocative-Video.

9. Kaitlyn Schallhorn, "Campaign Compares Clemson Athletics to Slavery, Accuses University of 'Whitewashing' History," *Campus Reform*, August 22, 2014, accessed November 10, 2019, https://www.campusreform.org/?ID=5851.

10. A.D. Carson, "My South Carolina University Is Whitewashing Its Complex Racial History," *Guardian*, July 9, 2015, accessed November 10, 2019, https://www.

theguardian.com/commentisfree/2015/jul/09/clemson-confederate-flag-rac-ist-tillman-hall.

11. "Barker, Bostic to Receive Clemson Medallion," *Greenville News*, May 2, 2016, accessed December 17, 2019, https://www.greenvilleonline.com/story/news/local/pickens-county/2016/05/02/barker-bostic-receive-clemson-medallion/83819308/; and Julia Sellers, "Clemson Honors Barker and Bostic with University's Highest Public Honor," *ClemsonWorld*, September 3, 2016, accessed December 17, 2019, https://clemson.world/the-clemson-medallion-2/.

12. Angela Nixon, "Clemson University Dedicates the 'Building That Teaches,'" *Newsstand*, Clemson University, Clemson, SC, April 13, 2012, accessed November 10, 2019, http://newsstand.clemson.edu/mediarelations/clemson-university-dedi-cates-the-building-that-teaches/.

13. Marina Koren, "A Brief History of Die-In Protests," CityLab, December 4, 2014, accessed November 10, 2019, https://www.citylab.com/equity/2014/12/a-brief-history-of-die-in-protests/383439/.

14. "60 'Fearful' Negroes Return to Campus," *Philadelphia Inquirer*, October 28, 1969, 4, accessed November 10, 2019, https://www.newspapers.com/image/169161694.

15. "Black 'Panic' Off at Clemson," *Democrat and Chronicle* (Rochester, NY), October 28, 1969, accessed November 10, 2019, https://www.newspapers.com/image/136661674.

16. Mike Forth, "Petition For Flag, 'Dixie' Signed by 3,300 Students," *Tiger*, November 7, 1969, 1.

17. Forth.

18. Campus Climate Survey 2012: Executive Summary, Division of Student Affairs, Clemson University, Clemson, SC, accessed November 10, 2019, https://www.clemson.edu/centers-institutes/gantt/documents/campus-climate-sum-mary.pdf.

19. "Frat Suspended for 'Clemson Cripmas' Party in Wake of Ferguson Protests," *Gawker*, December 8, 2014, accessed November 10, 2019, https://gawker.com/frat-suspended-for-clemson-cripmas-party-in-wake-of-f-1668222467.

20. Bryan Wagner, *The Tar Baby: A Global History* (Princeton, NJ: Princeton University Press, 2017), ix.

21. Susanne M. Schafer, "Clemson University Probes Racist Party," *Washington Post*, January 30, 2007, accessed November 10, 2019, http://www.washingtonpost.com/wp-dyn/content/article/2007/01/30/AR2007013001479.html.

22. "NAACP Probes MLK Party at Clemson," *CBS News*, January 31, 2007, accessed April 9, 2020, https://www.cbsnews.com/news/naacp-probes-mlk-party-at-clemson/.

23. Jim Clements, email to the Clemson Family, December 7, 2014.

24. Campus Climate Survey 2012.

25. Social Media with National Impact: A Conversation with Young Activists, Clemson University Calendar, Clemson, SC, accessed November 10, 2019, https://

calendar.clemson.edu/event/social_media_with_national_impact_a_conversa-
tion_with_young_activists#.XNqe5i-ZPys.

26. For more information about #StudentBlackOut, see the Black Liberation
Collective website, http://www.blackliberationcollective.org. The collective was
organized for "Black students who are dedicated to transforming institutions of
higher education through unity, coalition building, direct action and political education."

27. See The Stripes—Grievances, https://phd.aydeethegreat.com/see-the-
stripes/see-the-stripes-grievances/.

28. "History on Edge," Annual Meeting of the National Council on Public
History, April 15–18, 2015, 25, accessed October 16, 2019, https://ncph.org/wp-con-
tent/uploads/2015-Annual-Meeting-Digital-Program-Web.pdf.

29. @monicalmercado, "How do your #publichistory projects interpret race?",
Twitter, April 16, 2015, 3:30 P.M., https://twitter.com/monicalmercado/sta-
tus/588784136971653121.

30. Central Register of Prisoners, Central Correctional Institution (S.C.), June
16, 1892–May 2, 1899. Prisoners 10928–14877, South Carolina Department of
Archives and History.

31. State v. Simon Davis, February 1, 1892, Abbeville County, Office of the Clerk,
Abbeville County Courthouse, Abbeville, South Carolina.

32. Jane Powers Weldon, "Calhoun," *New Georgia Encyclopedia*, December 17,
2003, accessed November 10, 2019, https://www.georgiaencyclopedia.org/articles/
counties-cities-neighborhoods/calhoun; and "History," *Historic Downtown Calhoun*,
accessed November 10, 2019, https://downtowncalhounga.com/history/.

33. "About," The Academic Minute, accessed April 23, 2020, https://www.aacu.
org/academic-minute.

34. Board of Trustees, Clemson Trustees Minutes, July 14–16, 1908, *TigerPrints*,
https://tigerprints.clemson.edu/cgi/viewcontent.cgi?article=1356&context=trust-
ees_minutes.

35. David Eagleman, "Metamorphosis, an excerpt from *Sum: Forty Tales from the
Afterlives*" David Eagleman, accessed November 10, 2019, https://www.eagleman.
com/sum/excerpt.

CALL: THE TWELVE-YEAR-OLD FELON

1. Simon Davis, Abbeville County, Office of the Clerk.
2. Simon Davis.
3. Simon Davis.
4. *Annual Report of the Board of Directors and Superintendent of the South Carolina
Penitentiary for the Fiscal Year Ending October 31, 1893,* The Board (Columbia, SC:
Charles A. Calvo Jr., State Printer, 1893), 6.
5. *Annual Report, SC Penitentiary.*
6. Board of Trustees, Clemson University, "Third Annual Report of the Board

of Trustees of Clemson Agricultural College to the General Assembly of South Carolina, 1892," *Annual Reports* 9, 5–6, *TigerPrints,* https://tigerprints.clemson.edu/trustees_reports/9.

7. Board of Trustees, Clemson University, "Fifth Annual Report of the Board of Trustees, President and Officers of Clemson Agricultural College, Including the Seventh Annual Report of the South Carolina Experiment Station, 1894," *Annual Reports 11,* 6, *TigerPrints,* https://tigerprints.clemson.edu/trustees_reports/11.

8. "Angela Davis on Race in America," PBS American Portrait, accessed January 15, 2020, http://www.pbs.org/now/news/308-transcript.html.

9. *Simon Davis*, Abbeville County, Office of the Clerk.

10. *Simon Davis*.

11. *Simon Davis*.

CHAPTER 3

1. President's Commission on Slavery and the University, University of Virginia, https://slavery.virginia.edu.

2. Farah Stockman, "Monticello Is Done Avoiding Jefferson's Relationship with Sally Hemings," *New York Times,* June 16, 2018, accessed May 10, 2020, https://www.nytimes.com/2018/06/16/us/sally-hemings-exhibit-monticello.html.

3. Edward P. Alexander, "Washington and Lee University Historic District," National Register of Historic Places Inventory–Nomination Form, December 18, 1970, accessed April 22, 2020, https://www.dhr.virginia.gov/wp-content/uploads/2018/04/117-0022_WashingtonLeeHD_1970_NRHP_Final.pdf.

4. "African Americans at Washington and Lee," President's Office Issues and Initiatives, Washington and Lee University, Lexington City, VA, accessed November 11, 2019, https://www.wlu.edu/presidents-office/issues-and-initiatives/timeline-of-african-americans-at-wandl.

5. Rick Clark, email to Rhondda Robinson Thomas, July 1, 2015.

6. Rick Clark, email to Rhondda Robinson Thomas, March 5, 2019.

7. Eva Hester Martin, personal interview, March 9, 2015.

8. "About StoryCorps," StoryCorps, accessed November 11, 2019, https://story-corps.org/about/.

9. *StoryCenter: Listen Deeply. Tell Stories*, StoryCenter, Berkeley, CA, accessed November 11, 2019, www.storycenter.org.

10. Rhondda Thomas, email to StoryCenter Representative, March 22, 2019.

11. S. Epatha Merkerson, *Finding Your Roots with Henry Louis Gates Jr.*, season 5, episode 5, "Freedom Tales," aired February 5, 2019, accessed November 11, 2019, https://www.pbs.org/weta/finding-your-roots/about/season-5-episode-guide/episode-5/.

12. Elias Kibler, 1880 United States Federal Census, accessed November 11, 2019, https://search.ancestry.com/cgi-bin/sse.dll?dbid=6742&h=42349915&indiv=try&o_cvc=Image:OtherRecord.

13. Kibler, 1900 United States Federal Census, accessed November 11, 2019, https://search.ancestry.com/cgi-bin/sse.dll?dbid=7602&h=59304495&indiv=try&o_cvc=Image:OtherRecord.

14. Kibler, 1910 United States Federal Census, accessed November 11, 2019, https://search.ancestry.com/cgi-bin/sse.dll?dbid=7884&h=26678816&indiv=try&o_cvc=Image:OtherRecord.

15. Kibler, 1920 United States Federal Census, accessed November 11, 2019, https://search.ancestry.com/cgi-bin/sse.dll?dbid=6061&h=52764176&indiv=try&o_cvc=Image:OtherRecord.

16. Kibler, 1940 United States Federal Census, https://search.ancestry.com/cgi-bin/sse.dll?dbid=2442&h=138438959&indiv=try&o_cvc=Image:OtherRecord.

17. Elias L. Kibler, *Find a Grave*, accessed November 11, 2019, https://www.findagrave.com/memorial/155590563.

18. "Prominent Negro Addresses Cadets," *Tiger*, November 28, 1923, 1.[[verify date]]

19. Reel, "Riggs's Last Years, 1917–1924," in *The High Seminary*, 1:219.

20. Crystal Boyles, "Letters from George Washington Carver to a Clemson Cadet Shed New Light on University's Past," February 4, 2011, *Newsstand*, Clemson University, Clemson, SC, 2019, accessed November 11, 2019, http://newsstand.clemson.edu/george-washington-carver-letters/.

21. Boyles.

22. George Washington Carver, letter to Kelly E. Traynham, December 26, 1933, Tuskegee Normal and Industrial Institute, Tuskegee, Alabama, George Washington Carver Papers, 11–87, Clemson University Libraries' Special Collections & Archives.

23. Joseph A. Opala, "The Gullah: Rice, Slavery, and the Sierra Leone–American Connection," Yale University, accessed November 11, 2019, https://glc.yale.edu/sites/default/files/files/South%20Carolina%20Rice%20Plantations.pdf.

24. William A. Sinclair, *The Aftermath of Slavery: A Study of the Condition and Environment of the American Negro* (Boston: Small, Maynard, 1905), 187.

25. "Servants' Toilets," President's Report to Board of Trustees, Clemson Agricultural College of South Carolina, March 27, 1936, *TigerPrints*, accessed November 11, 2019, https://tigerprints.clemson.edu/cgi/viewcontent.cgi?article=1061&context=pres_reports.

26. Call My Name: African Americans in Clemson U History, accessed April 23, 2020, https://www.facebook.com/callmynamecu/.

27. Marjorie Campbell, email to David Blakesley, May 28, 2015; David Blakesley, email to Marjorie Campbell, May 28, 2015.

28. Matthew Bundrick, email to Rhondda Thomas, July 23, 2015.

29. Campbell, email to Rhondda Thomas, October 13, 2015.

30. Jan Lay, email to Rhondda Thomas, November 9, 2016.

31. Sam Hoover, email to Marjorie Campbell and Rhondda Thomas, June 22, 2016.

32. Rhondda R. Thomas, *Call My Name: Clemson University Black Heritage Tour*, Knight Lab, accessed November 10, 2019, https://uploads.knightlab.com/story-mapjs/06b0bcfd9cb34234a093636a1683146c/black-clemson/index.html.

33. *Taps* yearbook, Clemson University, 1965, 476, and 1967, 26–27, 120, Clemson University, *TigerPrints*, accessed November 11, 2019, https://tigerprints.clemson.edu/yearbooks/.

34. Carmen V. Harris, "A Ray of Hope: Blacks in the South Carolina Extension Service, 1915–1970 (PhD diss., Michigan State University, 2002).

35. William C. Hine, *South Carolina State University: A Black Land-Grant College in Jim Crow America* (Columbia: University of South Carolina Press, 2018).

CALL: LOYAL SLAVE OR DANGEROUS TRICKSTER?

1. Margaret L. Coit, *John C. Calhoun: American Portrait* (Norwalk, CT: Easton, 1993), 9.

2. Starke, William Pinckney, - 1886. Social Networks and Archival Context, University of Virginia Library and National Archives and Records Administration, February 3, 2019, accessed November 11, 2019, http://snaccooperative.org/ark:/99166/w68w6ssc.

3. Irving H. Bartlett, *John C. Calhoun: A Biography* (New York: W.W. Norton, 1993), 282.

4. Winifred Morgan, *The Trickster Figure in American Literature* (New York: Palgrave Macmillan, 2013), 16, 17.

5. "The African American Experience at Fort Hill," Department of Historic Properties, Clemson University, 2020, accessed April 22, 2020, https://www.clemson.edu/about/history/properties/fort-hill/african-americans.html.

6. Bartlett, 282.

7. Floride Calhoun to Patrick Calhoun, April 3, 1843, Pendleton District, John C. Calhoun Papers.

8. The Deed to the Fort Hill Farm, Thomas Green Clemson Papers, Box 1, Folder 25, and the Fort Hill Slave Inventory, Thomas Green Clemson Papers, Box 5, Folder 2, Clemson University Libraries' Special Collections & Archives.

9. Daniel Kelly, "Clemson University's Hunnicutt Creek to Be Restored," *Environmental Monitor,* December 5, 2012, accessed November 11, 2019, https://www.fondriest.com/news/clemson-universitys-hunnicutt-creek-to-be-restored.htm.

10. Kemp, personal interview, March 17, 2019.

11. Jonathan Veit, "Clemson to Launch Weekly Farm Market and Expand Research at Campus Farm," *Newsstand,* Clemson University, Clemson, SC, December 3, 2018, accessed November 11, 2019, http://newsstand.clemson.edu/mediarelations/clemson-to-launch-weekly-farm-market-and-expand-research-at-campus-farm/.

1. Coit, 9.
2. Coit.
3. Bartlett, 282.

CHAPTER 4

1. See, for example, "Hillary Clinton on Race and Gender in America," *NBC Nightly News with Lester Holt*, September 13, 2017, accessed November 10, 2019, https://www.facebook.com/watch/?v=2012725312080822.

2. "About," *Black Lives Matter*, accessed November 10, 2019, https://blacklives-matter.com/about/.

3. Monica Anderson and Paul Hitlin, "Social Media Conversations about Race," *Pew Research Center: Internet and Technology*, August 15, 2016, accessed April 16, 2020, https://www.pewresearch.org/internet/wp-content/uploads/sites/9/2016/08/PI_2016.08.15_Race-and-Social-Media_FINAL.pdf.

4. Nathaniel Cary, "Clemson Students Vote to Rename Tillman," *Greenville News*, January 30, 2015, accessed November 10, 2019, https://www.greenvilleonline.com/story/news/education/2015/01/30/clemson-student-group-votes-rename-tillman-hall/22593921/.

5. Minutes of the Meeting of the Clemson University Board of Trustees, February 6, 2015, accessed November 10, 2019, http://media.clemson.edu/bot/Minutes/2015/020615.pdf.

6. Nathaniel Cary, "Clemson Faculty Want Tillman Changed," *Greenville News*, February 10, 2015, accessed November 10, 2019, https://www.greenvilleonline.com/story/news/education/2015/02/10/clemson-faculty-want-tillman-halls-name-changed/23200235/.

7. Nathaniel Cary, "Clemson Won't Rename Tillman Hall, Board Chairman Says," *Greenville News*, February 11, 2019, accessed November 10, 2019, https://www.greenvilleonline.com/story/news/education/2015/02/11/clemson-rename-tillman-hall-board-chair-says/23238993/.

8. "Protection of Certain Monuments and Memorials," Title 10—Public Buildings and Property, South Carolina Code of Laws, Section 10-1-165, accessed November 10, 2019, https://www.scstatehouse.gov/code/t10c001.php.

9. "Protection of Certain Monuments and Memorials."

10. James W. Loewen, "What Learning about Slavery Can Teach Us about Ourselves," *Teaching Tolerance* 55 (Spring 2017), accessed November 10, 2019, https://www.tolerance.org/magazine/spring-2017/what-learning-about-slavery-can-teach-us-about-ourselves.

11. Nathaniel Cary, "Debate Looks at Pros, Cons of Renaming Tillman," *Greenville News*, March 11, 2015, accessed April 22, 2020, https://www.greenvilleonline.com/story/news/local/2015/03/10/debate-looks-pros-cons-renaming-tillman-hall/24735369/.

12. Past Presidents of the Faculty Senate, "We Have the Appetite to Rename Tillman Hall. Do You?", *Free Speech and Open Forum*, Faculty Senate, Clemson University, July 2015, accessed November 10, 2019, https://www.clemson.edu/faculty-staff/faculty-senate/documents/free-speech/rename-tillman.pdf.

13. "See The Stripes—Grievances," 2019, accessed November 10, 2019, https://aydeethegreat.com/see-the-stripes/see-the-stripes-grievances/.

14. "Sense of the Board Regarding Accurately Portraying Clemson University's History," 2015, accessed November 10, 2019, http://media.clemson.edu/bot/documents/resolution-clemson-history-16Q1.pdf.

15. Recommendations from the Task Force on the History of Clemson to the Board of Trustees, February 5, 2016, accessed November 10, 2019, http://media.clemson.edu/bot/documents/clemsonhistoryTF-final-020416.pdf.

16. "Yale University," Advocating History for Justice at Duke, accessed April 26, 2020, https://www.activatinghistoryatduke.com/yale.html.

17. Rudolph Lee, "Suggestion for the Restoration of Colonial Farm Life at Clemson College," Rudolph Edward Lee Papers, Clemson University Libraries' Special Collections & Archives.

18. Recommendations from the Task Force on the History of Clemson.

19. Lynn Rainville, *Invisible Founders: How Two Centuries of African American Families Transformed a Plantation into a College* (New York: Berghahn, 2019).

20. "Founders and Key Historical Figures," About, Clemson University, 2019, accessed November 10, 2019, https://www.clemson.edu/about/history/bios/index.html; and "Notable People," About Clemson University, accessed November 10, 2019, https://www.clemson.edu/about/history/notable-people.html. Founders and Key Historical Figures include Thomas Green Clemson, Anna Maria Calhoun Clemson, John Caldwell Calhoun, Floride Bonneau Colhoun Calhoun, Richard Wright Simpson, and Benjamin Ryan Tillman.

21. "Clemson: The Complete Story," Clemson University, https://www.clemson.edu/about/history/taskforce/.

22. Recommendations from the Task Force on the History of Clemson.

23. "Universities Studying Slavery," *President's Commission on Slavery and the University*, University of Virginia, Charlottesville, VA, accessed November 10, 2019, https://slavery.virginia.edu/universities-studying-slavery/.

24. Fred Holder, "First Annual South Carolina Archeology Week, September 19–26, 1992," *News Notes of the Oconee County Historical Society*, June 22, 2006, accessed November 10, 2019, https://sites.rootsweb.com/~scoconee/archived-txt/history/h-53.txt.

25. "Clemson University Black History Project," Clemson University Black History Project Papers, Clemson University Libraries' Special Collections & Archives.

26. "Project CUB Advisory Committee," Clemson University Black History Project Papers, Clemson University Libraries' Special Collections & Archives.

27. "Race, Memory and Memorialization," Center for the Study of Slavery and

Justice, Brown University, accessed April 22, 2020, https://www.brown.edu/initiatives/slavery-and-justice/race-memory-and-memorialization.

28. Abel Bartley, "Race, Reconstruction, and Post-Bellum Education in Thomas Green Clemson's Life and World," in *Thomas Green Clemson*, ed. Alma Bennett (Clemson, SC: Clemson Digital Press, 2009), 159–86.

29. James Barker, review of *The High Seminary: Clemson Agricultural College of South Carolina, 1894–1964*, vol. 1, *TigerPrints*, Clemson Libraries, Clemson, SC, accessed November 10, 2019, https://tigerprints.clemson.edu/restricted/2/.

30. James Barker, review of *The High Seminary: Clemson University, 1964–2000*, vol. 2, *TigerPrints*, Clemson Libraries, Clemson, SC, accessed November 10, 2019, https://tigerprints.clemson.edu/restricted/1/.

31. Leslie Wallace Skinner, review of *The High Seminary, vol. 2, A History of Clemson University, 1964—2000*, by Jerome V. Reel, *South Carolina Historical Magazine* 115, no. 1 (January 2014): 73–75.

32. Cathy Sams, "Markers Signal New Effort to Share Clemson's Full History," *Newsstand*, Clemson University, Clemson, SC, May 17, 2016, accessed November 10, 2019, http://newsstand.clemson.edu/markers-signal-new-effort-to-share-clemsons-full-history/.

33. James P. Clements, email to Clemson University faculty, staff, and students, April 11, 2016; and James P. Clements, email to Clemson University faculty, staff, and students, April 14, 2016.

34. Nathaniel Cary, "Clemson Student Arrested in Yik Yak Threat Case," *Greenville News*, April 21, 2015, accessed April 22, 2020, https://www.greenville-online.com/story/news/crime/2016/04/20/clemson-student-arrested-yik-yak-threats/83305754/.

35. For more information about the sit-in, please see Matt Vasilogambros, "Five Arrested in Clemson University Racism Protests," *Atlantic*, April 15, 2016, accessed April 13, 2020, https://www.theatlantic.com/national/archive/2016/04/clemson-university-arrests/478455/; and Josh Logue, "9-Day Sit-In Ends," *Inside Higher Education*, April 25, 2016, accessed April 13, 2020, https://www.insidehighered.com/news/2016/04/25/clemson-students-end-lengthy-sit.

36. A.D. Carson, "A Timeline of Campus, Community, and National Events," *Owning My Masters*, accessed April 22, 2020, https://phd.aydeethegreat.com/timeline-of-campus-community-and-national-events/.

37. Wanda Johnson, "Clemson Students Hope to Dig Up the Past at Fort Hill Archaeological Site," *Newsstand*, Clemson University, June 14, 2018, accessed November 10, 2019, http://newsstand.clemson.edu/mediarelations/clemson-students-hope-to-dig-up-the-past-at-fort-hill-archeological-site/.

38. Mollie R. Simon and Eric Connor, "Clemson University Students Petition to Remove John C. Calhoun Name from Honors College," *Greenville News*, February 11, 2019, accessed November 10, 2019, https://www.greenvilleonline.com/story/news/2019/02/11/clemson-petition-calhoun-honors-college/2830130002/.

39. Dahvier Alston and Matthew Innocenti, "A Resolution to Denounce

the Public Display of Confederate Flags at Clemson University," Clemson Undergraduate Student Government, August 30, 2018, accessed April 16, 2020, https://bloximages.newyork1.vip.townnews.com/thetigercu.com/content/tncms/assets/v3/editorial/d/0b/d0b4e502-afdf-11e8-87c6-438bbf61b9ca/5b8ddc788434a.pdf.pdf.

40. Elizabeth Tucker, "Secessionists Respond to CUSG's Confederate Flag Resolution, Challenge Clemson Students to Debate," *Tiger*, September 5, 2018, http://www.thetigercu.com/news/secessionists-respond-to-cusg-s-confeder-ate-flag-resolution-challenge-clemson-students-to-debate/article_70da9d60-b15c-11e8-afa1-ab858acea94f.html.

41. Jewel Amoah, "Narrative: The Road to Black Feminist Theory," *Berkeley Journal of Gender, Law & Justice* 12, no. 1 (1997): 84.

42. Toni Morrison, Nobel Lecture, December 7, 1993, accessed December 19, 2019, https://www.nobelprize.org/prizes/literature/1993/morrison/lecture/.

CALL: POST-DESEGREGATION CLEMSON

1. "60 'Fearful' Negroes Return to Campus," *Philadelphia Inquirer*, October 28, 1969.

2. James Forth, "Black Students Vacate Campus for Protection," *Tiger*, October 31, 1969, 1.

3. Jim Clements (@ClemsonPrez), Twitter, January 28, 2019, 10:38 A.M., https://twitter.com/clemsonprez/status/1089910697566322689.

4. The Constitution and Bylaws of the Student League for Black Identity, R. C. Edwards Papers, Series 12, Box 26, Folder 385, Clemson University Libraries' Special Collections & Archives.

5. Questions for Discussion, Student League for Black Identity, Robert C. Edwards Papers, Series 12, Box 26, Folder 385, Clemson University Libraries' Special Collections & Archives.

6. *Tiger*, February 14, 1969, 2.

7. Student League for Black Identity, Questions for Discussion, R. C. Edwards Papers, Series 12, Box 26, Folder 385, Clemson University Libraries' Special Collections & Archives.

8. *Taps* yearbook, Clemson University, 1965, 476, and 1967, 26–27, 120.

9. John Richards and Sandy Edge, letter to the editor, *Tiger*, October 31, 1969, 2.

10. Reggie Harper, "SLBI Program: 'White Problem' Discussed Here," *Tiger*, February 14, 1969, 1.

11. Clemson Black Student Union, *Tigerquest*, accessed November 16, 2019, https://clemson.campuslabs.com/engage/organization/CBSU.

RESPONSE: A TALE OF PARALLELS

1. Clemson president Jim Clements, "Message to the Clemson Family," email to the Clemson faculty, staff, and students, December 7, 2014.

CODA

1. Julian E. Nixon, email to Rhondda Robinson Thomas, December 21, 2018.

2. Margaret Walker, "For My People," *This Is My Century: New and Collected Poems* (Athens, GA: University of Georgia Press, 1989), 6–7.

CALL: RECONCILING MY LINEAGE TO STROM THURMOND

1. AmeriCorps VISTA, accessed November 11, 2019, https://www.nationalservice.gov/programs/americorps/americorps-programs/americorps-vista.

2. "A Bold Mission," South Carolina Collaborative for Race and Reconciliation, Office of Diversity and Inclusion, University of South Carolina, Columbia, SC, April 15, 2020, https://sc.edu/about/offices_and_divisions/diversity_and_inclusion/race_reconciliation/index.php.

RESPONSE: WHERE THERE'S A WILL . . .

1. "Cheered Confederate Flag: Students of South Carolina College Displeased Their Commandant," *New York Times*, 18 March 1904.

2. Thomas Green Clemson, The Will of Thomas Green Clemson, Clemson University, Clemson, SC, accessed November 17, 2019, https://www.clemson.edu/about/history/tgc-will.html.

3. South Carolina General Assembly, *Report and Resolutions of the General Assembly of the State of South Carolina at the Regular Session Commencing November 23, 1886, Part I* (Columbia, SC: Charles A. Calvo Jr., State Printer, 1887), 6.

4. Board of Trustees, Minutes of the Meeting of the Board of Trustees of the Clemson Agricultural College held in the President's Office, Clemson, S.C., June 18, 1948, 754–56. *TigerPrints*, accessed December 24, 2019, https://tigerprints.clemson.edu/cgi/viewcontent.cgi?article=1431&context=trustees_minutes.

5. Thomas Green Clemson to William Wilson (W. W.) Corcoran, October 29, 1878, Thomas Green Clemson Papers, Box 5, folder 14.

6. Clemson to Corcoran.

7. Alice Fahs and Joan Waugh, eds., *The Memory of the Civil War in American Culture* (Chapel Hill: University of North Carolina Press, 2004), 143–45.

8. Thomas Green Clemson to Mary Amarinthia Snowden, November 23, 1873, The Mary Amarinthia Snowden Papers, The South Caroliniana Library, University of South Carolina, Columbia, SC.

9. Clemson to Snowden.

10. Clemson to Snowden.

11. For more insights into the development of the convict leasing system, see David Blackmon, *Slavery by Another Name: The Re-enslavement of Black Americans from the Civil War to World War II* (New York: Anchor Books, 2009).

12. "About Clemson World," *Clemson World*, Fall 2019, Clemson University, Clemson, SC, accessed November 19, 2019, https://clemson.world/about/.

13. Replies, Karen Land, "The Power of Calling a Name," *ClemsonWorld*, Fall 2019, accessed December 19, 2019, https://clemson.world/callinganame/#comments.

14. History Task Force Implementation Team Final Report, October 2019, Clemson University, Clemson, SC, accessed November 19, 2019, https://www.clemson.edu/about/history/taskforce/documents/HistoryProjectFinalReport.pdf.

15. "Clemson Honored for Preserving, Sharing History," *Newsstand*, September 4, 2018, accessed November 17, 2019, https://newsstand.clemson.edu/mediarelations/clemson-honored-for-preserving-sharing-history/.

16. Thomas Green Clemson, Will.

17. Clemson, Will.

18. Alma Har'el, "Documenting the Process," *Time*, March 16–23, 2020, 6.

Bibliography

LIBRARIES AND ARCHIVES

Clemson University Libraries' Special Collections & Archives
  Black Heritage in the Upper Piedmont of South Carolina Project
  Board of Trustees Papers
  George Washington Carver Papers
  Central Dance Association Papers
  Thomas Green Clemson Papers
  Clemson University Black History Project Papers
  R. C. Edwards Papers
  Rudolph Edward Lee Papers
  President Robert F. Pool Committee Files
  Tiger newspaper
Clerk of the Court, Abbeville County, South Carolina
Library of Congress, Washington, DC
Henry Kirke Brown Papers
National Museum of African American History and Culture
Recorder of Deeds, Anderson County, South Carolina
Recorder of Deeds, Pickens County, South Carolina
South Carolina Department of Archives and History
  South Carolina State Penitentiary Records
  South Carolina Court of General Sessions Court Records
  Governor Benjamin Tillman Papers

MEDIA

ClemsonWorld, Clemson University, Clemson, South Carolina
Greenville News, Greenville, South Carolina
Newsstand, Clemson University, Clemson, South Carolina

Academical Village, University of Virginia
Aiken-Rhett House, Charleston, South Carolina
Ashtabula Plantation, Pendleton, South Carolina
Cape Coast Castle, Cape Coast, Ghana, West Africa
Drayton Hall Plantation, Charleston, South Carolina
Elmina Castle, Elmina, Ghana, West Africa
Fort Hill Plantation, Clemson, South Carolina
Colonial Williamsburg, Virginia
Thomas Jefferson's Monticello, Charlottesville, Virginia
Kingsley Plantation, Fort George Island, Florida
Laura Plantation, Vacherie, Louisiana
James Madison's Montpelier, Montpelier Station, Virginia
Oak Alley Plantation, Vacherie, Louisiana
Nathaniel Russell House, Charleston, South Carolina
George Washington's Mount Vernon, Mount Vernon, Virginia
Whitney Plantation, Edgard, Louisiana
Woodburn Plantation, Pendleton, South Carolina

SOURCES

Allen, Trent, and Kevin Bray, eds. *Clemson: There's Something in These Hills*. Clemson, SC: Fort Hill Press, 2006.
Amoah, Jewel. "Narrative: The Road to Black Feminist Theory." *Berkeley Journal of Gender, Law & Justice* 12, no. 1 (1997): 84–102.
Angelou, Maya. "Still I Rise." *And Still I Rise: A Book of Poems*. New York: Random House, 1978. *The Poetry Foundation*. Accessed January 15, 2020. https://www. poetryfoundation.org/poems/46446/still-i-rise.
Ashton, Susanna. "Texts of Our Institutional Lives: Don't You Mean 'Slaves,' Not 'Servants?': Literary and Institutional Texts for an Interdisciplinary Classroom." *College English* 69, no. 2 (November 2006): 156–72.
Barker, James. "The Sacred Soil of Bowman Field." In *Clemson: There's Something in These Hills*, edited by Trent Allen and Kevin Bray, 182–83. Clemson, SC: Fort Hill Press, 2006.
Bartlett, Irving H. *John C. Calhoun: A Biography*. New York: W.W. Norton, 1993.
Bartley, Abel. "Race, Reconstruction, and Post-Bellum Education in Thomas Green Clemson's Life and World." In *Thomas Green Clemson*, edited by Alma Bennett, 159–86. Clemson, SC: Clemson Digital Press, 2009.
Blackmon, Douglas A. *Slavery by Another Name: The Re-enslavement of Black Americans from the Civil War to World War II*. New York: Anchor Books, 2009.
Burton, Orville Vernon. "African American Status and Identity in a Postbellum Community: An Analysis of the Manuscript Census Returns." *Agricultural History* 72, no. 2 (Spring 1998): 213–40.

Calhoun, John C. "Document: Slavery a Positive Good, February 6, 1837." Teaching American History. Accessed September 24, 2019. teachingamericanhistory.org/library/document/slavery-a-positive-good/.

Callahan, John F. *In the African-American Grain: Call-and-Response in Twentieth-Century Black Fiction.* Urbana: University of Illinois Press, 2001.

Clifton, Lucille. *Quilting: Poems, 1987–1990.* Brockport, NY: BOA Editions, 1991.

Cohen, Harvey G. *Duke Ellington's America.* Chicago: University of Chicago Press, 2010.

Coletu, Ebony. "Biographic Mediation." *Auto/Biography Studies* 32, no. 2 (2017): 384–85.

Coit, Margaret L. *John C. Calhoun: American Portrait.* Norwalk, CT: Easton, 1993.

Cook, Harriet Hefner. *Fort Hill, John C. Calhoun Shrine, Clemson University, Clemson, S.C.* Clemson, SC: John C. Calhoun Chapter, United Daughters of the Confederacy, 1970.

Eisiminger, Skip, ed. *Integration with Dignity: A Celebration of Harvey Gantt's Admission to Clemson.* Clemson, SC: Clemson University Press, 2003.

Ernest, John. "Life beyond Biography: Black Lives and Biographical Research." *Commonplace* 17, no. 1 (Fall 2016). Accessed November 22, 2017. http://commonplace.online/article/life-beyond-biography/.

Fahs, Alice, and Joan Waugh, eds. *The Memory of the Civil War in American Culture.* Chapel Hill: University of North Carolina Press, 2005.

Fuller, Elizabeth Belser. *Anderson County Sketches.* Anderson, SC: Anderson County Tricentennial Committee, 1969.

Carmen V. Harris, "A Ray of Hope: Blacks in the South Carolina Extension Service, 1915–1970 (PhD diss., Michigan State University, 2002).

Hartman, Saidiya. *Lose Your Mother: A Journey along the Atlantic Slave Route.* New York: Farrar, Straus and Giroux, 2007.

Hawkins, Billy. *The New Plantation: Black Athletes, College Sports, and Predominantly White NCAA Institutions.* New York: Palgrave Macmillan, 2010.

Hine, William C. *South Carolina State University: A Black Land-Grant College in Jim Crow America,* Columbia: University of South Carolina Press, 2018.

Hunter, Jane Edna. *A Nickel and a Prayer.* Edited by Rhondda Robinson Thomas. Morgantown: West Virginia University Press, 2011.

Hurston, Zora Neale. *Their Eyes Were Watching God.* New York: Harper & Row, 1990.

Ingersoll, Ernest. "The Calhoun Summer Home." *Century Magazine* (April 1881): 892–94. Accessed December 3, 2017. http://www.unz.org/Pub/Century-1881apr-00892?View=PDF&apages=0084.

Jackson, Vince. *The Littlejohn's Grill Story: Blues, Jazz and Rock 'n' Roll in Clemson, SC.* Clemson, SC: SugarCane, 2008.

Johnson, James Weldon, ed. *The Book of American Negro Poetry.* New York: Harcourt, Brace, 1922.

Loewen, James W. "What Learning about Slavery Can Teach Us about Ourselves." *Teaching Tolerance* 55 (Spring 2017). Accessed November 10, 2019. https://www.

tolerance.org/magazine/spring-2017/what-learning-about-slavery-can-teach-us-about-ourselves.

McElya, Micki. *Clinging to Mammy: The Faithful Slave in Twentieth-Century America.* Cambridge, MA: Harvard University Press, 2009.

Megginson, W. J. *African American Life in South Carolina's Upper Piedmont, 1780–1900.* Columbia: University of South Carolina Press, 2006.

Morgan, Winifred. *The Trickster Figure in American Literature.* New York: Palgrave Macmillan, 2013.

Morrison, Toni. Nobel Lecture, December 7, 1993. The Nobel Prize in Literature 1993. Accessed January 15, 2020. https://www.nobelprize.org/prizes/literature/1993/morrison/lecture/.

Moyers, Bill. "Lucille Clifton." In *The Language of Life: A Festival of Poets*, edited by James Haba, 81–83. New York: Doubleday, 1995.

Norrell, Robert Jefferson. *Up from History: The Life of Booker T. Washington.* Cambridge, MA: Harvard University Press, 2009.

Prince, Mary. *The History of Mary Prince, a West Indian Slave. Related by Herself. With a Supplement by the Editor. To Which Is Added, the Narrative of Asa-Asa, a Captured African.* London: F. Westley and A. H. Davis, 1831.

Rainville, Lynn. *Invisible Founders: How Two Centuries of African American Families Transformed a Plantation into a College.* New York: Berghahn, 2019.

Reel, Jerome. *The High Seminary: A History of the Clemson Agricultural College of South Carolina, 1889–1964.* Vol. 1. Clemson, SC: Clemson University Press, 2009.

———. *The High Seminary: A History of Clemson University, 1964–2000.* Vol. 2. Clemson, SC: Clemson University Press, 2018.

Rhoden, William C. *Forty Million Dollar Slaves: The Rise, Fall, and Redemption of the Black Athlete.* New York, Crown, 2006.

Ryan, Abram J. *Poems: Patriotic, Religious, Miscellaneous.* New York: P. J. Kenedy & Sons, 1896.

Sheriff, G. Anne, Robert Dodson, and W. J. Megginson. *African American Cemeteries of Pickens County, SC.* Privately published, 2007. http://www.oldpendleton.scgen.org/Surnames/PDF%20Survey%20Scans/Book-7%20Blacks/Blk_Cemeteries.pdf.

Sinclair, William A. *The Aftermath of Slavery: A Study of the Condition and Environment of the American Negro.* Boston: Small, Maynard, 1905.

Skinner, Leslie Wallace. Review of *The High Seminary, vol. 2, A History of Clemson University, 1964–2000*, by Jerome V. Reel. *South Carolina Historical Magazine* 115, no. 1 (January 2014): 73–75.

Trethewey, Natasha. "Elegy for the Native Guards." In *Native Guard.* Boston: Houghton Mifflin, 2006.

Wagner, Bryan. *The Tar Baby: A Global History.* Princeton, NJ: Princeton University Press, 2017.

Index

Humanities and Public Life